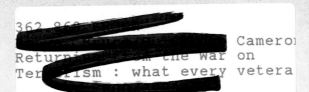

RETURNING *from the*

WAR
ON TERRORISM

What Every Veteran Needs to Know to Receive Your Maximum Benefits

BY BRUCE C. BROWN

RETURNING FROM THE WAR ON TERRORISM
What Every Veteran Needs to Know to Receive Your Maximum Benefits

Copyright © 2008 by Atlantic Publishing Group, Inc.
1405 SW 6th Ave • Ocala, Florida 34471 • 800-814-1132 • 352-622-1875–Fax
Web site: www.atlantic-pub.com • E-mail: sales@atlantic-pub.com
SAN Number: 268-1250

ISBN-13: 978-1-60138-150-7   ISBN-10: 1-60138-150-6

Library of Congress Cataloging-in-Publication Data

Brown, Bruce C. (Bruce Cameron), 1965-
  Returning from the War on Terrorism: What every veteran needs to know
to receive your maximum benefits / by Bruce C. Brown.
      p. cm.
  Includes bibliographical references and index.
  ISBN-13: 978-1-60138-150-7 (alk. paper)
  ISBN-10: 1-60138-150-6 (alk. paper)
 1. Military pensions--Law and legislation--United States. 2.
Veterans--Legal status, laws, etc.--United States. 3.
Veterans--Loans--Law and legislation--United States. 4.
Veterans--Medical care--Law and legislation--United States. I. Title.

  KF7745.B76 2008
  362.86'80973--dc22
                                    2008010975

INTERIOR LAYOUT DESIGN: Vickie Taylor • vtaylor@atlantic-pub.com

Printed in the United States

Printed on Recycled Paper

DEDICATION

This book is dedicated to my wife Vonda. I know the decision to marry you was the smartest choice I have made in my life; the jury is still out on my decision to postpone retirement from the Coast Guard! Thanks for being the most supportive and loving wife I could ever have hoped for. I know I drive you crazy a majority of the time, but despite that, you still love me unconditionally!

"Freedom itself was attacked this morning by a faceless coward. Freedom will be defended!"
— **George W. Bush, President of the United States**

"Our enemies have made the mistake that America's enemies always make. They saw liberty and thought they saw weakness. And now, they see defeat."
— **George W. Bush, President of the United States**

"It is fatal to enter any war without the will to win it."
George W. Bush, President of the United States

We recently lost our beloved pet "Bear," who was not only our best and dearest friend but also the "Vice President of Sunshine" here at Atlantic Publishing. He did not receive a salary but worked tirelessly 24 hours a day to please his parents. Bear was a rescue dog that turned around and showered myself, my wife Sherri, his grandparents Jean, Bob and Nancy, and every person and animal he met (maybe not rabbits) with friendship and love. He made a lot of people smile every day.

We wanted you to know that a portion of the profits of this book will be donated to The Humane Society of the United States. — *Douglas & Sherri Brown*

The human-animal bond is as old as human history. We cherish our animal companions for their unconditional affection and acceptance. We feel a thrill when we glimpse wild creatures in their natural habitat or in our own backyard.

Unfortunately, the human-animal bond has at times been weakened. Humans have exploited some animal species to the point of extinction.

The Humane Society of the United States makes a difference in the lives of animals here at home and worldwide. The HSUS is dedicated to creating a world where our relationship with animals is guided by compassion. We seek a truly humane society in which animals are respected for their intrinsic value and where the human-animal bond is strong.

Want to help animals? We have plenty of suggestions. Adopt a pet from a local shelter, join The Humane Society, and be a part of our work to help companion animals and wildlife. You will be funding our educational, legislative, investigative, and outreach projects in the U.S. and across the globe.

Or perhaps you'd like to make a memorial donation in honor of a pet, friend, or relative? You can through our Kindred Spirits program. If you'd like to contribute in a more structured way, our Planned Giving Office has suggestions about estate planning, annuities, and even gifts of stock that avoid capital gains taxes.

Maybe you have land that you would like to preserve as a lasting habitat for wildlife. Our Wildlife Land Trust can help you. Perhaps the land you want to share is a backyard — that's enough. Our Urban Wildlife Sanctuary Program will show you how to create a habitat for your wild neighbors.

So you see, it's easy to help animals, and The HSUS is here to help.

THE HUMANE SOCIETY
OF THE UNITED STATES.

2100 L Street NW • Washington, DC 20037 • 202-452-1100

www.hsus.org

TABLE OF

CONTENTS

INTRODUCTION

This book has become a personal crusade of mine to educate the millions of veterans on what they are entitled to. The key word is entitled. Veterans serve their country, and in return are granted entitlements under United States law. This book sets the record straight on what those entitlements are, explains how to maximize veterans' benefits, and contains a wealth of veterans' benefits information in a single source, rather than leaving the veteran to navigate the myriad of disconnected systems, Web sites, and information sources available. Our armed forces have a good program for transitioning active duty and reserve military members to retirement. However, the transitional benefits programs are often less than adequate for those who are discharged, released from active duty, medically disabled, and those who choose to leave the military after their service commitment.

I want to be clear that this book is primarily written for those who served (or are currently serving) in Afghanistan and Iraq and all other active duty, Reserve and National Guard members who are leaving the military in the future, have recently left the military, are preparing for retirement, or are under a medical discharge. I will discuss veterans' benefits for Vietnam, Korea, World War II, and other era veterans; however, this book is predominately geared for present-day veterans.

According to the U.S. Census Bureau, there are about 26 million veterans in the United States. As of January 2007, more than 1.6 million U.S. servicemen and women had tours of duty in Afghanistan and Iraq. When not on active duty, more than 20 percent of these vets do not have health-care coverage, and many more are unaware of the hundreds of benefits to which

they have access. As a result, many are suffering financial strain during and after deployment.

This is a discouraging statistic, because the federal and state governments and private foundations have scholarships and military discounts available only to veterans. There are billions of dollars in aid available, waiting to be claimed, but the problem is finding and properly applying for these programs.

This is the sixth book I have written for publication, and unlike my previous five books, this one is not related to online marketing, the Internet, search engines, blogging, e-mail, or how to succeed with establishing an online business. I am a military veteran with just under 24 years of active duty service in the U.S. Coast Guard. I had an approved retirement for the spring of 2008, and I was just beginning the transition process from military to civilian life. This is a stressful time for most career military persons because they are leaving the comfort zone that they have known for the better part of their life and are entering the "unknown," the often unstable and always competitive civilian workforce environment.

A last-minute job offer from the Coast Guard for a position in Miami was presented to me, and I opted to "extend" my military career a few more years. This opportunity gave me the window to write a resource guide that would help veterans navigate the veterans' benefits programs, help them maximize the benefits received, and help them achieve success in a post-military career. My sincere desire is that this finds its way into each veteran's backpack, onto his or her desk, or into his or her home and becomes a comprehensive resource he or she will use often.

These are trying times, especially for our deployed servicemen and servicewomen currently serving in the global war on terrorism in Iraq, Afghanistan, and other locations around the world.

THIS BOOK'S MISSION

This book provides candid, no-nonsense advice and practical information you can use to maximize your benefits while simplifying the often-confusing bureaucratic veterans' benefits system.

The mission of the Veterans Benefits Administration (VBA), in partnership with the Veterans Health Administration (VHA) and the National Cemetery Administration (NCA), is to provide benefits and services to the veterans and their families in a responsive, timely, and compassionate manner in recognition of their service to the nation. The Veterans Benefit Administration is part of the Veterans Administration.

The Board of Veterans' Appeals (also known as "BVA" or "the Board") is a part of the VA, located in Washington, District of Columbia. Members of the board review benefit claims determinations made by local VA offices and issue decisions on appeals. These law judges, attorneys experienced in veterans' law and in reviewing benefit claims, are the only ones who can issue board decisions. Staff attorneys, also trained in veterans' law, review the facts of each appeal and assist the board members. {38 U.S.C. §§ 7103, 7104}

Anyone who is not satisfied with the results of a claim for veterans' benefits (determined by a VA regional office, medical center, or other local VA office) should read the "How do I Appeal" pamphlet (**http://www.va.gov/vbs/bva/010202A.pdf**). It is intended to explain the steps involved in filing an appeal and to serve as a reference for the terms and abbreviations used in the appeal process.

VETERANS ADMINISTRATION ORGANIZATION

Veterans Health Administration

With 157 hospitals nationwide, VHA manages one of the largest healthcare systems in the United States. VA medical centers within a Veterans Integrated Service Network (VISN) work together to provide efficient, accessible healthcare to veterans in their areas. The VHA also conducts research and education and provides emergency medical preparedness.

Veterans Benefits Administration (VBA)

The Veterans Benefits Administration (VBA) provides benefits and services to the veteran population through 58 VA regional offices. Some of the benefits and services provided by VBA to veterans and their dependents include compensation and pension, education, loan guaranty, and insurance.

National Cemetery Administration (NCA)

The National Cemetery Administration (NCA) is responsible for providing burial benefits to veterans and eligible dependents. The delivery of these benefits involves managing 120 national cemeteries nationwide, providing grave markers worldwide, administering the State Cemetery Grants Program that complements the National Cemeteries Network, and providing Presidential Memorial certificates to next of kin of deceased veterans.

Board of Contract Appeals (BCA)

The Department of Veterans Affairs Board of Contract Appeals considers and determines appeals from decisions of contracting officers pursuant to the Contract Disputes Act of 1978.

Board of Veterans' Appeals (BVA)

The Board of Veterans' Appeals reviews benefit claims determinations made by local VA offices and issues decision on appeals. Only the board members can issue board decisions.

Center for Women Veterans

The mission of the Center for Women Veterans is to ensure women veterans have access to VA benefits and services; to ensure that VA healthcare and benefits programs are responsive to the gender-specific needs of women veterans; to perform outreach to improve women veterans' awareness of VA services, benefits, and eligibility; and to act as the primary advisor to the secretary for Veterans Affairs on all matters related to programs, issues, and initiatives for and affecting women veterans.

Office of Acquisition and Material Management (OAMM)

OAMM is responsible for overseeing the acquisition, storage, and distribution of supplies, services, and equipment used by VA facilities and other government agencies. OAMM manages pharmaceuticals, medical supplies and equipment, and nonperishable sustenance through its procurement system.

Office of Alternate Dispute Resolution (ADR) and Mediation

The Office of Alternate Dispute Resolution (ADR) and Mediation provides effective training and consulting in conflict resolution and ADR (emphasizing mediation) to VA organizations and employees.

Office of Budget

The Office of Budget is the focal point for the departmental budget formulation and execution, the Capital Investment Board, and for Performance Reporting.

Office of Public Affairs and Intergovernmental Affairs (OPAIA)

The Office of Public Affairs and Intergovernmental Affairs (OPAIA) has two major offices, Public Affairs and Intergovernmental Affairs. The primary mission of public affairs is to provide information through the news media to the nation's veterans and their eligible dependents and survivors, concerning available department benefits and programs. Intergovernmental Affairs interacts with federal, state, and local government agencies and officials in developing and maintaining a positive and productive relationship.

Office of Congressional Affairs (OCA)

The Office of Congressional Affairs (OCA) is the principal point of contact between the Department of Veterans Affairs and Congress and is the oversight and coordinating body for the department's congressional relations. The office serves in an advisory capacity to the secretary and deputy secretary and other VA managers concerning policies, programs, and legislative matters in which congressional committees or individual members of Congress have expressed an interest.

Office of Employment Discrimination Complaint Adjudication (OEDCA)

The Office of Employment Discrimination Complaint Adjudication (OEDCA) maintains a high-quality and high-performing work force and ensures fairness, integrity, and trust throughout the complaint adjudication phase of the equal employment opportunity complaint resolution process.

Office of Financial Management (OFM)

The Office of Financial Management (OFM) continually improves the quality of the VA's financial services through the development of sound financial policies and the promotion of efficient financial management systems, operations, policies, and practices.

Office of the General Counsel (OGC)

The Office of the General Counsel (OGC) identifies and meets the legal needs of the VA.

Office of Human Resources and Administration (OHRA)

The Office of Human Resources and Administration (OHRA)'s functional areas include human-resources management, administrative policies and functions, equal opportunity policies and functions, and security and law enforcement.

Office of Information and Technology (OIT)

The Office of Information and Technology (OIT) activities include integrated business and information technology (IT) planning; security and contingency planning to protect information and privacy across VA systems and networks; reviews to evaluate the performance of IT programs; review and approval of IT acquisitions; facilitation of intra- and intergovernmental partnerships; educating and informing the Department of IT initiatives and legislation; and sharing lessons learned.

Office of the Inspector General (OIG)

The Office of the Inspector General (OIG) provides service to veterans, VA employees, and citizens concerned with good government.

Office of Occupational Safety and Health

The staff of the Office of Occupational Safety and Health ensures that the VA complies with requirements of the federal Occupational Safety and Health Administration (OSHA), Joint Commission for Accreditation of Healthcare Organizations (JCAHO), and VA standards.

Office of Policy, Planning and Preparedness (OPPP)

The Office of Policy, Planning and Preparedness (OPPP) facilitates, coordinates, and validates the department's policy development and formulation processes; coordinates the VA's strategic planning process and implementation of the Government Performance and Results Act requirements; supports the identification, development, analysis, and review of issues affecting veterans' programs; links and supplements the actuarial and quantitative analysis capabilities of the VA in support of major policy inquiries; serves as the VA's focal point for access to and availability of official data; coordinates the independent evaluation of VA program performance; and fosters quality management techniques and procedures throughout the VA.

Office of Regulation Policy and Management (ORPM)

The Office of Regulation Policy and Management (ORPM) is responsible for the centralized management, control, and coordination of all VA regulations. ORPM supervises the VA's Regulation Rewrite Project, a comprehensive effort to review, reorganize, and rewrite VA regulations

lacking clarity, consistency, or logical organization. ORPM also is responsible for devising and implementing new procedures to centralize control and improve secretarial oversight, management, drafting efficiency, policy resolution, impact analysis, and coordination of diverse VA regulations.

Office of Small and Disadvantaged Business Utilization (OSDBU)

The Office of Small and Disadvantaged Business Utilization (OSDBU) advocates for the maximum practicable participation of small, small disadvantaged, veteran-owned, women-owned, and empowerment zone businesses in contracts awarded by the VA and in subcontracts, which are awarded by VA's prime contractors. The Empowerment Zone tax incentives are worth approximately $5.3 billion to small and large businesses in Empowerment Zones. These incentives encourage businesses to open and expand and to hire local residents. Empowerment Zone incentives include employment credits, low-interest loans through EZ facility bonds, reduced taxation on capital gains, and other incentives.

FEDERAL BENEFITS FOR VETERANS AND DEPENDENTS

During the Civil War, President Abraham Lincoln affirmed our nation's commitment "to care for him who shall have borne the battle, and for his widow and his orphan." His eloquent words live on today as the motto of the Department of Veterans Affairs, the federal agency responsible for honoring our nation's debt of gratitude to America's patriots.

Over the years, federal benefits for veterans have evolved to meet their changing needs. For example, VA has established a "seamless transition" program to ensure that service members returning from combat in Afghanistan and Iraq in support of the Global War on Terror receive the information they need about VA benefits and services before they leave the military and begin the transition to civilian life.

While much of our immediate attention focuses on our new generation of veterans, we certainly have not forgotten veterans who served in past wars. This publication is intended as a reference guide for all our nation's veterans, their spouses and family members, and those who help veterans access VA benefits and services.

It is said that the measure of a nation is gauged by the way its people honor their defenders. The decision to step forward to support and defend the Constitution, serving in harm's way when necessary, exacts a great toll. Yet our veterans do not hesitate to serve and bear the cost of freedom for all. In everything that we do here at VA, we strive to honor veterans — our nation's defenders — as they have honored us through their service and sacrifice.

Jim Nicholson
Secretary of Veterans Affairs

Veterans of the United States armed forces may be eligible for a broad range of programs and services provided by the federal Department of Veterans Affairs. These benefits are legislated in Title 38 of the United States Code. This booklet contains a summary of these benefits effective Jan. 1, 2007. For additional information, visit the VA Web page at **www.va.gov**.

GENERAL ELIGIBILITY

Eligibility for most VA benefits is based upon discharge from active military service under other than dishonorable conditions. Active service means full-time service, other than active duty for training, as a member of the Army, Navy, Air Force, Marine Corps, Coast Guard, or as a commissioned officer of the Public Health Service, Environmental Science Services Administration or National Oceanic and Atmospheric Administration, or its predecessor, the Coast and Geodetic Survey. Men and women veterans with similar service may be entitled to the same VA benefits.

Dishonorable and bad conduct discharges issued by general court-martial will almost always bar VA benefits. Veterans in prison and parolees must contact a VA regional office in order to determine eligibility. VA benefits will not be provided to any veteran or dependent wanted for an outstanding felony warrant.

WARTIME SERVICE

Certain VA benefits require wartime service. Under the law, VA recognizes these war periods:

Mexican Border Period: May 9, 1916, through April 5, 1917, for veterans who served in Mexico, on its borders or in adjacent waters.

World War I: April 6, 1917, through November 11, 1918; for veterans who served in Russia, April 6, 1917, through April 1, 1920; extended through July 1, 1921, for veterans who had at least one day of service between April 6, 1917, and Nov. 11, 1918.

World War II: Dec. 7, 1941, through Dec. 31, 1946.

Korean War: June 27, 1950, through Jan. 31, 1955.

Vietnam War: Aug. 5, 1964 (Feb. 28, 1961, for veterans who served "in country" before Aug. 5, 1964), through May 7, 1975.

Gulf War: Aug. 2, 1990, through a date to be set by law or Presidential Proclamation.

IMPORTANT DOCUMENTS

Those seeking a VA benefit for the first time must submit a copy of their service discharge form (DD-214, DD-215, or, for World War II veterans, a WD form), which documents service dates and type of discharge, or give their full name, military service number, and branch and dates of service. The veteran's service discharge form should be kept in a safe location that is accessible to the veteran and next of kin or designated representative.

OPERATIONS ENDURING FREEDOM AND IRAQI FREEDOM (OEF/OIF)

The VA has established a special Web page just for OEF/OIF returning veterans. The URL is **www.seamlesstransition.va.gov**. Detailed contact information for OEF/OIF veterans will be posted on this Web page.

Toll-free numbers for contacting the VA are:

VA Benefits: 1-800-827-1000

- Burial

- Civilian Health and Medical Program of the Department of Veterans Affairs (CHAMPVA)

- Death pension

- Dependency indemnity compensation

- Direct deposit

- Directions to VA benefits regional offices

- Disability compensation

- Disability pension

- Education

- Home loan guaranty

- Life insurance

- Medical care

- Vocational rehabilitation and employment

Education (GI Bill): 1-888-442-4551

Healthcare benefits: 1-877-222-8387

Income Verification and Means Testing: 1-800-929-8387

Life insurance: 1-800-669-8477

Mammography helpline: 1-888-492-7844

Special issues — Gulf War/Agent Orange/Project Shad/Mustard Agents and Lewisite/Ionizing Radiation: 1-800-749-8387

Status of headstones and markers: 1-800-697-6947

Telecommunications Device for the Deaf (TDD): 1-800-829-4833

For healthcare services, contact your nearest VA medical facility.

WHO IS A VETERAN?

I still find it amazing that most Americans do not understand what or who a veteran is. Often, it is believed that a veteran is someone who has been severely wounded or killed in battle. I felt it was important to clearly define what a veteran is early in this book, so everyone has a thorough understanding of who we are talking about when we use the term "veteran," or in relation to veterans' benefits. This book is primarily written for those who served (or are currently serving) in Afghanistan and Iraq and all active duty, Reserve, and National Guard members who are leaving the military in the near future, recently left the military, are preparing for retirement, or are either facing or were recently processed out of the military a medical discharge. I will discuss veterans' benefits for Vietnam, Korea, World War II, and other era veterans briefly; however, this book is predominately geared to present-day veterans.

One fact I have discovered in researching this book is that there is no universal definition of a veteran in relation to veterans' benefits. In each case there are standards and qualifying data, and you must prove your status to the Veterans Administration. Although this may be simple in the case of career military or military retirees, it becomes extremely complicated for single-term enlistees, reservists, and National Guard members.

DEFINITION OF A VETERAN

A veteran, as defined by U.S. federal law, is any person who has served for any length of time in any branch of the United States armed forces. As you will discover, there are different "types" of veterans, and depending on your veteran status, you have different types of veterans' benefits and entitlements and, in some cases, no benefits or entitlements. There is no "cookie-cutter" definition for a veteran which translates easily into veterans' benefits, but if you have served in the U.S. military and have a DD-214 (discharge paperwork) with anything other than dishonorable, you will likely qualify for all or some benefits. In each chapter of this book, I will include qualification data to determine if your service qualifies for the specific entitlements or benefits. When dealing with the Veterans Administration, the burden falls on you to prove your veteran status; therefore, start compiling information to document your service, discharge, and localities you served (such as war-related service) to help you document claims.

A war veteran is any person serving in any branch of the United States armed forces who was ordered to foreign soil or waters to participate in direct or non-direct support activity against any enemy of the United States.

A combat veteran is any person serving in any branch of the United States armed forces who experiences any level of hostility or engages in enemy combatant action for any duration of time resulting from offensive, defensive, or friendly fire military action involving a real or perceived enemy in a pre- or post-designated combat operations.

To begin the process to claim veterans' benefits, documentation of your service is critical, and a great deal of patience is necessary. The red tape is often long and frustrating. Patience, in this case, is a virtue, as it may take weeks or months for any significant action to be taken on your veteran's claim package, depending on what benefits you are trying to take advantage of. In defense of the Veterans Administration, many benefits are easy to obtain and are routinely given in an expeditious and relatively simple manner.

Here are a few things to remember when you start to deal with claiming your veterans' benefits. Many benefits have been around for years, and the eligibility requirements are clear and simple to understand. Others are much more complicated and can change based on congressional regulations, determinations of "honorable discharge" or "under honorable conditions" status, and changes in law as enacted through the legislative process. Or, the specific type or location of service (such as Afghanistan, Iraq, or global war on terrorism), can qualify you for certain benefits. This is particularly true for our Reserve and National Guard veterans.

A common myth is that a veteran is not a veteran until retired from the military. Although it is true that military retirees are veterans, the fact is they become veterans when they first enter the military (in most cases). Military retirees are veterans; however, there are many other current active duty service, Reserve, and National Guard members who are veterans, and even more who served their country for a specified time under their contract who have been discharged under honorable or general conditions. They are also veterans.

However, depending on when you served, for how long, what combat operations you participated in, and what your discharge status was — all factor into what veterans' benefits you may be eligible for and entitled to. At this point, do not be overly concerned or confused. We will examine which benefits you may qualify for in each chapter of the book and break it down into clear, easy-to-understand information.

TYPES OF VETERANS

- **Honorable or general discharged veteran**: A person who has served in the armed forces of the United States for any time, is not entitled to retirement benefits, and was discharged under general or honorable conditions is entitled to certain benefits through the Veterans Administration. Certain entitlements and benefits are based on length of service and type of service, such as combat-related duties.

- **Military retiree**: A person who has served in the armed forces of the United States for 20 plus years of military service and is eligible for a full military retirement package. Some services were offered early military retirement packages under President Bill Clinton, such as the U.S. Coast Guard, as an incentive to reduce the size of the military. These retirees are also entitled to military retirement pay and a comprehensive benefit package. This includes those persons in a medically retired status. Retirees are eligible for a wide array of benefits, entitlements, and privileges, and access to military bases for exchange, commissary, and medical benefits; however, some benefits and entitlements may be limited by Congressional regulation.

☸ **Disabled veteran**: A person who has served in the armed forces of the United States who has suffered wounds, physical ailments, medical conditions, or illness as a result of military service. Disabled veterans are entitled to a compensation package between 10 and 100 percent based on the severity of their condition. Additionally, the actual condition does not necessarily have to have been combat-related, such as a medical complication from an improvised explosive device. In other words, an off-duty sports injury while on active duty often qualifies as service-related. There is no requirement that the wound, injury, or illness be combat-related. This is one of the most widely claimed veteran benefits, since it qualifies you for financial and medical benefits. We will cover disability in depth in later chapters of this book.

HOW DO YOU TELL WHO IS A VETERAN?

Some veterans bear visible signs of their service — a missing limb, a jagged scar, a certain look in the eye. Others carry the evidence inside them — a pin holding a bone together, a piece of shrapnel in the leg, or perhaps another sort of steel, the soul's ally forged in the refinery of adversity.

Except in parades, however, the men and women who have kept America safe wear no badge or emblem. You cannot always recognize a veteran just by looking.

WHO IS A VETERAN?

He is the cop on the beat who spent six months in Saudi Arabia sweating two gallons a day making sure armored personnel carriers did not run out of fuel.

He is the barroom loudmouth, dumber than five wooden planks, whose overgrown frat-boy behavior is outweighed a hundred times on the cosmic scale by four hours of exquisite bravery near the 38th parallel.

She (or he) is the nurse who fought against futility and went to sleep sobbing every night for two solid years in Da Nang.

He is the POW who went away one person and came back another — or maybe did not come back.

He is the Parris Island drill instructor who has never seen combat but has saved countless lives by turning slouchy, no-account rednecks and gang members into Marines and teaching them to watch each other's backs.

He is the parade-riding Legionnaire who pins on his ribbons and medals with a prosthetic hand.

He is the career quartermaster who watched the ribbons and medals pass him by.

He is one of the anonymous heroes in the Tomb of the Unknowns, whose presence at Arlington National Cemetery forever preserves the memory of all anonymous heroes whose valor died unrecognized on the battlefield or in the ocean's sunless deep.

He is the old guy bagging groceries at the supermarket, palsied and aggravatingly slow, who helped liberate a Nazi death camp and who wishes all day long that his wife were still alive to hold him when the nightmares come.

He (or she) is an ordinary, yet an extraordinary, human being — a person who sacrificed his life's most vital years in the service of his country and who sacrificed his ambitions so others would not have to sacrifice theirs.

He is a soldier and a savior and a sword against the darkness, and he is nothing more than the finest, greatest testimony on behalf of the finest, greatest nation ever known.

So remember, each time you see someone who has served our country, just lean over and say "Thank you." That's all most people need, and in most cases it will mean more than any medals they were awarded or could have been awarded.

Two little words that mean a lot, "Thank you."

Nov. 11 is Veterans Day.

Author unknown. Submitted by Dr. Fred-Otto Egeler, Public Affairs Officer of Los Angeles District, U.S. Army Corp of Engineers.

Source: www.hq.usace.army.mil/cepa/pubs/nov00/story5.htm

SUMMARY OF ALL VETERANS' BENEFITS — WHO IS ELIGIBLE?

You may be eligible for VA benefits if you are:

- A veteran

- A veteran's dependent

- A surviving spouse, child, or parent of a deceased veteran

- An active duty military service member

- A member of the Reserve or National Guard

CHAPTER 3

PREPARING TO DEPART THE MILITARY

At some point in every military member's career, he or she must transition from military to civilian life. This may be by one of the following methods: retirement, discharge/release from active duty (honorable, dishonorable, or general), medical retirement, medical discharge or disability, or some component of Reserves or National Guard members who are transitioning from active duty back to their active or inactive reserve status. In all cases, these individuals are veterans. However, the degree of benefits to which they may be entitled varies significantly. This chapter is specifically written for all military service members who are preparing to transition out of the military to civilian life in any of the above categories. I have chapters dedicated to providing detailed information on military retirement and medical retirement and medical discharge; however, all veterans must prepare to depart the military, regardless of the reason, circumstance, or type of discharge/retirement.

Departing the military, even with the peace of mind of having a retirement income to depend upon, is a stressful time for any veteran. Those who are departing the military due to a disability or combat-related injury face the biggest challenge, since they not only have to deal with the physical and mental challenges associated with their disability, but also do not receive a military retirement pension (unless they were retirement eligible) and must navigate the murky and confusing halls of the Veterans Administration for support, benefits, and treatment.

Transitioning from the military to civilian workforce is a tremendous challenge. Many military members have not held civilian jobs in years, many military skills do not easily transition to the civilian sector, and senior officers and enlisted military members may be junior to much younger individuals in the corporate environment. Even with military retirement, there is a definite drop in pay. Those who are simply leaving the military after serving their commitment will go from a steady paycheck to no paycheck from the military. Luckily, for all us in uniform, each service has a wealth of programs designed to assist military members with their transition to civilian life.

TRANSITION ASSISTANCE PROGRAM

All military branches have a transition program. This program was created under the Veterans Administration and is administered through all military services. All services offer transition programs, and although most are not mandated, I highly recommend you carve out the time to participate in the course. Here is a sample of what is covered:

The Transition Assistance Program (TAP) was created to help out departing military members prepare for and enter civilian life after their military service. TAP offers advice on finances, résumés, job search and placement, benefits during transition to civilian life, assistance, and related services.

TAP was created by law and is supported by the Departments of Defense, Veterans Affairs, Homeland Security, and the Department of Labor's Veterans' Employment and Training Service (VETS). The TAP program is designed for military service members within 180 days of separation or retirement.

TAP is designed to assist military service members and their spouses successfully make the transition from military service to the civilian workplace more easily, at less cost to both the military member and the government.

TAP is provided in three- to five-day sessions, held at military installations nationwide. Attendees learn about how to perform a job search, complete a résumé, and dress for success; career decision making; labor market conditions; and interview techniques. One of the most valuable things attendees receive is an honest appraisal of employability relative to the current job market and their skills so they may set realistic expectations for future employment. Of course, veterans' benefits are covered in detail. Here are some answers to frequently asked questions:

How do I get a quota for a TAP class?

This depends on the service you are in, but often TAP classes are announced routinely throughout the year and are easy to attend. Your family service center, command career counselors, servicing personnel office, or other administrative support units should have application information and procedures readily available for you. Federal law requires a pre-separation counseling interview for all officers and enlisted members no later than 90 days before separation or retirement.

How long before my end of obligated service (EAOS) should I sign up for TAP?

Title 10, United States Code states that for all anticipated retirements, pre-separation counseling will begin as soon as possible during the 24-month period preceding the anticipated retirement date. In the case of a separation other than a retirement, pre-separation counseling should begin as soon as possible during the 12-month period preceding the anticipated separation date. Ideally, the service member will attend the workshop no later than six to nine months before completion of the military obligation.

Do I have to attend the Transition Assistance Program?

TAP was established in November 1990 to comply with federal law, which requires all separating and retiring service members, both officer and enlisted, to have access to permanent transition assistance services. The U.S. Navy mandates attendance, as do some other services. Attendance is highly encouraged but optional for Coast Guard service members. Personnel should complete a TAP workshop no later than 90 days before separation/ retirement. The Marine Corps Separation and Retirement Manual stipulates that a retiring/separating Marine will attend the three-day TAP seminar. Spouses are encouraged to attend.

Where can I find information about TAP locations and class dates?

DOD has created a Web portal for military transitioners located at **http:// www.dodtransportal.dod.mil/dav/lsnmedia/LSN/dodtransportal/**. This site features a brief overview of the DOD Transition Assistance Program, locations and phone numbers of all transition assistance offices, and job search information and assistance.

The following Web sites provide information related to the Transition Assistance Program:

- **www.va.gov**

- **www.careermag.com:** Free résumé posting, job searches, career magazine articles

- **www.careerpath.com**: Free résumé posting, job searches, articles, interview questions and answers, salary wizard

- **www.monster.com**: Résumé center, free résumé posting, job searches

- **www.usajobs.opm.gov**: Official Federal Government job listings by the Office of Personnel Management

- **www1.va.gov/opa/vadocs/current_benefits.asp**: Federal Benefits for Veterans and Dependents

DISABLED TRANSITION ASSISTANCE PROGRAM

The Disabled Transition Assistance Program is provided to all military members determined to be disabled in any capacity. There are varying degrees of disability, which I will cover in depth later in this book. Disabled military members have additional entitlements and preferences that are not afforded to others. It is often complicated and confusing to determine entitlements; therefore, the Disabled Transition Assistance Program was created. DTAP was created for military members who may be released (or medically retired) because of a disability or who believe they have a disability qualifying them for VA's Vocational Rehabilitation and Employment Program (VR&E). DTAP assists eligible military members with decision making about the VA's Vocational Rehabilitation and Employment Program. Additionally, it is designed to expedite the delivery of vocational rehabilitation services by assisting veterans with the application process. Due to the complexity of the programs, DTAP may be offered by the Veterans Administration in the local area and not directly through the military service. In the past, sessions have been conducted extensively at veterans' or military hospitals.

Although challenging, most military members enjoy a successful transition into retirement, second careers, or future government service in the civilian government employee sector.

TRANSITION ASSISTANCE IN THE VA MILITARY SERVICES PROGRAM

Fact Sheet from the Department of Veterans Affairs — Operation Iraqi Freedom & Enduring Freedom

The Department of Veterans Affairs has a long history of special efforts to bring information on VA benefits and services to active duty military personnel.

These efforts include counseling about VA benefits through the Transition Assistance Program (TAP), a nationally coordinated federal effort to assist military men and women to ease the transition to civilian life through employment and job training assistance. A second component of the program, the Disabled Transition Assistance Program (DTAP), helps separating service members with disabilities.

VA also has launched special efforts to provide a seamless transition for those returning from service in Operations Iraqi Freedom and Enduring Freedom. Internal coordination was improved, and efforts currently focus on reducing red tape and streamlining access to all VA benefits. Each VA medical facility and benefits regional office has identified a point of contact to coordinate activities locally to help meet the needs of these returning combat service members and veterans. In addition, the VA increased the staffing of benefits counselors at key military hospitals where severely wounded service members from Iraq and Afghanistan are frequently sent. Further details about the initiatives for today's veterans of the war on terrorism are described at **www.seamlesstransition.va.gov/index.asp**, and general information for these newest veterans is available on a special VA Web page at **www.seamlesstransition.va.gov**.

Even before beginning the TAP pilot program, VA put a high priority on outreach to military members nearing separation from active duty. From its inception, VA has applied a broader definition to its military services outreach, called the VA Military Services Program. Although TAP and DTAP are the centerpieces, the broader definition encompasses pre-separation and retirement briefings, outreach to Reserve and National Guard units, and liaison and counseling services with various military post activities such as personal affairs, community affairs, and education offices.

The VA operates a longstanding Veterans Assistance at Discharge System from which all veterans recently separated or retired from active duty, including Reserve and National Guard members, receive a letter from the secretary of Veterans Affairs with information on VA benefits and services. Special mailings are also sent concerning VA education, the home loan guaranty, and insurance benefits.

The VA also operates a Benefits Delivery at Discharge program that assists service members at participating military bases with development of VA disability compensation claims before their discharge. This fosters continuity of care between the military and VA systems and speeds up the VA's processing of their application for compensation. The pre-discharge physical is conducted under VA disability examination protocols either by VA medical centers, contract medical examiners, or military personnel.

The Veterans' Benefits Amendments of 1989 provided for a three-year pilot program of transition assistance conducted jointly by the VA, the Department of Defense, and the Department of Labor (DOL). The TAP program provides separating service members employment assistance, job training assistance, and other transitional services, including counseling on VA benefits and services.

The DTAP program for disabled service members offers personalized vocational rehabilitation and employment assistance, and is located at major military medical centers where such separations occur, as well as at other military installations.

During fiscal year 2004, VA representatives conducted more than 7,000 briefings, which were attended by more than 261,000 active duty personnel and their families residing in the United States. Included were 1,400 briefings for more than 88,000 Reserve and National Guard members for whom VA provides pre- and post-deployment briefings. In fiscal year 2005 to date, the VA has conducted nearly 4,000 transition briefings attended by more than 157,000 participants in the United States. Nine hundred seventy-four of those briefings were for more than 68,000 Reserve and National Guard members.

The Army has implemented its own version of transition services, the Army Career and Alumni Program (ACAP). There are dozens of ACAP sites in the United States and overseas.

The U.S. Army Wounded Warrior Program assists severely wounded, ill, and injured soldiers and their families by providing support and advice during medical treatment, rehabilitation, and transition back into the Army or a civilian community. For more information on the Wounded Warrior Program, visit **www.aw2.army.mil**.

The VA's goal for TAP services is to ensure that service members are aware of their VA benefits and to provide assistance as needed. For those leaving active duty due to medical problems, the outreach effort is intensified to ensure a full understanding of the VA compensation process and Vocational Rehabilitation and Employment Program.

TAP participation is voluntary and consists of three- to five-day seminars conducted by the VA, DOD, and DOL at military installations for personnel within one year of separation or two years of retirement. It provides a number of services to assist military personnel in making a smooth transition to civilian life, including employment assistance, such as résumé writing and skills marketing and job referral.

In addition, VA military services coordinators (MSCs) are in place at each VA regional office. Some coordinators are placed near large military populations, and some are based on military installations. Some of them work full-time on military coordinating duties.

MSCs and other VA benefits counselors participate in TAP and DTAP seminars and conduct personal interviews. They also conduct benefit briefings at other military pre-separation and retirement programs, and are involved in outreach to members of Reserve and National Guard units. The MSCs and counselors work directly with offices on military installations and provide education, medical, family and personal counseling, and casualty assistance. Returning Reserve and National Guard members also can elect to attend a formal TAP workshop and DTAP.

Concerned that military personnel overseas have less access to information about veterans' benefits than their stateside counterparts, the VA and DOD began in 1992 to provide briefings to personnel stationed in Europe, the Far East, Panama, and Guantanamo Bay, Cuba. In the years that followed, VA transition activities in Europe were expanded, as were visits to the Far East. The VA currently has counselors assigned in Germany, England, Italy, Korea, and Japan. A circuit-traveling service provides periodic briefings in Spain, Iceland, the Azores, and Guantanamo Bay.

In addition to the transition briefings conducted in the United States, in fiscal year 2004 the VA conducted 625 overseas transition briefings for more than 15,180 service members. To date this fiscal year, the VA has conducted 232 overseas transition briefings for more than 5,600 service members. VA and DOL staff conducted TAP briefings on board the USS Constellation, USS Enterprise, and USS George Washington on their return to the United States from extended deployments. VA expects to continue to support additional requests from the Navy for TAP briefings onboard ships.

This joint VA-DOD initiative is helping service members file for and receive service-connected disability compensation benefits more quickly than in the past. The VA, on average, adjudicates these claims within 60 to 70 days of discharge by examining service members under VA protocols as part of the discharge process. By comparison, VA's national average processing time is about 170 days for claims requiring a disability rating.

In the Benefits Delivery at Discharge program, the medical information needed to begin the VA file carries over from the DOD to VA seamlessly. In addition, if a service member is found to be disabled, additional applicable vocational rehabilitation and employment services may be initiated in a timely manner. This expedited BDD process is used by service members applying for benefits within 180 days of discharge.

Currently, 140 military installations worldwide participate in this program, including sites in Germany and in Korea. In fiscal year 2003, the VA processed just under 26,000 BDD claims and in fiscal year 2004, the VA processed 39,000 claims under the program.

VA SERVICES FOR RETURNING COMBAT VETERANS OF OPERATION IRAQI FREEDOM AND OPERATION ENDURING FREEDOM

The Department of Veterans Affairs has developed special programs to serve the nation's newest veterans — the men and women who served in Iraq and Afghanistan — by assisting them with a smooth transition from active duty to civilian life. The VA's goal is to ensure that every seriously injured or ill serviceman and woman returning from combat receives easy access to benefits and world-class service. Combat veterans have special healthcare eligibility. Their contact with the VA often begins with priority scheduling for care and, for the most seriously wounded, VA counselors visiting their bedside in military wards before separation to ensure their VA disability payment coverage will be ready the moment they leave active duty. Through enhanced programs and new policies, the VA is striving to ensure it holds open doors to a seamless transition from soldier to citizen.

For two years after discharge, these veterans have special access to VA healthcare, even those who have no service-connected illness. Veterans can become "grandfathered" for future access by enrolling with VA during this period. This covers not only regular active-duty personnel who served in Iraq or Afghanistan, but also Reserve or National Guard members serving in the combat theaters. Veterans with service-related injuries or illnesses always have access to VA care for the treatment of their disabilities without any time limit, as do lower-income veterans. Hospital care, outpatient treatment, and nursing home services are offered at 1,400 locations. Additional information about VA medical eligibility is available at **www. va.gov/healtheligibility**.

The VA's broad range of benefits includes disability compensation and pension, vocational rehabilitation and employment, education and training, home loan guarantees, automobile and specially adaptive equipment grants, home modification programs for the disabled, life insurance and traumatic injury protection, and survivor benefits. Information on these programs is available at **www.vba.va.gov/benefit_facts/index.htm**.

The VA launched an ambitious outreach initiative to ensure separating combat veterans know about VA benefits and programs available to them, including compensation for service-related disabilities. Each veteran with service in Iraq or Afghanistan receives a letter from the secretary of Veterans Affairs introducing the veteran to the VA and its benefits and providing phone numbers and Web sites for more information.

As with all military members, transition briefings before discharge also acquaint them with benefits, as do additional pamphlet mailings following separation. Brochures, wallet cards, and videos have been produced, and briefings are being conducted at town hall meetings and family readiness groups and during unit drills near the homes of returning National Guard members and reservists. Because of the large number of reservists and National Guard members mobilized in this conflict, the VA has made a special effort to work with their units to reach transitioning service members at demobilization sites and has trained recently returned veterans to serve as National Guard Bureau liaisons in every state to assist their fellow combat veterans.

Suicide Prevention Lifeline

The National Suicide Prevention Lifeline has been enhanced to provide a new service for veterans in crisis. Call 1-800-273-TALK (8255) and press 1 to be connected immediately to VA suicide prevention and mental health service professionals.

Seamless Transition Liaisons for the Severely Wounded

In an effort to assist wounded military members and their families, the VA has placed workers at key military hospitals where severely injured service members from Iraq and Afghanistan are frequently sent. These include benefit counselors who help the service member obtain VA services and social workers who facilitate healthcare coordination and discharge as well as planning a service member's transition from military to VA care. Under this program, VA staff members serve at Walter Reed Army Medical Center in Washington, D.C.; National Naval Medical Center in Bethesda, Maryland; Eisenhower Army Medical Center at Ft. Gordon, Georgia; Brooke Army Medical Center at Ft. Sam Houston, Texas; Madigan Army Medical Center at Tacoma, Washington; Darnall Army Medical Center at Ft. Hood, Texas; Evans Army Hospital at Ft. Carson, Colorado; and Camp Pendleton Naval Medical Center in San Diego, California.

The VA and the Department of Defense have improved collaboration and communication. VA employees based at military treatment facilities brief service members about VA health benefits, disability compensation, vocational rehabilitation, and employment. Coordinators at each VA benefits regional office and VA medical center work with VA counselors and military discharge staff to ensure a smooth transition to VA services at locations nearest to the veteran's residence after discharge. At the VA facilities serving the veteran's hometown, the hospital is alerted when the seriously wounded service member is being discharged so that the continuity of his or her medications and therapy is ensured when he or she arrives home.

Patterns of disease shown in diagnoses of recent combat veterans who have come to the VA for care have not suggested significant differences from the types of primary care, chronic conditions, or mental health issues seen in earlier combat veterans. However, careful studies will be required to draw appropriate comparisons using control groups of similar veterans, representative samplings, and other scientific methods. An early neurological study tested 654 Army veterans before deployment to Iraq in 2003 and again after returning in 2005, finding mild impairments in memory and attention lapses but significantly faster reaction times when compared to other veterans not deployed to the theater. These warrant further investigation. The VA also will analyze combat veterans' deaths from diseases in hopes of publishing mortality studies in the future.

Nationally automated data from the VA's payment system for service-connected diseases and disabilities does not distinguish between combat-related injuries and those incurred or worsened while the service member was in non-hostile locations. Some of the most common service-connected conditions among those who served at some point in the Iraq and Afghanistan theaters include musculoskeletal conditions and hearing disorders.

Improvised explosive devices and rocket-propelled grenades often result in devastating injuries, including amputations, sensory loss, and brain injury. Modern body armor and advances in front-line trauma care have enabled combat veterans to survive severe attacks that in prior wars were fatal. In response to the demand for specialized services, the VA expanded its four traumatic brain injury centers in Minneapolis, Palo Alto, Richmond, and Tampa to become polytrauma centers encompassing additional specialties to treat patients for multiple complex injuries. This is being expanded into a network of 21 polytrauma network sites and polytrauma clinic support teams around the country, providing state-of-the-art treatment closer to injured veterans' homes.

These centers treat traumatic brain injury alone or in combination with amputation, blindness, or other visual impairment, complex orthopedic injuries, auditory and vestibular disorders, and mental health concerns. The VA has added clinical expertise to address the special problems that the multi-trauma combat injured patient may face. This can include intensive psychological support treatment for both patient and family, intensive case management, improvements in the treatment of vision problems, and rehabilitation using the latest high-tech specialty prostheses. Polytrauma teams bring together experts to provide innovative, personalized treatment to help the injured service member or veteran achieve optimal function and independence.

Because brain injury is being recognized as the signature injury of the current conflict, the VA launched an educational initiative to provide its clinicians a broad base of knowledge with which to identify potential traumatic brain injury patients, mechanisms for effective care, and a better understanding of patients who experience this condition. The VA has made training mandatory for physicians and other key staff in primary care, mental health, and rehabilitation programs.

About one-third of these combat veterans who seek care from the VA have a possible diagnosis of a mental disorder, and the VA has significantly expanded its counseling and mental health services. The VA has launched new programs, including dozens of new mental health teams based in VA medical centers, focused on early identification and management of stress-related disorders and the recruitment of about 100 combat veterans in its Readjustment Counseling Service to provide briefings to transitioning servicemen and women regarding military-related readjustment needs.

Many of the challenges facing soldiers returning from Afghanistan and Iraq are stressors that have been identified and studied in veterans of previous wars. The VA has developed world-class expertise in treating chronic mental health problems, including posttraumatic stress disorder (PTSD).

Posttraumatic stress involves a normal set of reactions to a trauma such as war. Sometimes it becomes a disorder with the passage of time when feelings or issues related to the trauma are not dealt with and are suppressed by the individual. This can result in problems readjusting to community life following the trauma. Since the war began, the VA has activated dozens of new PTSD programs around the country to assist veterans in dealing with the emotional toll of combat. In addition, 207 readjustment counseling vet centers provide easy access in consumer-friendly facilities apart from traditional VA medical centers.

One early scientific study indicated the estimated risk for PTSD from service in the Iraq war was 18 percent, while the estimated risk for PTSD from the Afghanistan mission was 11 percent. Data from multiple sources now indicate that about 10 to 15 percent of soldiers develop PTSD after deployment to Iraq and another 10 percent have significant symptoms of PTSD, depression, or anxiety and may benefit from care. Alcohol misuse and relationship problems add to these rates. Combat veterans are at higher risk for psychiatric problems than military personnel serving in noncombat locations, and more frequent and more intensive combat is associated with higher risk. With military pre- and post-deployment health assessment programs seeking to destigmatize mental health treatment, coupled with simplified access to VA care for combat veterans after discharge, experts believe initial high rates likely will decrease.

Studies of PTSD patients have suggested as many as half may enjoy complete remission, and most of the remainder will improve. Research has led to scientifically developed treatment guidelines covering a variety of modern therapies with which clinicians have had success. Treatments range from psychological first aid to cognitive behavioral therapy. Psychopharmacology may include drugs such as Zoloft or Paxil — with newer drugs under studies now in progress. More information about VA's PTSD programs is available at **www.ncptsd.va.gov**.

CHECKLIST OF ITEMS TO COMPLETE BEFORE YOU DEPART THE MILITARY

This can grow to be an exhaustive list, and your military service transition staff will walk you through the entire process; however, here are some key items to consider:

    Travel: You are entitled to travel expenses from your last permanent duty station to your place of retirement or home of record. The personnel office will instruct you on your entitlements. Note that you are not entitled to Dislocation Allowance upon discharge or retirement.

Household goods shipment: You are entitled to a HHG shipment from your last permanent duty station to your place of retirement or home of record. The transportation staff will assist you. Note that currently, all HHG shipments are automatically insured at full replacement value. The Defense Department began full replacement value coverage October 1, 2007, on international shipments and November 1, 2007, on domestic shipments. Congress mandated that the coverage be fully in place by March 1, 2008. Previously, troops could be reimbursed at a rate of $1.25 multiplied by the weight of their shipment, up to $40,000 — and the government paid for depreciated replacement cost, not full replacement value. Now, moving companies can be liable for up to $5,000 per shipment, or $4 multiplied by the net weight of the shipment in pounds, up to $50,000, whichever is greater. Weight does not become a factor until a shipment goes over the $5,000 threshold.

Final pay/pay: Your personnel office will have computed your final pay and/or retirement pay benefits. Keep your current direct deposit accounts open until your transition pay/retirement pay is processed. Shifting banks during retirement is often problematic when it comes to getting your pay and travel in a timely manner.

Health insurance: This is covered in depth later in this book; however, you should have been counseled on your entitlements.

Physical: You must have a physical before discharge or retirement. This is your last chance to document any ailments, injuries, chronic pain, problems, or illnesses before you depart active duty. You are highly recommended to document everything while on active duty, as it is much more difficult to connect service-related injuries/disabilities after you depart the military without any significant documentation in your active duty health record.

Document everything, and get a complete copy of your health record before you depart the service.

8 **Healthcare from the VA**: The previous chapter outlined eligibility, and I will provide in-depth information on VA healthcare later in this book.

8 **Dental Care**: This is an area that leaves quite a bit to be desired. Even the Retiree Dental Plan is not great. Often, you are eligible for one dental exam and treatment in a VA dental facility. To obtain this, you must apply within 90 days of your discharge date, and the actual treatment must be completed within 180 days from your discharge date.

8 **Terminal leave and administrative absence**: Retirement is the only time officers can sell leave; however, all service members may take terminal leave (at command discretion) when departing the military. You are also authorized (with command approval) up to 21 days of administrative absence in connection with retirement. This is subject to rules, which differ by each military service, and is designed to give you additional time to transition to civilian life. You will need to determine and calculate the benefits of selling leave versus terminal leave (or a combination of both).

8 **Permissive orders**: Most services allow for up to five days of permissive orders for house or job seeking. This is not allowed in conjunction with administrative absence, travel, or terminal leave and is entirely at the expense of the service member.

This is a short list of some of the main issues you will need to understand before you depart the military. There are obviously many more. All should be thoroughly presented, discussed, and understood by you from your transition and personnel/administration staff.

VETERANS' PREFERENCE

Many of us will be entering the civilian workforce and/or applying for government civil service positions. It is important that you understand what your veterans' preferences are before you begin the process of job-hunting. Veterans' preference can improve your odds of competing for jobs, particularly civil service positions.

Why Preference Is Given

Since the time of the Civil War, veterans of the armed forces have been given some degree of preference in appointments to federal jobs. Recognizing their sacrifice, Congress enacted laws to prevent veterans seeking federal employment from being penalized for their time in military service. Veterans' preference recognizes the economic loss suffered by citizens who have served their country in uniform, restores veterans to a favorable competitive position for government employment, and acknowledges the larger obligation owed to disabled veterans.

Veterans' preference in its present form comes from the Veterans' Preference Act of 1944, as amended, and is codified in various provisions of Title 5, United States Code. By law, veterans who are disabled or who served on active duty in the armed forces during certain specified time periods or in military campaigns are entitled to preference over others in hiring from competitive lists of eligibles and in retention during reductions in force.

In addition to receiving preference in competitive appointments, veterans may be considered for special noncompetitive appointments for which only they are eligible.

When Preference Applies

Preference in hiring applies to permanent and temporary positions in the competitive and excepted services of the executive branch. Preference does not apply to positions in the Senior Executive Service or to executive branch positions for which Senate confirmation is required. The legislative and judicial branches of the federal government also are exempt from the Veterans' Preference Act unless the positions are in the competitive service (Government Printing Office, for example) or have been made subject to the Act by another law.

Preference applies in hiring from civil service examinations conducted by the Office of Personnel Management (OPM) and agencies under delegated examining authority for most excepted service jobs including Veterans Recruitment Appointments (VRA) and when agencies make temporary, term, and overseas limited appointments. Veterans' preference does not apply to promotion, reassignment, change to lower grade, transfer, or reinstatement.

Veterans' preference does not require an agency to use any particular appointment process. Agencies have broad authority under law to hire from any appropriate source of eligibles, including special appointing authorities. An agency may consider candidates already in civil service from an agency-developed merit promotion list, or it may reassign a current employee, transfer an employee from another agency, or reinstate a former federal employee. In addition, agencies are required to give priority to displaced employees before using civil service examinations and similar hiring methods.

Civil service examination: Title 5, United States Code (U.S.C.) 3304-3330, Title 5 Code of Federal Regulations (CFR) Part 332, OPM Delegation Agreements with individual agencies, OPM Examining Handbook, OPM Delegated Examining Operations Handbook; Excepted service appointments, including VRAs: 5 U.S.C. 3320; 5 CFR Part 302; Temporary and term employment: 5 CFR Parts 316 and 333; Overseas limited employment: 5 CFR Part 301; Career Transition Program: 5 CFR Part 330, Subparts F and G.

Types of Preference

(Note: The National Defense Authorization Act for fiscal year 2006 clarified the scope of the term "veteran" for the purposes of determining who is entitled to veterans' preference. OPM is in the process of revising its regulations to conform to this clarification. In the interim, agencies should rely upon the statute and this guidance in determining who is entitled to veterans' preference.)

To receive preference, a veteran must have been discharged or released from active duty in the armed forces under honorable conditions (such as with an honorable or general discharge). As defined in 5 U.S.C. 2101(2), armed forces means the Army, Navy, Air Force, Marine Corps, and Coast Guard. The veteran must also be eligible under a preference category below (also shown on the Standard Form [SF] 50, Notification of Personnel Action).

Military retirees at the rank of major, lieutenant commander, or higher are not eligible for preference in appointment unless they are disabled veterans. (This does not apply to reservists who will not begin drawing military retired pay until age 60.)

For nondisabled users, active duty for training by National Guard or Reserve soldiers does not qualify as active duty for preference. For disabled veterans, active duty includes training service in the Reserves or National Guard, per the Merit Systems Protection Board decision in Hesse v. Department of the Army, 104 M.S.P.R.647(2007).

For purposes of this chapter and 5 U.S.C. 2108, war means only those armed conflicts declared by Congress as war and includes World War II, which covers the period from December 7, 1941, to April 28, 1952.

When applying for federal jobs, eligible veterans should claim preference on their application or résumé. Applicants claiming 10 point preference must complete Standard Form (SF) 15, Application for 10-Point Veteran Preference, and submit the requested documentation.

The following preference categories and points are based on 5 U.S.C. 2108 and 3309 as modified by a length of service requirement in 38 U.S.C. 5303A(d). (The letters following each category, such as "TP," are a shorthand reference used by OPM in competitive examinations.)

Five-Point Preference (TP)

Five points are added to the passing examination score or rating of a veteran who served:

- During a war

- During the period of April 28, 1952, through July 1, 1955

- For more than 180 consecutive days, other than for training, any part of which occurred after January 31, 1955, and before October 15, 1976

- During the Gulf War from August 2, 1990, through January 2, 1992

- For more than 180 consecutive days, other than for training, any part of which occurred beginning September 11, 2001, and ending on the date prescribed by presidential proclamation or by law as the last day of Operation Iraqi Freedom

- In a campaign or expedition for which a campaign medal has been authorized. Any Armed Forces Expeditionary medal or campaign badge, including El Salvador, Lebanon, Grenada, Panama, Southwest Asia, Somalia, and Haiti, qualifies for preference

A campaign medal holder or Gulf War veteran who originally enlisted after September 7, 1980, (or began active duty on or after October 14, 1982, and has not previously completed 24 months of continuous active duty) must have served continuously for 24 months or the full period called or ordered to active duty. The 24-month service requirement does not apply to 10-point preference eligibles separated for disability incurred or aggravated in the line of duty or to veterans separated for hardship or other reasons under 10 U.S.C. 1171 or 1173.

A Word About Gulf War Preference

The Defense Authorization Act of Fiscal Year 1998 (Public Law 105-85) of November 18, 1997, contains a provision (section 1102 of Title XI) that accords veterans' preference to everyone who served on active duty during the period beginning August 2, 1990, and ending January 2, 1992, provided, of course, the veteran is otherwise eligible.

This means that anyone who served on active duty during the Gulf War, regardless of where or for how long, is entitled to preference if otherwise eligible (such as separated under honorable conditions and served continuously for a minimum of 24 months or the full period for which called or ordered to active duty). This applies not only to candidates seeking employment, but also to federal employees who may be affected by reduction in force.

Questions and Answers About Gulf War Preference

Public Law 105-85 of November 18, 1997, contains a provision (section 1102 of Title XI) that accords veterans' preference to anyone who served on active duty, anywhere in the world, for any length of time between August 2, 1990, and January 2, 1992, provided the person is otherwise eligible. What does "otherwise eligible" mean, here?

It means the person must have been separated from the service under honorable conditions and have served continuously for a minimum of 24 months or the full period for which called or ordered to active duty. For example, someone who enlisted in the Army and was serving on active duty when the Gulf War broke out on August 2, 1990, would have to complete a minimum of 24 months service to be eligible for preference. A reservist who was called to active duty for a month and spent all his time at the Pentagon before being released would also be eligible. What the law did was to add an additional paragraph (C) covering Gulf War veterans to 5 U.S.C. 2108(1) (on who is eligible for preference). But, significantly, the law made no other changes to existing law. In particular, it did not change paragraph (4) of section 2108 (the Dual Compensation Act of 1973), which severely restricts preference entitlement for retired officers at the rank of Major and above. When the Dual Compensation Act was under consideration, there was extensive debate in Congress as to who should be entitled to preference. Congress basically compromised by giving preference in appointment to most retired military members (except for high-ranking officers who were not considered to need it), but severely limiting preference in Reduction In Force (RIF) for all retired military because they had already served one career and should not have preference in the event of layoffs.

So, otherwise eligible means that the individual must be eligible under existing law.

Which provision of the new law contains the 24-month service requirement for regular military service members on active duty as opposed to reservists who are called or ordered to active duty?

The 24-month service requirement provision is found in Section 5303A of Title 38, United States Code, which defines the minimum active-duty service requirement for those who initially enter active duty after the date of September 7, 1980.

Can an applicant claim preference based on Gulf War service after January 2, 1992?

The law specifies that only those on active duty during the period beginning August 2, 1990, and ending January 2, 1992, are eligible for preference. Applicants who served on active duty exclusively after these dates would have to be in receipt of a campaign badge or expeditionary medal.

Are there any plans to extend veterans' preference to any other groups of individuals who served on active duty during times of conflict that may not have served in specific theaters of operation?

We are not aware of any plans to extend veterans' preference to any other group of individuals.

An applicant is claiming preference based on service in Bosnia, but has no DD Form 214 to support this claim. Can we give him/her preference?

A service member whose record appears to show service qualifying for veterans' preference (for example, there is an indication that the person served in Bosnia in 1996), may be accorded five points tentative preference on that basis alone. However, before the person can be appointed, he or she must submit proof of entitlement to preference. That proof may be an amended DD Form 214 showing the award of the Armed Forces Expeditionary Medal (AFEM) for Bosnia in the case of service members who served there and were released before enactment of the recent veterans' preference amendments, or it may be other official documentation showing award of the Armed Forces Expeditionary Medal.

How are we to know that a reservist was (a) called to active duty, and (b) served the full period for which called? Do not some reservists just receive a letter telling them they are being placed on active duty?

A reservist will always have orders placing him (or her) on active duty — it is the only way the reservist can be paid. Although the individual may also have a letter saying that he or she is being called up, there will always be orders backing this up. Similarly, when the reservist is released from active duty, he or she will always have separation or demobilization orders.

Several employees have come to the agency personnel office claiming they should have preference under the new law, but they have no proof of service during the specified period. We are getting ready to issue Reduction In Force notices. Should we take the employees' word for it, or wait until they have proof?

The employees cannot be given veterans' preference without required documentation. The agency should work with the employee and the appropriate military service record organizations to obtain this documentation as soon as possible to avoid having to rerun the Reduction In Force at the last minute.

If our agency has "frozen" personnel actions and issued Reduction In Force notices but the Reduction In Force effective date has not arrived, how can we account for changes in veterans' preference status?

Regardless of where you are in the process of carrying out the Reduction In Force, you must correct the veterans' preference of employees who will now be eligible as a result of the statute. Veterans' preference cannot be "frozen" like qualifications or performance appraisals — it must be corrected right up until the day of the Reduction In Force. If a change in preference results in a different outcome for one or more employees, amended Reduction In Force notices must be issued. If such a change results in a worse offer, the affected employee must be given a full 60/120-day notice period required by regulation. This may require the agency to use a temporary exception to keep one or more employees on the rolls past the Reduction In Force effective date to meet this obligation.

What if an employee would have been registered as an I-A on the agency's Reemployment Priority List due to the new law but has been listed as a I-B? What is the agency's obligation to make up for any lost consideration as a result?

The employee's registration status on the Reemployment Priority List should be corrected immediately so that the employee will be considered as an I-A for the remainder of his or her time on the Reemployment Priority List. If the agency finds that a lower-standing person was selected over the employee, the agency must notify the employee of the selection and a right to appeal to Merit Systems Protection Board. If the employee files an Reemployment Priority List appeal, Merit Systems Protection Board may order a retroactive remedy that could include extending the employee's time period for consideration under the Reemployment Priority List.

Ten-Point Compensable Disability Preference (CP)

Ten points are added to the passing examination score or rating of a veteran who served at any time and who has a compensable service-connected disability rating of at least 10 percent but less than 30 percent.

Ten-Point 30 Percent Compensable Disability Preference (CPS)

Ten points are added to the passing civil service examination score or rating of a veteran who served at any time and who has a compensable service-connected disability rating of 30 percent or more.

Ten-Point Disability Preference (XP)

Ten points are added to the passing examination score or rating of:

- A veteran who served at any time and has a present service-connected disability or is receiving compensation, disability retirement benefits, or pension from the military or the Department of Veterans Affairs but does not qualify as a CP or CPS

- A veteran who received a Purple Heart

Ten-Point Derived Preference (XP)

Ten points are added to the passing examination score or rating of spouses, widows, widowers, or mothers of veterans as described below. This type of preference may be referred to as derived preference because it is based on service of a veteran who is not able to use the preference.

Both a mother and a spouse (including widow or widower) may be entitled to preference on the basis of the same veteran's service if they both meet the requirements. However, neither may receive preference if the veteran is living and is qualified for federal employment.

Spouse

Ten points are added to the passing examination score or rating of the spouse of a disabled veteran, disqualified for a federal position along the general lines of usual occupation because of a service-connected disability. Such disqualification is presumed when the veteran is unemployed and:

- Is rated by appropriate military or Department of Veterans Affairs authorities to be 100 percent disabled and/or unemployable.

- Has retired, been separated, or resigned from a civil service position on the basis of a disability that is service-connected in origin.

- Has attempted to obtain a civil service position or other position along the lines of his or her usual occupation and has failed to qualify because of a service-connected disability.

Preference may be allowed in other circumstances, but anything less than the above warrants a more careful analysis.

(Note: Veterans' preference for spouses is different than the preference the Department of Defense is required by law to extend to spouses of active duty members in filling its civilian positions. For more information on that program, contact the Department of Defense.)

Widow/Widower

Ten points are added to the passing examination score or rating of the widow or widower of a veteran who was not divorced from the veteran, has not remarried, or the remarriage was annulled, and the veteran either:

- Served during a war or during the period April 28, 1952, through July 1, 1955, or in a campaign or expedition for which a campaign medal has been authorized

- Died while on active duty that included service described immediately above under conditions that would not have been the basis for other than an honorable or general discharge

Mother of a Deceased Veteran

Ten points are added to the passing examination score or rating of the mother of a veteran who died under honorable conditions while on active duty during a war or during the period of April 28, 1952, through July 1, 1955, or in a campaign or expedition for which a campaign medal has been authorized; and

- She is or was married to the father of the veteran.

- She lives with her totally and permanently disabled husband (either the veteran's father or her husband through remarriage).

- She is widowed, divorced, or separated from the veteran's father and has not remarried.

꙰ She remarried but is widowed, divorced, or legally separated from her husband when she claims preference.

Mother of a Disabled Veteran

Ten points are added to the passing examination score or rating of a mother of a living disabled veteran if the veteran was separated with an honorable or general discharge from active duty, including training service in the Reserves or National Guard; performed at any time; and is permanently and totally disabled from a service-connected injury or illness; and the mother:

꙰ Is or was married to the father of the veteran

꙰ Lives with her totally and permanently disabled husband (either the veteran's father or her husband through remarriage)

꙰ Is widowed, divorced, or separated from the veteran's father and has not remarried

꙰ Remarried but is widowed, divorced, or legally separated from her husband when she claims preference

(Note: Preference is not given to widows or mothers of deceased veterans who qualify for preference under 5 U.S.C. 2108 (1) (B), (C) or (2). Thus, the widow or mother of a deceased disabled veteran who served after 1955 but did not serve in a war, campaign, or expedition, would not be entitled to preference.)

THE "RULE OF THREE" AND VETERAN PASSOVERS

Selection must be made from the highest three eligibles on the certificate who are available for the job — the "rule of three." However, an agency may not pass over a preference eligible applicant to select a lower-ranking nonpreference eligible applicant or nonpreference eligible applicant with the same or lower score.

ADDITIONAL RESOURCES

- Combat veterans' information: **www.va.gov/Environagents/page.cfm?pg=16**

- Survivors' benefits: **www.vba.va.gov/survivors/index.htm**

- Women veterans' information: **www.vba.va.gov/bln/21/Topics/Women**

- The United States Department of Labor has an outstanding reference guide of information and Web links of veterans guides and training services located at: **www.youth2work.gov**

MILITARY RETIREMENT

One of the biggest incentives to join the military is its robust retirement benefit. You are eligible for retirement after just 20 years of service, meaning an individual who signs up at 18 can retire at only age 38. There are several retirement plans determined by the date you entered active duty service. For information on medical retirement and discharges, see the next chapter.

How you request your retirement is based on service-specific policy, but often, retirement requests may be submitted any time a member is retirement eligible and often no more than one year in advance, nor less than six months in advance of the requested retirement date. Once approved by your service, you are issued retirement "orders" that contain the accounting information, retirement date, and specific instructions to prepare for your retirement. Let us look at some of the items you will have to consider and complete:

- **Counseling**: Before your retirement, it is important that you participate in briefings, counseling sessions, administrative guidance, and of course attend a Transition Assistance Program (TAP). The decisions you make at the time of retirement directly affect your entitlements, benefits, and the amount of your pay and survivor benefits. You will find some decisions, once made, are impossible to change, so give careful thought and consideration to this and take the time to discuss your options with family.

Documentation: The following documents/events form the basis for the establishment of your retired account and are to be completed as part of your pre-retirement preparation. This is, of course, service specific, and your branch of service may have slightly different forms and/or procedures:

- **Data for Payment of Retired Personnel (DD 2656)**: This form is available in your disbursing office (Navy), Military Personnel Flight (Air Force), your installation's RSO (Army), or sent to Marines and Coast Guard with your retirement orders. It requires you to provide the Defense Financial Accounting Service (DFAS) with dependency information, your Survivor Benefit Plan (SBP) election, beneficiary information to whom unpaid retired pay will be paid at the time of your death, and withholding information for federal and state tax purposes. All this information is used to build your retired pay account. Please note that the DOD uses the DFAS for retired pay, while the Coast Guard uses the Department of Agriculture's Finance Center.

- **SBP Election Statement for Former Spouse Coverage (DD 2656-1)**: In addition to the DD 2656, if you elect some type of Former Spouse SBP coverage, you must also complete a DD 2656-1.

- **Allotment Authorization**: You can start, stop, or change current allotments by requesting action by the office that takes care of your active duty pay account. Ensure that your allotment total will not exceed your retirement pay. All necessary adjustments to your allotments should be made at least 30 days before retirement.

The following allotments cannot be carried forward to your retired accounts: charity allotments, except contribution to Navy/Marine Corps Relief Society, Army Emergency Relief, or Air Force Assistance Fund, and Education allotments.

The following allotments may be carried forward to your retired pay account if at least one month's payment was made while on active duty (this may differ for the Coast Guard): loan repayment to Red Cross, saving allotment, home loans, U.S. saving bonds, dependency allotment (to spouse, former spouse[s], children, grandmother, and/or anyone having a permanent residence other than your own), National Service Life Insurance, Commercial Life Insurance, Navy/Marine Corp Mutual Aid Insurance, repayment of a debt to a federal agency and tax levy assignment to the Internal Revenue Service (IRS), charitable contributions to Navy/ Marine Corps Relief Society, Army Emergency Relief, Air Force Assistance Fund, Coast Guard Mutual Assistance, repayment of loan to Navy Relief Society, Army Emergency Relief, Air Force Aid Society or Coast Guard Mutual Assistance, Veterans Group Life Insurance, and the TRICARE Retired Dental Program.

The following is information for starting/changing allotments after your retirement:

- The dollar amount of allotment may not exceed your gross retired pay less deduction for SBP, federal withholding tax, and any other deduction.

- Your net retired/retainer pay should be sent to your financial institution by direct deposit unless you reside in a foreign country in which direct deposit is not available. Your retired pay will be deposited to your account on the first business day of the month following the end of the month. Direct deposit enables your payment to be deposited directly to the bank, saving and loan association, or credit union of your choice. Direct deposit has the following advantages:

  - It eliminates the possibility of your check being lost, stolen, forged, or destroyed in delivery. Treasury Department statistics show that more than one million checks are either lost or stolen each year.

  - It eliminates the inconvenience of cashing and depositing your check, and it assures deposit of your pay on the first business day of the month following the month for which payment is due and assures delivery, deposit, and availability of your pay while you travel.

HOW RETIREMENT PAY IS CALCULATED

Navy and Marine Corps members are considered to be a retired member for classification purposes if you are an enlisted member with more than 30 years of service or a warrant or commissioned officer. Enlisted Navy and Marine Corps members with less than 30 years of service are transferred to the Fleet Reserve/Fleet Marine Corps Reserve, and their pay is referred to as retainer pay. Air Force, Army, and Coast Guard members with more than 20 years of service are all classified as retired. When a Navy or Marine Corps member completes 30 years, including time on the retired rolls in receipt of retainer pay, the Fleet Reserve status is changed to retired status. Retired pay amounts are determined by multiplying your service factor (normally referred to as your multiplier) by your active duty base pay at the time of retirement). By law, the gross retired pay must be rounded down to a whole dollar amount.

(1) **Service Factor (Multiple)**: If you are a retiree with 30 or more years of service, your multiple is 75 percent. If you are a retiree/Fleet reservist with less than 30 years, this factor is determined by taking 2.5 percent times your years of service. Years of service include credit for each full month of service as one-twelfth of a year. Years of service for officers includes all active service, periods of inactive reserve service before June 1, 1958, ROTC active duty time before October 13, 1964, constructive service credit for Medical and Dental Corps, and drills performed while in the inactive reserve after May 31, 1958. Years of service for Fleet reservists and all other enlisted retirements include all active service, active duty for training performed after August 9, 1956, and any constructive service earned for a minority or short-term enlistment completed before December 31, 1977, and drills performed while in the Active Reserves.

(2) **Base Pay at Time of Retirement**: If you entered the service before September 8, 1980, your base pay for retirement is the same as your last

active duty pay. (Your allowances are not considered.) An example of this type of retired pay calculation is as follows:

- A Navy or Marine E-8 is transferring to Fleet Reserve on July 31, 2000, with 22 years, 8 months service

- 2.5 percent x 22.67 years = 56.68 percent

- 56.68 percent x $3,161.10 (July 1, 2000, active duty rate for an E-8 over 22 years) = $1,791.71 or $1,791

For those who entered the armed forces on or after September 8, 1980, the base pay is the average of the highest 36 months of active duty base pay received. The base pay for members having less than three years service is the average monthly active duty basic pay during their period of service. For certain retirees who entered the armed forces on or after September 8, 1980, the initial cost-of-living adjustment (COLA) is reduced.

For those who entered the armed forces on or after August 1, 1986, the base pay is computed in the same way as it is computed for retirees identified in section (2) above. However, there are differences in how cost-of-living adjustments are computed.

Tower Amendment: In addition to the computation explained previously, your pay will be computed according to provisions of the Tower Amendment if it applies to your situation. The Tower Amendment was enacted to ensure that you will not receive a lesser amount of retired pay than you would have received if you had retired on a prior date. The Tower eligibility date may be the day before the effective date of an active duty pay increase. Tower pay is computed by using the active duty pay rates in effect on that date, your rank/rate on that date, total service accumulated on that date, and all applicable cost-of-living increases.

(1) Using the previous example, the member was an E-8 and had 22 years, 1 month, service on December 31, 1999. The member's pay would be computed as follows:

- 2.5 percent x 22.08 years = 55.20 percent

- 55.20 percent x $3,119.40 (January 1, 1998, active duty rate for an E-8 over 22 years) = $1,721.90 + 2.8 percent (Cost of Living Adjustment [COLA]) = $1,769

(2) Since E-8 was eligible to transfer to the Fleet Reserve on December 31, 1998, it would also compute the entitlement as of that date, when the E-8 had 21 years, 1 month service. The pay would be computed as follows:

- 2.5 percent x 21.08 = 52.70 percent

- 52.70 percent x $2,976.60 (1/1/99 active duty rate for an E-8 over 21 years) = $1,568+ 1.3 percent (COLA) = $1,588+ 2.8 percent (COLA) = $1,632

(3) In this situation therefore, this Fleet reservist would receive monthly retainer pay of $1,791 since the Tower Amendment computations are not more beneficial than the current pay computation.

You can estimate your monthly retirement pay at **www.defenselink.mil/ militarypay/retirement/calc/index.html** and a military compensation calculator is available here at **www.dod.mil/cgi-bin/rmc.pl**.

To decide which system applies to you, you must determine the date that you first entered the military. This date is called the DIEMS (Date of Initial Entry to Military Service) or DIEUS (Date of Initial Entry to Uniformed Services). The date you first entered the military is the first time you enlisted or joined the active or reserves. This date is fixed — it does not change. Departing the military and rejoining does not affect your DIEMS.

Some individuals have unique circumstances that complicate determining their DIEMS. Here are a few examples:

- The DIEMS for academy graduates who entered the academy with no prior service is the date they reported to the academy, not the date they graduated.

- Beginning an ROTC scholarship program or enlisting as a Reserve in the Senior ROTC program sets the DIEMS.

8 Members who entered the military, separated, and then rejoined the military have a DIEMS based on entering the first period of military service.

8 The DIEMS for members who enlisted under the delayed entry program is when they entered the delayed entry program, not when they initially reported for duty.

8 For those who joined the Reserves and later joined the active component, their DIEMS is the date they joined the Reserves.

Be aware that your pay date may be different than your DIEMS. Also, your DIEMS does not determine when you have enough time in the service to retire — it determines only which retirement system applies to you.

Not all services have their DIEMS dates properly defined in their personnel records. If you have unusual circumstances and are unsure of when your DIEMS date is or believe your records show an incorrect DIEMS date, contact your personnel office to discuss your particular situation.

Now, based upon the date you initially entered the military, you can determine which retirement system applies to you.

RETIREMENT SYSTEM	CRITERIA TO RECEIVE
Final Pay	Entry before September 8, 1980
High-3	Entry on or after September 8, 1980, but before August 1, 1986, or entered on or after August 1, 1986, and did not choose the Career Status Bonus (CSB) and REDUX retirement system
CSB/REDUX	Entered on or after August 1,1986, and elected to receive the Career Status Bonus (if you do not elect to receive the Career Status Bonus, you will be under the High-3 retirement system)

FINAL PAY RETIREMENT SYSTEM

Final Pay applies to those who entered the Service before September 8,

1980. Each year of service is worth 2.5 percent toward the retirement multiplier. Hence, 2.5 percent x 20 years = 50 percent and 2.5 percent x 30 years = 75 percent. The longer an individual stays on active duty, the higher the multiplier and the higher the retirement pay, up to the maximum of 75 percent.

Years of Service	20	21	22	23	24	25	26	27	28	29	30
High-3	50%	52.5%	55%	57.5%	60%	62.5%	65%	67.5%	70%	72.5%	75%

This multiplier is applied against the final basic pay of the individual's career. Also, only basic pay is used in retirement calculations in all retirement systems. Allowances and special pays do not affect retired pay.

Cost-of-living adjustments are given annually based on the increase in the Consumer Price Index (CPI), a measure of inflation. Under the Final Pay system, the annual COLA is equal to CPI. This is a different index than the one used for active duty annual pay raises. The index used for active duty pay raises are based upon average civilian wage increases. Thus, retirement pay COLAs and annual active duty pay raises will differ.

HIGH-3 YEAR AVERAGE RETIREMENT SYSTEM

The High-3 system applies to members who first entered Service after September 8, 1980, but before August 1, 1986. It also applies to individuals who entered on or after August 1, 1986, who do not elect the REDUX retirement with the Career Status Bonus at their 15th year of service.

Each year of service is worth 2.5 percent toward the retirement multiplier. Hence, 2.5 percent x 20 years = 50 percent and 2.5 percent x 30 years = 75 percent. The longer an individual stays on active duty, the higher the multiplier becomes and the higher the retirement pay, up to the maximum of 75 percent.

Years of Service	20	21	22	23	24	25	26	27	28	29	30
High-3	50%	52.5%	55%	57.5%	60%	62.5%	65%	67.5%	70%	72.5%	75%

This multiplier is applied against the average basic pay for the highest 36 months of the individual's career. This often, though not always, equals the average basic pay for the final three years of service. Also, only basic pay is used in retirement calculations in all retirement system options. Allowances and special pays do not affect retired pay.

Cost-of-living adjustments are given annually based on the increase in the Consumer Price Index, a measure of inflation. Under the High-3, the annual COLA is equal to CPI. This is a different index than the one used for active duty annual pay raises. The index used for active duty pay raises are based upon average civilian wage increases. Thus, retirement pay COLAs and annual active duty pay raises will differ.

CSB/REDUX RETIREMENT SYSTEM

The Military Reform Act of 1986 created the REDUX retirement system, and it applies to all members who joined on or after August 1, 1986. The National Defense Authorization Act (NDAA) for FY2000 amended this system. The NDAA made two major changes: (1) it allows those in this group to choose between the High-3 retirement system and the REDUX retirement system, and (2) it added a $30,000 Career Status Bonus as part of the REDUX retirement system.

The CSB/REDUX retirement system applies to those who entered the service on or after August 1, 1986, and who elected to receive the $30,000 Career Status Bonus at their 15th year of service.

The REDUX retirement system and Career Status Bonus is a package deal. It is the combination of these two items that can be advantageous to many individuals. The REDUX portion determines retirement income (the longer one's career, the higher that income) and the $30,000 Career Status Bonus provides current cash — available for investing, major purchases, or setting up a business after retirement.

The REDUX multiplier calculation and annual cost-of-living adjustments differ from the other systems. Also, REDUX has a catch-up increase at age 62 that brings the REDUX retired pay back to the same amount paid under the High-3 System. REDUX is the only military retirement system with a readjustment feature.

Each of the first 20 years of service is worth 2.0 percent toward the retirement multiplier. But each year after the 20th is worth 3.5 percent. Hence, 2.0 percent x 20 years = 40 percent. But a 30-year career is computed by 2.0 percent times the first 20 years plus 3.5 percent for the 10 years beyond 20, resulting in the maximum of 75 percent. The table below summarizes the initial multiplier at various years of service under REDUX.

Years of Service	20	21	22	23	24	25	26	27	28	29	30
REDUX	40%	43.5%	47%	50.5%	54%	57.5%	61%	64.5%	68%	71.5%	75%

Under REDUX, the longer an individual stays on active duty, the closer the multiplier is to what it would have been under High-3 up to the 30-year point where the multipliers are equal.

In precisely the same way as High-3, this multiplier is applied against the average basic pay for the highest 36 months of the individual's basic pay. This often, though not always, equals the average basic pay for the final three years of service. Also, this is basic pay; allowances and special pays do not affect retired pay.

Cost-of-living adjustments for retired pay are given annually based on the increase in the Consumer Price Index, a measure of inflation. Under REDUX, the COLA is equal to CPI minus 1 percent.

A feature unique to REDUX is a re-computation of retirement pay at age 62. Two adjustments are made. The first adjusts the multiplier to what it would have been under High-3. For example, a 20-year retiree's new multiplier would become 50 percent, a 24-year retiree's multiplier would become 60 percent, but a 30-year retiree's would remain 75 percent. This new multiplier is applied against the individual's original average basic pay for his or her highest 36 months. Then the second adjustment is done. Full CPI for every retirement year is applied to this amount to compute a new base retirement salary. At age 62, the REDUX and High-3 retirement salaries are equal. But, REDUX COLAs for later years will again be set at CPI minus 1 percent.

Those members who elect the CSB/REDUX retirement system at their 15th year of service receive a $30,000 Career Status Bonus. To receive this bonus, the member must agree to complete a 20-year active duty career with length-of-service retired pay under the 1986 Military Retirement Reform Act — 1986 MRRA or REDUX. Continuation beyond 20 years is possible, subject to service personnel management actions. However, the member's commitment with the CSB is only to the 20-year point. The entire $30,000 bonus, or first installment payment for those electing a multi-year payment option, is paid shortly after the member makes the CSB/REDUX election and commits to the 20 years of service obligation. Exact mechanics should be provided by your service near the point you have 14 and 1/2 years of service.

If the member does not complete the obligation of the 20-year career, the member must repay a pro-rated share of the bonus.

RETIREMENT CHOICE

Members who entered the service after July 31, 1986, will be given a choice of retirement plans at their 15th year of service. There are two options:

(1) Take the pre-1986 retirement system (High-3 Year Average System).

(2) Elect the post-1986 retirement system (Military Retirement Reform Act [MRRA] of 1986, commonly referred to as REDUX) and take a $30,000 Career Status Bonus (CSB).

Both options have their own merits. Neither is universally better than the other. Which option is more advantageous can only be determined by each individual for his or her own unique circumstances and preferences. The following provides more depth to this discussion.

The following fictitious story, about twin brothers Harry and Richard, shows the differences between the High-3 and CSB/REDUX retirement systems, the potential worth of the Career Status Bonus and insight of the lifetime value of the two retirement options. How this story plays out for you depends on your personal situation and assumptions about your career and the economy. A planning calculator is available on the Web for you to make some comparisons of your own.

In August 1986, Harry and Richard, 20-year-old twins, enlisted in the military. As Harry and Richard had always done everything together, they continued to do so by being promoted with identical dates for their entire career. But, one event made their careers and futures different.

In 2001, Harry and Richard faced a choice. They were nearing their 15th year of service and could retain the High-3 retirement plan or they could take a $30,000 Career Status Bonus and the REDUX retirement system.

Harry chose High-3, and Richard chose the single lump sum CSB/REDUX option. Immediately, their finances changed. Richard now had $30,000 more in cash. This money was his to spend as he wished — a down payment on a house, college tuition for the children, a new car, or to invest for use later.

This $30,000 is taxable unless placed into the Thrift Savings Plan (TSP) or other qualified investment. TSP has been authorized, and an open season for military members to start participating in the program began October 2001, with first contributions to the system to be made from pay in January 2002. Under current rules, Richard may place a maximum of $10,500 in a TSP account. Taxes would not be paid on this $10,500 or its earnings until withdrawal. This is a positive feature that Richard would be well advised to consider. To simplify this story, however, Richard decided not to invest in the TSP but instead to pay tax on the entire amount now and invest the entire after-tax balance in a mutual fund earning 8 percent annually. As the $30,000 is taxable income and Richard is in the 28-percent tax bracket, he will pay $8,400 in taxes on this bonus, leaving $21,600 to invest.

In 2006, Harry and Richard retire with 20 years of service. Since they both had an average (highest three years) base pay of $3,000 per month, Harry, under High-3, gets 50 percent or $1,500 per month, and Richard, under REDUX, gets 40 percent or $1,200. Although Harry has a larger retirement check than Richard, Richard has been building up the savings on his $21,600 of Career Status Bonus for the past five years — it is now worth $28,600 (after paying taxes on its earnings). (Note: Retirement income may be taxable. Tax implications on the retirement income are not reflected in this story.)

Each year during their retirement, Harry and Richard will receive cost-of-living adjustments based upon the consumer price index (CPI), which measures inflation. Harry's High-3 COLA is the full CPI (3.5 percent each year in our story) so Harry gets a 3.5 percent raise. Richard, however, gets a 2.5 percent raise because COLAs under the REDUX system are equal to CPI minus 1 percent. But, Richard's Career Status Bonus is still growing in his mutual fund.

This story continues the same way until 2028 as they near their 62nd birthday. Up to this point, Harry has received nearly $582,000 in retirement income, and his current monthly amount is now about $3,100. Richard has collected $415,000 total and now gets a bit more than $2,000 each month. But, Richard is still saving that Career Status Bonus — it is now worth $98,000. Counting both the mutual fund value and what he has collected in retirement, selecting the CSB/REDUX plan netted him $513,600 — close, but $68,300 less than Harry has received.

Their 62nd birthday also brings retirement adjustment for Richard. Richard's retirement pay is recomputed as if he had been under High-3 all these years. This means that he will now get 50 percent of his original base pay plus full 3.5 percent COLAs added to it for his past retirement years. So, for one year, Harry and Richard receive the same retirement pay — about $3,200 per month. This is for only one year because the following year, Harry gets his 3.5 percent COLA and Richard gets his 2.5 percent COLA, but it is added to his newly adjusted retirement salary of $3,200. This catch-up adjustment affects Richard's total accumulation, and by the end of the year, his total is within $63,000 of Harry's total accumulation. The following year Richard's total retirement accumulation and the balance of his mutual fund begin to surpass Harry's total accumulation.

By now, some people would have spent the money that Richard put in the mutual fund on vacations, cars, or as an augmentation of their retirement income, but Richard wants to pass the money to his heirs and keeps saving. When they are 75, Harry has received more than $1,260,000 in retirement income; his current monthly amount is $5,000. Richard has collected more than $1,049,000 in retirement income and now earns $4,400 each month. But, Richard is still saving that Career Status Bonus — it is worth more than $214,600. Counting both the mutual fund value and what he has collected in retirement, selecting the CSB/REDUX retirement option is worth $1,264,000, surpassing Harry's total amount by $4,000. From this point forward, Richard will continue to outpace Harry's total accumulation.

The following chart summarizes Harry and Richard's story. This is an example that shows what the differences between the CSB/REDUX and High-3 options. These results are dependent upon the assumptions built into the story and the choices that Richard made.

POINTS OF COMPARISON	HARRY (HIGH-3)	RICHARD (CSB/REDUX)
15th Year of Service		
Bonus	$0	$30,000
Taxes	$0	-8,400
Total	$0	$21,600
Time of Retirement		
Savings	$0	$28,600
Cumulative Retired Pay	$0	$0
Total	$0	$28,600
End of First Retirement Year		
Savings	$0	$30,200
Cumulative Retired Pay	$18,000	$14,400
Total	$18,000	$44,600
Retirement pay for the year	$18,000	$14,400

POINTS OF COMPARISON	HARRY (HIGH-3)	RICHARD (CSB/REDUX)
Age 61		
Savings	$0	$98,000
Cumulative Retired Pay	$581,000	$415,600
Total	$581,000	$513,600
Retirement pay for the year	$37,100	$24,200
Age 62 — REDUX Readjustment		
Savings	$0	$103,600
Cumulative Retired Pay	$620,300	$454,000
Total	$620,300	$557,600
Retirement pay for the year	$38,400	$38,400
Age 75		
Savings	$0	$214,600
Cumulative Retired Pay	$1,260,000	$1,049,000
Total	$1,260,000	$1,264,000
Retirement pay for the year	$60,000	$52,900

Now, on the other hand, if Richard had bought that new car in 2001..???

Many individual differences — age, salary, and years of service at retirement, spending and saving habits — will and should influence your decision and will make your story with a fictitious twin different than Harry and Richard's. A calculator that allows you to enter your personal situation is available at **www.defenselink.mil/militarypay/retirement/calc/04_compare.html**.

TEMPORARY EARLY RETIREMENT AUTHORIZATION (TERA)

A law has been passed that granted all branches of service temporary authority to approve retirements for members with more than 15 but less than 20 years of service. This is also known as the Voluntary Separation Incentive Program and has not been authorized by law since 2001. To compute retired pay under this provision of law, a retiree is assessed a reduction factor. The reduction factor is computed as 1 minus one/twelve hundredth of the difference between 240 (the number of months for a standard 20-year retirement) and the number of months of creditable service for retired pay. The reduction factor is assessed upon the standard retired pay computation, which provides for 2.5 percent for each year of service, multiplied by the final base pay on active duty or the average of the highest 36 months of base pay.

(1) **Service entry date before September 8, 1980**: For example, an E-7 with exactly 19 years of service (228 months) for retirement is granted a TERA retirement. Pay is computed as follows:

- Reduction Factor = 1.0 - (240-228)/1,200 = 1.0 - (12/1,200) = 1.0 - .01 = .99

- Unreduced Retired Pay in this example would be computed as $2,588.10 (Active Duty Pay Rates for E-7 over 18 years) x 19 x .025 = $1,229.34

- Multiply Unreduced Retired Pay by Reduction Factor and round to next lower whole dollar. $1,229.34 x .99 = $1,217

(2) **Service entry date on/after September 8, 1980**: An E-7 who entered the service on or after September 8, 1980, retiring with exactly 15 years of service (180 months), would have pay computed as follows:

- Reduction Factor =1.0 - (240-180)/1,200 = 1.0 - (60/1,200) = 1.0 - 0.5 = .95

- Unreduced Retired Pay in this example would be computed as $2,350 (Average of the highest 36 months of basic pay received) x 15 x .025 = $881.25

- Multiply Unreduced Retired Pay by Reduction Factor and round to next lower whole dollar. $881.25 x .95 = $837.18 or $837

(3) Another portion of TERA affords a retiree the opportunity to obtain credit for military retired pay by performing public and community service during the time from the retirement date under TERA through the date that 20 years of service would have attained. To get credit for community service, you must sign up on the Public Community Service Registry (see your retirement counselor for specific details). Retired pay in this situation would be recomputed when the retiree reaches age 62 and, based on the amount of community service, may give the retiree active duty pay rates at a higher number of years' service (not to exceed 20) and a lower or eliminated Reduction Factor. Using the E-7 example, if the retiree earned an additional six months of service, retired pay would be based on E-7 active duty rates of more than 18, or $2,588.10.

- Reduction Factor = 1.0 - (240-234/1,200) = 1.0 - (6/1,200) = 1.0 - 5 = .995

- Unreduced Retired Pay would be $2,588.10 x 19.5 x .025 = $1,261.70

- Multiply Unreduced Retired Pay by Reduction Factor and round to next lower whole dollar

DEDUCTIONS TO RETIRED PAY

Military retirement pay is not exempt from taxes and other withholding. You will see the following deductions to your pay:

(1) **Federal Withholding Tax**: Usually, retired pay is fully taxable. The amount of taxable income is reduced by SBP costs and any waiver for VA compensation. The amount deducted from your pay for federal withholding tax is based on the number of exemptions indicated on your pay data form or W-4 after retirement. To change withholding tax status or request an additional withholding amount after retirement, send an IRS Form W-4 to the DFAS or the Coast Guard Personnel Service Center, as appropriate.

Disability retirement payments are taxable for those members with either total military service after September 24, 1975, or who were in the service before this date but were not on active military service or under binding written commitment to become a member of the armed services on September 24, 1975. Disability retirement payments are nontaxable for those members with total military service before September 24, 1975; members who were on active military duty or under binding written commitment to a member of the armed services on September 24, 1975, or members whose disability retirement has been deemed as combat related, regardless of their active military service. If your calculation is based on the first method, only that portion of your pay that would have been received under the actual percentage of disability calculation is taxable.

The amount of taxable income may be further reduced by any SBP cost. If, after retirement, you waive a portion of your pay in favor of VA compensation, your taxable income will be reduced by the amount of VA compensation or the amount of percentage of disability calculation, whichever is greater.

(2) **State Withholding Tax**: State tax withholding is on a voluntary basis and must be in whole dollar amounts. The minimum monthly amount is $10. Before making your written request, you must contact the taxing authority in the state in which you have established residence to determine if you are required to pay state income tax.

(3) **Federal Insurance Contribution Act (Social Security)**: Retired/retainer pay is not subject to FICA deductions, nor is your retired pay reduced when you become entitled to Social Security payments.

CHANGES IN BENEFITS & ENTITLEMENTS

The following may affect your benefits and entitlements:

Tax levies: All services must tax levies for delinquent taxes issued by the Internal Revenue Service (IRS). As in the case of garnishments, the collection action is mandatory and any rebuttal concerning the levy must be addressed to the IRS. Levies are continuous, and collection will run until the entire amount is either collected or the IRS informs your servicing pay office that it is released from collecting the levy amount.

Cost-of-living adjustments: Current provisions of law authorize periodic increases to retired pay. These increases were intended to reflect rises in the Consumer Price Index. The increases affect the amounts of gross monthly pay, federal withholding tax, Survivor Benefit Plan (SBP) costs, and annuities. Retired members who entered the armed forces on or after September 8, 1980, and who became entitled to retired pay on or after January 1, 1996, will receive an initial cost-of-living adjustment computed, using the quarter of the retirement date, minus 1 percent. Cost-of-living adjustments thereafter for members meeting the above conditions will not be reduced. Cost-of-living adjustments for retired members who entered the armed forces on or after August 1, 1986, will be reduced by 1 percent.

Federal civil service retirement: If you subsequently retire from federal civilian service and wish to waive your military retired pay (to include your military service in the computation of your civil service annuity), you must contact your servicing pay office, in writing, at least 60 days before your planned civilian retirement date. It is suggested that you contact your civilian personnel office before the submission of your waiver request to ensure that you are aware of all the available options. If you elect survivor coverage from your civil service annuity, your military Survivor Benefit Plan participation will be suspended while you receive the civil service annuity. If you want to retain military SBP, you may do so, but you must then decline survivor annuity from the Office of Personnel Management. If your pay is subject to court-ordered distribution, you must authorize an allotment in an amount equal to the distribution to include military service in the civil service annuity computation.

Garnishment: Your retired pay is subject to garnishment for payment of child support or alimony upon the issue of a writ of garnishment by a state or federal court. Any action to rebut the writ of garnishment or to restrain its execution must be taken through the court that issued it.

Payments to a former spouse: Your retired pay is subject to court-ordered distribution to a spouse or former spouse where the parties were married to each other for at least 10 years during which you performed at least 10 years of creditable military service. The distribution can consist of a division of disposable retired pay. This division may include community property or payments of alimony and/or child support. The total amount payable under this provision of law cannot exceed 50 percent of the disposable retired pay. In cases where there is both a division of pay and a garnishment, the total amount payable cannot exceed 65 percent of the disposable retired pay. You will be notified should a distribution be applied to your retired pay. Any action to rebut the court order or to restrain its execution must be taken through the court that issued it. Payment of these monies is not automatic. Former spouses must apply to your pay office to receive this benefit.

COMBAT-RELATED SPECIAL COMPENSATION (CRSC)

Combat-Related Special Compensation (CRSC) may entitle you to additional funds that are designed to compensate you for the reduction of your military retired pay due to the receipt of Department of Veterans Affairs compensation (also known as the VA waivers). With CRSC, you can receive either partial or full concurrent receipt of your military retirement pay and your VA disability compensation.

How Is the Amount of My CRSC Calculated?

CRSC pay is based on the combined disability rating of combat-related disabilities as determined by your branch of service. Additionally, only combat-related disabilities for which you receive Department of Veterans Affairs compensation will be considered. Use the following formula to obtain your combined VA rating of multiple combat-related disabilities:

(1) Subtract each disability percent from 100 percent to obtain the remaining efficiencies.

(2) Multiply the remaining efficiencies together.

(3) Subtract the result from 100 percent.

(4) Round to the nearest 10 percent (round up for 5 percent or above).

Example (using three disabilities of 50 percent, 40 percent, and 30 percent)

    (1) [100 - 50 = 50 percent] / [100 - 40 = 60 percent] / [100 - 30 = 70 percent]

    (2) 50 percent x 60 percent x 70 percent = 21 percent

    (3) 100 percent - 21 percent = 79 percent

    (4) 79 percent rounds up to an 80 percent combined disability

Even though you may not have qualified for CRSC in the past, the National Defense Authorization Act of 2003 expanded CRSC eligibility to retired military personnel who have a combat-related Department of Veterans Affairs disability rating between 10 percent and 50 percent, effective January 1, 2004. Your branch of service will determine which disabilities (if any) qualify as combat-related.

With the inception of the CRSC program on June 1, 2003, the following eligibility requirements were established:

- Retirees must apply to their respective branch of service to be approved for CRSC.

- Retirees must be in receipt of VA compensation.

- Retirees must be in receipt of military retired pay or be in a suspended pay status due to receipt of VA compensation.

- Retirees must have an approved combat-related VA disability rating of 60 percent or greater. Retirees having an approved combat-related disability associated with a Purple Heart have to have a rating of 10 percent or greater.

- Retirees must have 20 years of active service or, for reservists, 7,200 reserve points to be eligible.

- Retirees who have waived their retired pay in lieu of a civil service retirement are not eligible for CRSC.

Effective January 1, 2004, CRSC eligibility was extended to retirees with combat-related VA disability ratings between 10 and 50 percent. Additionally, reservists needed only 20 years of qualifying service (supported by documentation from the applicable branch of service, such as a 20-year letter, retirement orders, or a statement of service) to be eligible. The other eligibility requirements remained unchanged. Note that qualified reservists will not receive CRSC until they begin to receive retired pay at age 60.

Temporary Early Retirement Authorization retirees are not eligible to receive CRSC unless they have returned to active duty and accumulated enough service time to meet the 20-year requirement before retiring a second time.

CRSC Frequently Asked Questions

Do all retirees with a combat-related disability qualify?

No. The law stipulates that retirees must have 20 or more years of active duty (20 years of service for the purposes of computing retired pay) to qualify. National Guard and Reserve retirees must have 20 or more years of qualifying service. Retirees under Temporary Early Retirement Authority and disability retirees with less than 20 years of service are not eligible to receive Combat-Related Special Compensation. Retirees who combine their military and civil service retirements are not eligible for CRSC.

I have a disability retirement for military service, but have not applied for a VA disability rating. Would I qualify for the new compensation?

You may be eligible for the new compensation because you have a combat-related disability, but to be paid the compensation you must have an offset to your retired pay for VA disability compensation. Therefore, you must have a VA rating and be receiving disability compensation to qualify, and you must have completed 20 years of service.

I have a Purple Heart for a combat wound, but I have a VA disability that is not combat-related. Do I qualify?

No. To qualify, you must have a VA-rated disability of at least 10 percent directly related to a combat/operations-related disability as approved by your branch of service.

I do not have a Purple Heart, but I have a VA disability rating of 60 percent, of which only 30 percent is combat-related. Do I qualify?

Yes. The law extended eligibility from 60 percent down to a minimum 10 percent combat-related disability, and the Purple Heart decoration is no longer a criteria.

MILITARY SERVICE AND SOCIAL SECURITY

Although you are in military service, you pay Social Security taxes just as civilian employees do. In 2008, the tax rate is 7.65 percent, up to a maximum of $97,500. If you earn more, you continue to pay the Medicare portion of the tax (1.45 percent) on the rest of your earnings.

How Your Work Qualifies You for Social Security

To qualify for benefits, you must have worked and paid Social Security taxes for a certain length of time. In 2007, you received four credits if you earned at least $4,000. The amount needed to get credit for your work goes up each year. The number of credits you need to qualify for Social Security benefits depends on your age and the type of benefit for which you are eligible. No one needs to have worked for more than 10 years.

Your Social Security benefit depends on your earnings, averaged over your entire working lifetime. The higher your earnings, the higher your Social Security benefit. Under certain circumstances, special earnings can be credited to your military pay record for Social Security purposes. These extra earnings are for periods of active duty or active duty for training. These extra earnings may help you qualify for Social Security or may increase the amount of your Social Security benefit. Social Security will add these extra earnings to your earnings record when you file for benefits.

If you served in the military from 1940 through 1956, including attendance at a service academy, you did not pay Social Security taxes. However, the Social Security Administration will credit you with $160 a month in earnings for military service from September 16, 1940, to December 31, 1956, if:

- You were honorably discharged after 90 or more days of service.

- You were released because of a disability or injury received in the line of duty.

- You are applying for survivors' benefits based on a veteran's work and the veteran died while on active duty.

You cannot receive these special credits if you are receiving a federal benefit based on the same years of service, unless you were on active duty after 1956. If you were on active duty after 1956, you can get the special credit for 1951 through 1956, even if you are receiving a military retirement based on service during that period.

If you served in the military from 1957 through 1977, you are credited with $300 in additional earnings for each calendar quarter in which you received active duty basic pay.

If you served in the military from 1978 through 2001, you are credited with an additional $100 in earnings, up to a maximum of $1,200 a year, for every $300 in active duty basic pay. After 2001, additional earnings are no longer credited.

If you began your service after September 7, 1980, and did not complete at least 24 months of active duty or your full tour, you may not be able to receive the additional earnings.

In addition to retirement benefits, Social Security pays survivors' benefits to your family when you die. You also can get Social Security benefits for you and your family if you become disabled. For more information about these benefits, ask the Social Security Administration for the pamphlet *"Understanding The Benefits"* (Publication No. 05-10024).

When you apply for Social Security benefits, you will be asked for proof of your military service (DD Form 214) or information about your Reserve or National Guard service.

When You Are Eligible for Medicare

If you have healthcare insurance from the Department of Veterans Affairs or under the TRICARE or CHAMPVA program, your health benefits may change or end when you become eligible for Medicare. See the chapter later in this book on TRICARE and healthcare entitlements.

You Can Work and Get Retirement Benefits

You can retire as early as age 62. But, if you do, your Social Security benefits will be reduced permanently. If you decide to apply for benefits before your full retirement age, you can work and still get some Social Security benefits. There are limits on how much you can earn without losing your retirement benefits. These limits change each year. When you reach your full retirement age, you can earn as much as you are able and still get all your Social Security benefits.

The full retirement age in 2007 was 65 and 10 months, but it will gradually increase until it reaches age 67 for people born in 1960 and later. To help you decide the best time to retire, contact the Social Security Administration for a copy of *"Retirement Benefits"* (Publication No. 05-10035). There is no offset for receiving both military retirement pay and your full social security benefit.

REPORTING THE DEATH OF A MILITARY RETIREE

Retirement pay benefits stop upon the death of the retiree, except as provided for in the Survivor Benefit Plan (if participation was elected). The Survivor Benefit Plan is covered in depth later in this book. In the event of a death of a retiree, survivors must immediately notify the Defense Finance and Accounting Service or the agency pay office. In all cases, you must provide a cause of death, death certificate, and location of death.

The pay office will take steps to close out the pay account to prevent any overpayments. If the decedent was a retiree enrolled in the Survivor Benefit Plan and/or the Retired Serviceman's Family Protection Plan (RSFPP), additional steps will be taken by the pay office to initiate pay accounts for eligible survivors.

Designated beneficiaries of retirees should expect to receive a Standard Form 1174 (SF-1174) and, if applicable, SBP/RSFPP-related forms within seven to 10 business days of reporting the death. Additionally, you should:

- Notify the Social Security Administration at (800) 772-1213.

- Notify the Defense Enrollment Eligibility Reporting System (DEERS) at (800) 538-9552.

- If the member was receiving disability compensation or Dependency Indemnity Compensation (DIC), notify the Department of Veterans Affairs (DVA) at (800) 827-1000.

- If the member was a civil servant or retired civil servant, notify the Office of Personnel Management (OPM) toll-free at (888) 767-6738.

- If the member enrolled in DVA-sponsored insurance such as National Service Life Insurance (NSLI) or Service Members' Group Life Insurance (SGLI), notify them at (800) 669-8477.

If you live near a military installation, you may be able to receive help with administrative matters from a Casualty Assistance Officer (CAO), Decedent Affairs Officer or Retired Activities/Affairs Office (RAO).

Additional toll-free numbers you may find useful, if applicable, are:

Armed Forces Benefit Association (AFBA)
(800) 776-2322

Army & Air Force Mutual Aid Association (AAFMAA)
(800) 522-5221

Burial at Sea
(888) 647-6676 (option 4)

Funeral Honors
(877) 645-4667

Military Benefit Association
(800) 336-0100

Officers Benefit Association
(800) 736-7311

Uniformed Service Benefit Association
(800) 368-7021

MILITARY STOP-LOSS

Presidential authority may suspend any provision of law pertaining to separation and retirement from the military. The military may legally keep you in uniform past your planned separation or retirement dates in times of national emergency. Stop-loss implementation authority was delegated to the secretary of defense by executive order on September 14, 2001. It was in turn delegated to the secretaries of the services.

A stop-loss order can affect an entire branch of service or specific military operations. At one time or another in the past few years, members of all services have had their terms of service extended to meet operational requirements, although as of early 2007, only the Army was still using stop-loss, with about 10,000 soldiers affected.

MEDICAL RETIREMENT & DISCHARGE

Medical retirement is significantly different than a medical discharge. In short, if you are retirement eligible but have a medical condition that prohibits you from performing your military service, you will go through a medical board and be medically retired, often with a retirement and some veterans' benefits in the form of disability or other entitlements. Medical discharge is for those who are not eligible for retirement but have a medical condition that prohibits them from service on active duty. Depending on the condition and whether it is service connected or combat related, there may be benefits through the Veterans Administration.

The process to determine medical fitness for continued duty involves two boards — the Medical Evaluation Board (MEB) and the Physical Evaluation Board (PEB). Both may result in a medical retirement or discharge.

Title 10, U.S.C., chapter 61, provides the secretaries of the military departments with authority to retire or separate members when the secretary finds that they are unfit to perform their military duties because of physical disability.

Most Medical Evaluation Boards or Physical Evaluation Boards are a result of a military member reporting a condition to a military hospital or

Military Treatment Facility (MTF). Under these circumstances, medical officers may require a complete physical examination to determine fitness and ultimately refer the veteran to a Medical Evaluation Board when the member's medical condition or ailment renders him or her unfit for duty or incapable of performing their duties.

Physical or mental health issues that prohibit the performance of military duties or cause a disqualification from worldwide deployment for a period of more than 12 months will initiate a Medical Evaluation Board. This process is the same regardless of retirement eligibility. A Medical Evaluation Board consists of active duty physicians who review the clinical case file and decide whether the individual should be returned to duty or should be separated or retired from the service, using medical standards for performing military service.

If the MEB makes the determination that a service member has a medical condition or ailment that is not compatible with continued military service, it refers the case to a Physical Evaluation Board (PEB). The PEB determines fitness and/or disability and may recommend one of the following:

- Return the member to duty (with or without assignment limitations)

- Place the member on the temporary disabled/retired list (TDRL)

- Separate the member from active duty

- Medically retire the member

The standard used by the PEB for determining fitness is whether the medical condition precludes the member from reasonably performing the duties of his or her office, grade, rank, or rating. The DOD and Coast Guard have published standards for deployability and readiness, which the PEB evaluation is based upon.

In all cases of a recommendation for discharge, the service member is given an appeal process, with assigned legal counsel.

Four factors determine whether disposition is fit for duty, separation, permanent retirement, or temporary retirement. These are:

- Can the service member perform his job/rating/MOS?

- What is the member's rating percentage?

- How stable is the disabling condition?

- How many years of active service for preexisting conditions?

Fit for duty: The member is judged to be fit when he can reasonably perform the duties of his grade and military job. If the member is medically unfit to perform the duties of his/her current job, the PEB can recommend medical retraining into a job he/she will be medically qualified to perform such as administrative type duties, although this is not common.

Disability rating percentage: Once a determination of physical unfitness is made, the PEB is required by law to rate the disability using the Department of Veterans Affairs Schedule for Rating Disabilities. Ratings can range from 0 to 100 percent, rising in increments of 10.

Separation without benefits: Separation without benefits occurs if the disability is determined to be preexisting or not service connected, was not caused by or aggravated by military service, and the member has less than eight years of active service. Additionally, it occurs if the disability was incurred while the member was absent without leave (AWOL) or while engaged in misconduct or willful negligence. If the member has more than eight years of active service, he/she may be medically retired (if eligible) or medically separated with severance pay, even if the condition was preexisting or hereditary. This is a key fact.

Separation with severance pay: Separation with disability severance pay occurs if the member is found not fit for continued military service, has less than 20 years of service (not retirement eligible), and has a disability rating of less than 30 percent. Disability severance pay equals two months basic pay for each year of service not to exceed 12 years (a maximum of 24 months basic pay). The member may also be eligible to apply for

monthly disability compensation from the Veterans Administration if the VA determines the disability is service-connected.

Permanent disability retirement: Permanent disability retirement occurs if the member is found not fit for continued military service, the disability is determined to be permanent and stable and rated at a minimum of 30 percent, or the member has 20 years of military service.

Temporary disability retirement: Temporary disability retirement occurs if the member is found not fit for continued military service and entitled to permanent disability retirement except that the disability is not stable for rating purposes (for the VA disability percentage). "Stable for rating purposes" is when the condition will likely change (degrade or improve) within the next five years — which will ultimately result in a different disability rating. When a service member is placed on the Temporary Disability Retirement List (TDRL), he or she must undergo a periodic medical examination within 18 months (minimum) followed by another PEB evaluation. At that time, he or she may be retained on the TDRL, or a final disability determination will be made.

Retirement pay computation: Compensation is based on the higher of two computations: disability rating times retired pay base; or 2.5 x years of service x retired pay base. Service members on the TDRL receive no less than 50 percent of their retired pay base.

If you have been found to be physically unfit for further military service and meet certain standards specified by law, you will be granted a disability retirement. Your disability retirement may be temporary or permanent. If temporary, your status should be resolved within a five-year period. The amount of your disability retirement pay must also be determined.

The amount of your disability-retired pay is determined by one of the following two methods:

- The first method is to multiply your base pay or average of highest 36 months of active duty pay at the time of retirement, by the percentage of disability, which has been assigned. Members who entered the service September 8, 1980, or later, must use the highest average formula. The minimum percentage for temporary disability retirees will equal 50 percent. The maximum percentage for any type of retirement is 75 percent. This computation is sometimes referred to as "Method A."

§ The second method is to multiply only your years of active service at the time of your retirement by 2.5 percent by your base pay or average of highest 36 months of active duty pay at the time of retirement. This computation is sometimes referred to as "Method B."

DIFFERENCES BETWEEN MILITARY AND VA DISABILITY RATINGS

Although both the Department of Defense and the Department of Veterans Affairs use the Department of Veterans Affairs Schedule for Rating Disabilities, not all the general policy provisions set forth in the rating schedule apply to the military. Consequently, disability ratings may vary between the two departments. The military rates only those conditions determined to be physically unfitting, thereby compensating for loss of a military career. The VA may rate any service-connected impairment, thus compensating for loss of civilian employability. Another difference in the two is the term of the rating. The military's ratings are permanent upon final disposition. VA ratings may fluctuate with time, depending upon the progress of the condition. Further, the military's disability compensation is affected by years of service and basic pay, while VA compensation is a flat amount based upon the percentage rating received.

Veterans whose service-connected disabilities are rated at 30 percent or more are entitled to additional allowances for dependents. Depending upon the disability rating of the veteran, monthly allowances for a spouse range from $39 to $94 and for a dependent child, $26 to $88. Additional amounts are provided for each additional child, and there is a higher scale for children in school after age 18.

OTHER MAJOR FACTORS AFFECTING PAYMENT LEVELS

Adjustments to rates are based on a number of factors in addition to dependents. Factors that can have a significant effect on amounts are:

- Veterans with severe service-connected disabilities may receive compensation at a basic rate as high as $6,576 per month. Special monthly compensation rates apply when a veteran experiences loss or loss of use of one or more limbs; loses one or more of the senses (sight, hearing, or speech); loses a reproductive organ or its use; or loss of breast tissue by a female veteran.

- Allowances may be made for veterans requiring aides, such as bedridden individuals who need assistance with eating, bathing, or certain other activities of daily living. This adjustment is referred to as aid and attendance.

- Veterans whose service-connected disability leaves them unable to maintain gainful employment may meet criteria for allowances at the 100 percent compensation rate under a benefit called individual unemployability. A veteran with a single service-connected disability may be eligible if the veteran's disability is rated at 60 percent or more. A veteran with multiple disabilities may be eligible if the veteran has a combined rating of 70 percent or more and at least one of the disabilities is individually rated 40 percent or higher.

FACTS ABOUT VA DISABILITY COMPENSATION

- Disability compensation for veterans is not subject to federal or state income tax. About 80 percent of veterans receive VA benefits by direct deposit, which VA recommends for security reasons.

- Veterans are rated at increments of 10 percent reflecting degree of disability. As federal regulations summarize the underlying principle, "The percentage ratings represent as far as can practicably be determined the average impairment in earning capacity resulting from such diseases and injuries and their residual conditions."

- The largest category of veterans on the compensation scale is at 10 percent disability ($108 per month), with 783,000 veterans at this rate at the beginning of fiscal year 2005 among the total of 2.6 million veterans receiving disability compensation.

- The criteria for rating the severity of various disabilities are available online at **www.access.gpo.gov/nara/cfr/waisidx_03/38cfr4_03.html**.

As medical knowledge, laws, and procedures change, VA regularly publishes proposed changes to these criteria in the Federal Register for public comment before a final regulation is adopted.

- Where a veteran has more than one disability, the percentages are not simply added together to produce a new rating. Instead, a formula described in federal regulations calculates the rating.

- A veteran may be rated at 0 percent, meaning there is evidence of the service-connected condition, but it does not impair the veteran. An example is a minor scar. This 0 percent rating, though not compensable, can be beneficial, since it may raise the veteran's priority in other VA programs such as healthcare eligibility. In addition, it may be reviewed for a higher rating if the condition worsens.

- A veteran may have a number of disabilities individually evaluated as 0 percent, which produces a 10 percent combined disability and entitles the veteran to disability compensation. At the beginning of fiscal year 2005, there were more than 15,000 veterans in the category of "compensable zero" ratings.

- In addition to the 2.6 million veterans on the compensation rolls, past studies have shown about 1.2 million veterans have overall (noncompensable) ratings of 0 percent, but because they do not receive payments from VA, the exact number is not known.

○ There were 771,000 new and reopened claims requiring a disability rating received from veterans in fiscal year 2004, an average of more than 64,000 claims filed per month.

○ Among veterans on the rolls, the largest category of service-connected disabilities is musculoskeletal problems, accounting for about 40 percent of all disabilities. This includes such problems as impairment of the knee and arthritis due to trauma. Data on the number and type of disabilities are published annually. This information can be found at **www.vba.va.gov/reports.htm**.

Annual Cost-of-Living Adjustment

A proposed cost-of-living adjustment is included in the president's budget proposal released early each calendar year. It is part of the spending forecast and appropriations request for the ensuing fiscal year, a starting point for legislative discussion. The actual percentage increase is set through a separate bill debated by Congress and often signed into law the following fall.

Legislators are not bound by any specific annual Consumer Price Index formula but historically have chosen to mirror the percentage given to Social Security recipients. The Social Security increase, in turn, is based on a Bureau of Labor Statistics calculation of the rise in the Consumer Price Index for urban wage earners and clerical workers (CPI-W).

Cost-of-living adjustments become effective December 1 each year and are reflected in the payment received by veterans on or about the first day of the New Year. Whenever a payment falls on a holiday or weekend, as is the case with the January 1 payment each year, that month's payment is issued the last prior business day.

Finding Help with Disability Compensation/Discharge and Retirement

In all cases, your best source of guidance and information is through your military service. Your military treatment facility, health benefits advisors, servicing personnel and pay office, family support center, and career advisors will assist you as you navigate the Medical and Physical Evaluation Board processes and disability compensation determinations. This is a critical time for you to fight for your rights, document everything, and push for your maximum benefit determination.

MILITARY DISABILITY EVALUATION: ENSURING CONSISTENT AND TIMELY OUTCOMES

In April 2006, the Government Accounting Office (GAO) produced a report titled "Military Disability Evaluation: Ensuring Consistent and Timely Outcomes for Reserve and Active Duty Service Members." Key information from this report is reproduced below:

The House Subcommittee on Military Personnel asked GAO to discuss the results of its recent study on the Military Disability Evaluation System. In this study, GAO determined (1) how current DOD policies and guidance for disability determinations compare for the Army, Navy, and Air Force, and what policies are specific to Reserve component members of the military; (2) what oversight and quality control mechanisms are in place at DOD and these three services of the military to ensure consistent and timely disability decisions for active and Reserve component members; and (3) how disability decisions, ratings, and processing times compare for active and Reserve component members of the Army, the largest branch of the service, and what factors might explain any differences.

GAO Recommends

In this report, GAO recommended that the secretary of defense take certain steps to improve DOD oversight of the military disability evaluation system, including evaluating the appropriateness of timeliness standards for case processing and assessing the adequacy of training for disability evaluation staff. The secretary concurred and indicated that our recommendations would be implemented.

In March 2006, GAO reported that policies and guidance for military disability determinations differ somewhat among the Army, Navy, and Air Force. DOD has explicitly given the services the responsibility to set up their own processes for certain aspects of the disability evaluation system and has given them latitude in how they go about this. As a result, each service implements its system somewhat differently. Further, the laws that govern military disability and the policies that the Department of Defense and the services have developed to implement these laws have led reservists to have different experiences in the disability system compared to active duty members. For example, because they are not on active duty at all times, it takes longer for reservists to accrue the 20 years of service that may be needed to earn monthly disability retirement benefits.

Although the DOD has issued policies and guidance to promote consistent and timely disability decisions for active duty and reserve disability cases, the DOD is not monitoring compliance. To encourage consistent decision making, DOD requires all services to use multiple reviewers to evaluate disability cases. Furthermore, federal law requires that they use a standardized disability rating system to classify the severity of the medical impairment. In addition, DOD periodically convenes the Disability Advisory Council, composed of DOD and service officials, to review and update disability policy and to discuss current issues. However, neither DOD nor the services systematically determine the consistency of disability decision making. DOD has issued timeliness goals for processing disability cases but is not collecting information to determine compliance. Finally, the consistency and timeliness of decisions depend, in part, on the training that disability staff receives. However, the DOD is not exercising oversight over training for staff in the disability system.

Although GAO's review of the military disability evaluation system's policies and oversight covered the three services, GAO examined Army data on disability ratings and benefit decisions from 2001 to 2005. After controlling for many of the differences between reserve and active duty soldiers, GAO found that among soldiers who received disability ratings, the ratings of reservists were comparable to those of active duty soldiers with similar conditions. GAO's analyses of the military disability benefit decisions for the soldiers who were determined to be unfit for duty were less definitive but suggest that Army reservists were less likely to receive permanent disability retirement or lump sum disability severance pay than their active duty counterparts. Data on possible reasons for this difference, such as whether the condition existed before service, was not available for our analysis. GAO did not compare processing times for Army Reserve and active duty cases because we found that the Army's data needed to calculate processing times was unreliable. Army statistics based on this data indicate that from fiscal year 2001 through 2005, reservists' cases took longer to process than active duty cases.

Under certain circumstances, both active duty and reserve component members of the military are entitled to receive compensation for service-incurred or -aggravated injuries or illnesses that render them unfit for continued military service. According to DOD regulations, a primary goal of the military disability evaluation system is to ensure consistent and timely decisions for active duty and Reserve component members.

Over the past five years, nearly half a million Reserve component members across all services have been mobilized to augment active duty military forces in conflicts and peacekeeping missions worldwide. In total, the Army, Navy, and Air Force evaluated 23,316 disability cases in fiscal year 2005. One in four of these was a reservist's case. Because Reserve component members represent a substantial proportion of the mobilized military force, it is incumbent on DOD and the military to ensure that disability decisions made in their cases are consistent with those made in the cases of active duty members and as timely.

According to DOD regulations, the process should include a Medical Evaluation Board, a Physical Evaluation Board, an appellate review process, and a final disposition. Each service member who goes through the system should be assigned a Physical Evaluation Board Liaison Officer (PEBLO) to help the service member navigate the system and prepare documents for the PEB.

The disability evaluation process has four possible outcomes. One of the following can be applied to a service member:

1. Found fit for duty

2. Separated from the service without benefits — service members whose disabilities were incurred while not on duty or as a result of intentional misconduct are discharged from the service without disability benefits

3. Separated from the service with lump sum disability severance pay

4. Retired from the service with permanent monthly disability benefits or placed on the Temporary Disability Retirement List (TDRL)

The disability evaluation process begins at a Military Treatment Facility (MTF) when a physician medically evaluates a service member's injury or condition to determine if the service member meets the military's retention standards and prepares a narrative summary describing the findings. This process is referred to as a Medical Evaluation Board. Service members who meet retention standards are returned to duty. Those who do not are referred to the Physical Evaluation Board.

The first step in the PEB stage of the process is the informal PEB — an administrative review of the case file without the presence of the service member. To arrive at its findings and recommendations regarding eligibility for disability benefits, the PEB determines if service members are fit for duty, if their injuries or conditions are compensable, and what disability rating their injuries or conditions should be assigned. The PEB also considers the stability of the condition in cases eligible for monthly disability retirement benefits. Service members with conditions that might improve or worsen are placed on TDRL and reevaluated by the PEB at least every 18 months to determine if their condition has stabilized. Those who continue to be unfit for duty after five years on TDRL are separated from the military with monthly retirement benefits, discharged with severance pay, or discharged without benefits, depending on their condition and years of service.

Service members have the opportunity to review the informal PEB's findings and may request a formal hearing with the PEB. Only those found unfit are guaranteed a formal hearing. If service members disagree with a formal PEB's findings and recommendations, they can, under certain circumstances, appeal to the PEB reviewing authority. Once the service member agrees with the findings and recommendations or exhausts all available appeals, the reviewing authority issues the final disposition.

The DOD explicitly gives the services responsibility for administering the military disability evaluation system. Although DOD regulations establish some parameters and guidelines for this system, the services have considerable latitude in how they interpret them. Consequently, across the services there are differences in MEB and PEB procedures and the use of counselors to help service members navigate the system.

The Air Force convenes an actual board of physicians who meet regularly and vote on whether service members meet retention standards. In contrast, the Army and Navy MEBs are informal procedures during which case files are separately reviewed by board members. Each branch of the service has established PEB to determine whether service members who do not meet medical retention standards are entitled to disability compensation. Makeup of the board differs by service. The Army allows the same individuals to sit on both the informal and formal PEB in the same case. The Air Force allows this only under certain circumstances. The Navy has no written policy on the matter, and one Navy PEB official indicated that the same individuals often served on both informal and formal PEBs in a case.

A service member's Physical Evaluation Board Liaison Officer is expected to counsel him or her on his or her rights, the effects of MEB and PEB decisions, and available disability benefits. Each service employs PEBLO counselors in accordance with these rules but has placed them under different commands, begins the counseling process at different points in the disability evaluation process, and provides PEBLOs with different levels of training.

Due to the part-time nature of Reserve service, some laws governing military disability compensation result in different experiences with the disability system for reservists. Under the law, to receive monthly disability retirement benefits, a service member determined unfit for duty must have at least 20 years of active duty service or a disability rated at least 30 percent. Because reservists are not on duty at all times, it takes longer for them to accrue the 20 years of service needed to qualify for monthly disability retirement benefits when their disability rating is less than 30 percent.

Part-time status also makes it more difficult for reservists with preexisting conditions to be covered by the eight-year rule and therefore eligible for disability compensation of any kind. By law, service members determined to be unfit for duty are automatically eligible for disability compensation if they have at least eight years of active duty service, even if their conditions existed before entry into the military or were not aggravated by their military service. This entitlement applies to reservists only when they are on ordered active duty. For reservists, accruing these eight years can be more difficult than for active duty service members.

Officials reported that commanders and others responsible for completing line of duty determinations were often uncertain as to when line of duty determinations were necessary for reservists and active duty members. Moreover, these officials noted that in some cases, the necessary line of duty determinations were not made, resulting in delays for service members. For example, Air Force officials we spoke with had different impressions as to whether line of duty determinations were always required for reservists, even though Air Force regulations state they are. Officials from the Army and Army National Guard similarly offered different perspectives on the need for line of duty determinations for reservists.

In the Army, deployed active duty soldiers return to their unit for service in a backup capacity when they are injured or ill and require medical treatment. Mobilized injured or ill Army reservists have no similar unit to return to. Consequently, their mobilization orders are often suspended; they are retained on active duty in medical holdover status and often assigned to a medical retention-processing unit while they receive medical treatment. While in medical holdover status, reservists may live on base, at a military treatment facility, at home, or at other locations. After their mobilization orders expire, they can elect to continue on active duty through a program such as medical retention processing, which allows them to continue receiving pay and benefits. According to the Army, about 26,000 reservists entered medical holdover status between 2003 and 2005.

Unlike most injured active duty soldiers, reservists in medical holdover must live away from their families while receiving medical treatment. In certain cases reservists in medical holdover may receive treatment and recuperate at home. The Army's Community Based Healthcare Organizations (CBHCO) provide medical and case management for these reservists. As of December 2005, about 35 percent of the reservists in medical holdover were being cared for in the CBHCO program. To be assigned to this program, reservists must meet a number of criteria. For example, reservists must live in communities where they can get appropriate care, and they must also be reliable in keeping medical appointments

To help ensure consistent decision making in disability cases, all services must use a common rating schedule, multiple reviews are required, and a disability advisory council was created to oversee administration of the system. The law requires all services to assign ratings to disabilities based on a common schedule: the Department of Veterans Affairs Schedule for Rating Disabilities (VASRD). The VASRD is a descriptive list of medical conditions associated with disability ratings. DOD regulations require each service to review service members' case files multiple times during the disability evaluation process by a number of officials with different roles. Military officials also regard the appeals process required by DOD as helping to ensure the consistency of disability evaluation decision making.

According to DOD officials, primary oversight of the disability evaluation system currently rests with the DOD Disability Advisory Council. The council is composed of officials from each of the three services' disability agency; DOD health affairs, reserve affairs, and personnel officials; and representatives from the Department of Veterans Affairs. According to DOD officials, the council serves as a forum to discuss issues such as changing rules and increasing coordination among the services.

Despite this policy guidance and the presence of the disability council, both DOD and the three services lack quality assurance mechanisms to ensure that decisions are consistent. Given that one of the primary goals of the disability system is that disability evaluations take place in a consistent manner, collecting and analyzing the service member's final disability determinations are critical for ensuring that decisions are consistent. DOD regulations recognize this and require that the agency establish necessary reporting requirements to monitor and assess the performance of the disability system and compliance with relevant DOD regulations. Yet DOD does not collect and analyze information from the services on the final disability determinations and personal characteristics of service.

To help ensure timely disability decisions, DOD regulations indicate that MEBs should normally be completed in 30 days or less; PEBs should normally be completed in 40 days or less. DOD does not regularly collect available data from the services on their MEB and PEB processing times, so it does not monitor compliance with its goals.

The Army and Navy may use the data they compile on their disability cases to track the timeliness of both MEB and PEB decisions. The Air Force tracks processing times only for PEB cases because it has no centralized database containing information from all its MEB cases. Data reported by the services shows disability case processing time goals are not being met. Some of the military officials we spoke with believe this is because the goals themselves are unrealistic, particularly when addenda to the MEB's findings are required, such as in orthopedic or psychiatric cases requiring certain medical tests.

The usefulness of data of disability case processing times may also be undermined by confusion among military officials and data entry staff regarding when the disability evaluation process begins. According to DOD, the process begins on the date a physician dictates the narrative summary for an MEB. When we compared original Army PEB case files to Army electronic data from both its MEB and PEB databases, for example, we found that the date entered in the electronic file was often not the date on the narrative summary. When we asked about these errors, Army officials said that increased training of data entry staff would help resolve this problem. Navy officials also noted that there was some confusion about when case processing begins if additional medical information is needed.

According to DOD regulations, the assistant secretary of defense for health affairs is given explicit instructions to develop and maintain a training program for MEB and PEB staff. When we spoke with officials from the Office of Health Affairs, however, they indicated they were unaware that they had the responsibility to develop such a training program. In addition, despite high turnover among military disability evaluation staff, the services do not have a system to ensure that all staff is properly trained. This turnover stems, in part, from the military requirement that personnel rotate to different positions to be promoted. Military officials told us that depending on the positions involved, some staff remain in their positions from one to six years, with most remaining about three years. This turnover and the resulting loss of institutional knowledge require that the services systematically track who has been properly trained. However, all the services lack data systems that would allow them to do so, an issue that was highlighted in a recent RAND report.

Our analyses of Army data from calendar years 2001 to 2005 indicated that after taking into account many of the differences between reserve and active duty soldiers, Army reservists and their active duty counterparts received similar disability ratings. The results of our analyses of military disability benefit decisions for soldiers suggest that Army reservists with impairments that made them unfit for duty were less likely to receive either permanent disability retirement or lump sum disability severance pay than their active duty counterparts. The results of our analysis of benefits are less definitive than those from our analysis of ratings, however, because data on all possible reasons for the difference in receipt of benefits, such as years of service and whether the condition existed before service, were not available for our analysis.

We did not conduct our own statistical analysis to determine if processing times for Army Reserve and active duty soldiers' cases were comparable. The electronic data needed to calculate these times were unreliable, so not of sufficient quality to warrant their use in our analysis. Nonetheless, the statistics the Army provided on PEB disability case processing times indicate that reservists' cases reviewed between fiscal years 2001 and 2005 took consistently longer than those of active duty soldiers. More than half (54 percent) of reserve soldiers' cases took longer than 90 days, while more than one-third (35 percent) of active duty soldiers' cases exceeded 90 days.

According to Army officials, there are a number of possible explanations for the differences in processing times in reservist and active duty cases. In reservists' cases, the MEB often must request medical records from private medical practitioners, which can cause considerable delays in the process. In addition, the personnel documents for reservists are stored in facilities around the United States and may take longer to retrieve than records for active duty soldiers.

Decisions affecting eligibility for military disability benefits have a significant impact on the future of service members dedicated to serving their country. Given the importance of these decisions and the complexity of the evaluation process and rules governing eligibility for benefits, it is essential that the services take adequate steps to ensure that decisions in reserve and active duty cases are consistent and timely. It is also incumbent on DOD to adequately oversee administration of its disability evaluation system and the fairness of the system's outcomes for both Reserve and active duty members of the military across all the services.

DOD is not adequately monitoring disability evaluation outcomes in reserve and active duty disability cases. The services are not systematically evaluating the consistency and timeliness of disability decisions nor compiling reliable data on all aspects of the system needed to statistically analyze disability evaluation outcomes. Military officials recognize that not all disability cases are processed within the time set by DOD and that reservist cases take longer to process than those of active duty members. They have suggested that the goals may not be appropriate in many cases. If timeliness goals do not reflect appropriate processing times, they may not be a useful program management tool. Finally, while the consistency and timeliness of decisions depend on the adequate training and experience of all those involved in evaluating disability cases, we found that DOD had little assurance that staff at all levels in the process are properly trained.

Based on these findings and conclusions, we recommended in our recent report that the secretary of defense take certain steps to improve DOD oversight of the military disability system, including evaluating the appropriateness of timeliness standards for case processing and assessing the adequacy of training for disability evaluation staff. The secretary concurred with our recommendations and indicated our recommendations would be implemented.

VETERANS' BENEFITS AND ENTITLEMENTS

It is important to understand both the process of a military disability retirement or discharge and the entitlements. The actual entitlements are based on a combination of factors and are based on the policies in place at the Veterans Administration for computing disability entitlements. Chapter 7 will cover disability benefits in detail.

Concurrent Retirement and Disability Payments (CRDP)

CRDP is a phased-in restoration of the retired pay deducted from military retirees' accounts due to their receipt of Department of Veterans Affairs (DVA) compensation. The phased-in restoration began January 1, 2004, with the first payments dated February 2, 2004.

Eligibility

You are eligible for CRDP if you have a DVA-rated, service-connected disability of 50 percent or higher and have 20 or more qualifying years of service for a normal retirement. For members of the Reserve components, this means that you must be in receipt of a "20 Year Letter" and be at least 60 years of age. If you combined your military time and civil service time to enhance your civil service retirement from OPM, you are eligible for CRDP payments; however, you will have to reinstate your retired pay by coordinating with OPM.

Taxability

CRDP payments are taxable according to your current retired pay Federal

Income Tax Withholding tax rate and may affect the amount you wish to have deducted for State Income Tax Withholding.

Collection Actions

CRDP payments are subject to collection actions for alimony, child support, community property, garnishment, and government debt.

Disability Compensation

To be eligible, the service of the veteran must have been terminated through separation or discharge under conditions other than dishonorable.

Veterans with disability ratings of at least 30 percent are eligible for additional allowances for dependents, including spouses, minor children, children between the ages of 18 and 23 who are attending school, children who are permanently incapable of self-support because of a disability arising before age 18, and dependent parents. The additional amount depends on the veteran's disability rating.

The VA offers three payment options to veterans eligible to receive benefit payments. Most veterans receive their payments by direct deposit to a bank, savings and loan, or credit union account. In some areas, veterans who do not have a bank account can open a federally insured Electronic Transfer Account, which costs about $3 a month, provides a monthly statement, and allows cash withdrawals. Other veterans may choose to receive benefits by check. To choose a payment method, call toll-free 1-877-838-2778, Monday through Friday, 7:30 a.m.-4 p.m., CST. See more on this topic in Chapter 7.

DOD PROGRAMS ADDRESSING THE ISSUE OF CONCURRENT RECEIPT

The Department of Defense is, and has been, making extra payments to retirees to overcome the offset from retired pay associated with receipt of disability compensation from the Department of Veterans Affairs. Retirees cannot receive benefits simultaneously under more than one of these three programs. The programs are:

(1) Concurrent Retirement and Disability Payment (CRDP): The FY 2004 NDAA provides a 10-year phase out of the offset to military retired pay due to receipt of VA disability compensation for members whose combined disability rating is 50 percent or greater. Members retired under disability provisions (10 U.S. Code chapter 61) must have 20 years of service. This entitlement is taxable.

Effective January 1, 2004: Payments were made to nearly 150,000 qualified retirees on February 2, 2004. Those who had significant complications in their accounts (such as former spouse divisions or retirement under chapter 61) were delayed until their account could be manually reviewed but were paid retroactively. Today, more than 158,000 retirees are receiving total CRDP payments of more than $57 million per month.

Effective January 1, 2005: Those individuals rated 100 percent disabled by the VA are eligible to receive all their formerly offset military retired pay without the offset phase out.

Effective October 1, 2009: Those individuals not rated 100 percent disabled by the VA but are paid at the 100 percent level as "Individual Unemployables" (IUs), were entitled to receive all their formerly offset military retired pay beginning October 1, 2009.

Initial rates: CRDP is part of retired pay and cannot exceed the amount that would be otherwise offset. During CY 2004, CRDP was paid to qualified retirees up to the following maximum amount based on the current monthly VA disability rating:

100 percent (total) $750

90 percent $500

80 percent $350

70 percent $250

60 percent $125

50 percent $100

Payments above are increased each year following 2004, based on a percentage of the remaining amount of retired pay still being offset for each individual until the offset is completely eliminated in 2014.

Applications for CRDP are neither required nor accepted. DFAS will determine CRDP benefits automatically. Retirees who are not receiving payments but believe they qualify should contact their military department or DFAS to determine the reason for nonpayment.

(2) Combat-Related Special Compensation (CRSC): The CRSC program pays added benefits to retirees who receive VA disability compensation for combat-related disabilities and have 20 years of service. This entitlement is nontaxable.

Effective June 1, 2003: Initially, benefits were payable to members with a combined combat-related disability rating of 60 percent or more, or with a combined rating of 10 percent or more for combat-related injuries for which they were awarded a Purple Heart.

Effective January 1, 2004: Eligibility was expanded to members with any combined percentage rating for combat-related disabilities compensated by the VA. Eligibility criteria was also relaxed with respect to the 20-year requirement to include any member otherwise qualified who is receiving Reserve retired pay (paid at age 60 based on points for Reserve participation with 20 "good" years).

Application Required: To receive CRSC benefits, retirees must apply with their branch of service on a DD Form 2860. The service will determine which disabilities, if any, qualify as combat related. DFAS will pay CRSC based on the current combined disability rating of combat-related disabilities as compensated for the current month by the VA. Benefits before January 2004 are based on the VA compensation rate for a "veteran alone" and applicable to only those disabilities determined as combat related.

Services may be contacted at the following addresses and toll-free numbers:

- **Army**: U.S. Total Army Personnel Command, U.S. Army Physical Disability Agency (CRSC), c/o The Adjutant General Directorate, 2461 Eisenhower Avenue, Alexandria, VA 22331-0470 (Toll-free 1-866-281-3254)

- **Navy and Marine Corps**: Department of Navy, Naval Council of Personnel Boards Combat-Related Special Compensation Branch, 720 Kennon Street SE, Suite 309, Washington Navy Yard, DC 20374-5023 (Toll-free 1-877-366-2772)

- **Air Force**: United States Air Force Personnel Center Disability Division (CRSC), 550 C Street West, Suite 6, Randolph AFB, TX 78150-4708 (Toll-free 1-800-616-3775)

(3) Special Compensation for Severely Disabled Retirees (SCSD): The SCSD program was repealed effective January 1, 2004, and replaced with more generous benefits under the CRDP program described above. Members had to have 20 years of service for the computation of retired pay. Those retired under disability retirement provisions (chapter 61, title 10, United States Code) were excluded from eligibility.

Effective October 1, 1999: SCSD became effective October 1, 1999, for qualified retirees with VA disabilities rated 70 percent or more within four years of retirement. The criteria were relaxed October 1, 2001, to include chapter 61 retirees so long as they had the required 20 years of service. Effective February 1, 2002, the criteria were again relaxed to include those with disabilities rated 60 percent or more within four years of retirement. 37,000 members were eventually compensated. Members not compensated who provide evidence of their qualifications may be retroactively compensated for any months in which they met the requirements of law.

VETERANS HEALTHCARE & VA HOSPITALS

Aside from disability benefits, one of the main benefits veterans enjoy is access to quality healthcare at little or no cost through the VA network of hospitals and Medical Treatment Facilities. Since the global war on terrorism began, Military Treatment Facilities, such as Walter Reed Army Medical Center, have enjoyed less than stellar press for the treatment of our wounded veterans. This is a travesty, which fortunately was recognized and I hope is being remedied. The string of Veterans Administration Hospitals across the United States is a welcome sanctuary for our veterans who enjoy great medical care for little or no cost. The benefit for free or low-cost access to healthcare for veterans is one of the (if not the) biggest benefit to being a veteran. Understand that VA healthcare is not just for retired military members. Under many other circumstances (I have outlined them all here for you), you are entitled to VA healthcare, if eligible, from two years to lifetime, depending on how long you served, disability status, combat-related duties, and several other factors. Often military members who plan to make a career in the military think about the TRICARE Retiree Medical Program and do not think about the VA benefits they are entitled to. You will be surprised at just how readily available VA facilities and VA hospitals may be for you. I live in Land O' Lakes, Florida, and a veterans' hospital is just three miles from my house.

The VA operates the nation's largest integrated healthcare system with more than 1,400 sites of care, including hospitals, community clinics, nursing homes, domiciliaries, readjustment counseling centers, and various other facilities. For additional information on VA healthcare, visit **www.va.gov/health_benefits**.

Benefits on the Go

VA enrollment allows healthcare benefits to become portable throughout the entire VA system. Enrolled veterans who are traveling or who spend time away from their primary treatment facility may obtain care at any VA healthcare facility across the country without having to reapply.

VETERANS' HEALTHCARE BENEFITS

The VA provides a number of healthcare services. These are:

- Hospital, outpatient medical, dental, pharmacy, and prosthetic services

- Domiciliary, nursing home, and community-based residential care

- Sexual trauma counseling

- Specialized healthcare for women veterans

- Health and rehabilitation programs for homeless veterans

- Readjustment counseling

- Alcohol and drug dependency treatment

- Medical evaluation for disorders associated with military service in the Gulf War, or exposure to Agent Orange, radiation, and other environmental hazards

Clinical Programs and Initiatives

The Veterans Administration offers wide variety of clinical programs and initiatives. Information on each of these may be obtained at **www1.va.gov/health/clinical.asp**. These include, but are not limited to:

- Agent Orange health effects and Vietnam veterans

- Blind rehabilitation services

- Cancer program

- Center for Women Veterans

- Cold injury

- Diabetes program

- Flu (influenza-pandemic)

- Gulf War veterans' health

- Healthcare programs for elderly veterans

- HIV/AIDS program

- Homelessness

- Kidney diseases program

- Mental health

- Mental Illness Research, Education and Clinical Centers (MIRECC)

- National Center for Posttraumatic Stress Disorder

- National Center Patient Safety

- Nursing

- Polytrauma

- Recreation/creative arts therapy service

- Social work

- War-Related Illness and Injury Study Center

Priority Scheduling for Service-Connected Veterans

VA will provide you priority access to care if you are a veteran who:

- Needs care of a service-connected disability

- Has a service-connected disability rated 50 percent or higher and need care for any condition

In this case, VA will schedule you for a primary care evaluation within 30 days of the desired date. If your outpatient appointment cannot be scheduled within this time, VA will arrange to have you seen within 30 days at another VA healthcare facility or obtain the services on a fee basis, under a sharing agreement or contract at VA expense.

All other veterans will be scheduled for a primary care appointment as soon as one becomes available.

Veterans Pharmacy/Prescription Benefits

Veterans enjoy free or low cost prescriptions (copay) from VA facilities. You can even get refills online through the HealtheVet Web site.

Emergency Care in Non-VA Facilities

Emergency care in non-VA facilities is provided as a safety net for veterans under specific conditions. You are eligible if the non-VA emergency care is for a service-connected condition or, if enrolled, you have been provided care by a VA clinician or provider within the past 24 months and have no other healthcare coverage. Also, it must be determined that VA healthcare facilities were not feasibly available, that a delay in medical attention would have endangered your life or health, and that you are liable for the cost of the services.

Extended Care

The VA provides institutional long-term care to eligible veterans through VA nursing homes, community nursing homes, state veterans homes, and domiciliaries. Other services include:

- Hospice

- Respite care

- Geriatric Evaluation and Management (GEM)

- Community residential care

- Home healthcare

- Adult day healthcare

- Homemaker/home health aide services

There is more on this topic later in the chapter.

Eyeglasses and Hearing Aids

You are eligible for hearing aids and eyeglasses if you:

- Receive increased pension for regular aid and attendance or are permanently housebound

- Receive compensation for a service-connected disability

- Are a former prisoner of war

- Received a Purple Heart medal

Otherwise, hearing aids and eyeglasses will be provided only in special circumstances and not for normally occurring hearing or vision loss.

Foreign Medical Program

The Foreign Medical Program (FMP) is a program for veterans who live or travel overseas. Under the FMP, the Department of Veteran Affairs will pay the VA allowable amount for treatment of a service-connected disability or medical services needed as part of a VA vocational rehabilitation program.

The VA's Health Administration Center (HAC), located in Denver, Colorado, handles the FMP program for medical services provided to eligible veterans in all foreign countries except the Philippines. For more information, contact the HAC toll free at 877-345-8179 or visit its Web site at **www.va.gov/hac/forbeneficiaries/fmp/fmp.asp**.

VA HEALTHCARE ELIGIBILITY

The VA provides a medical benefits package — a standard enhanced health benefits plan available to all enrolled veterans. This plan emphasizes preventive and primary care, and offers a full range of outpatient and inpatient services within the VA healthcare system.

The VA maintains an annual enrollment system to manage the provision of quality hospital and outpatient medical care and treatment to all enrolled veterans. A priority system ensures that veterans with service-connected disabilities and those below the low-income threshold are able to be enrolled in the VA's healthcare system.

All Veterans Are Potentially Eligible

- Eligibility for most veterans' healthcare benefits is based solely on active military service in the Army, Navy, Air Force, Marines, or Coast Guard (or Merchant Marines during World War II) and a discharge under any circumstance other than dishonorable conditions.

- Reservists and National Guard members who were called to active duty by a federal executive order may qualify for VA healthcare benefits. Returning service members, including reservists and National Guard members who served on active duty in a theater of combat operations, have special eligibility for hospital care, medical services, and nursing home care for two years following discharge from active duty.

- Healthcare eligibility is not just for those who served in combat.

- Veterans' healthcare is not just for service-connected injuries or medical conditions.

- Veterans' healthcare facilities are not just for men only. VA offers full-service healthcare to women veterans.

Determining VA Healthcare Eligibility

Eligibility for healthcare through VA is a two-step process:

1. VA must determine your eligibility status as a veteran by reviewing your Character of Discharge from active military service and your length of active military service.

2. VA must determine whether you qualify for one of the eight enrollment priority groups.

The number of veterans who can be enrolled in the healthcare program is determined by the amount of money Congress gives the VA each year. Because funds are limited, VA set up priority groups to make sure that certain groups of veterans can be enrolled before others.

Once you apply for enrollment, your eligibility will be verified. Based on your specific eligibility status, you will be assigned a priority group. The priority groups range from one to eight, with one being the highest priority for enrollment. Some veterans may have to agree to pay copay to be placed in certain priority groups.

ENROLLMENT PRIORITY GROUPS

Priority	Description
Priority 1	• Veterans with service-connected disabilities rated 50 percent or more disabling, or • Veterans determined by VA to be unemployable due to service-connected conditions. Note: A service-connected disability is a disability that VA determines was incurred or aggravated while on active duty in the military and in the line of duty. A service-connected rating is an official ruling by the VA that your illness/condition is directly related to your active military service. Service-connected ratings are established by VA regional offices located throughout the country.
Priority 2	Veterans with service-connected disabilities rated 30 percent or 40 percent disabling.
Priority 3	• Veterans with service-connected disabilities rated 10 percent or 20 percent disabling, • Veterans who are former POWs, • Veterans awarded the Purple Heart, • Veterans whose discharge was for a disability that began in the line of duty, or • Veterans who are disabled because of VA treatment or participation in VA vocational rehabilitation program.
Priority 4	• Veterans who are receiving aid and attendance or housebound benefits (on pension) from the VA or • Veterans who have been determined by the VA to be catastrophically disabled. Aid & Attendance: A VA compensation or pension benefit awarded to a veteran determined to be in need of the regular aid and attendance of another person to perform basic functions of everyday life. A veteran may qualify for aid and attendance benefits if he or she: • Is blind or so nearly blind as to have corrected visual acuity of 5/200 or less, in both eyes, or concentric contraction of the visual field to 5 degrees or less, or

ENROLLMENT PRIORITY GROUPS	
Priority	**Description**
Priority 4 cont.	• Is a patient in a nursing home because of mental or physical incapacity, or • Proves a need for aid and attendance under established criteria. Catastrophically Disabled: A veteran who has a permanent, severely disabling injury, disorder, or disease that compromises the ability to carry out the activities of daily living to such a degree that he/she requires personal or mechanical assistance to leave home or bed or requires constant supervision to avoid physical harm to self or others.
Priority 5	• Veterans receiving VA pension benefits, • Veterans who are eligible for Medicaid programs, or • Veterans with income and assets below VA Means Test Thresholds. Pension Benefit: VA pension is a monetary award paid on a monthly basis to veterans with low income who are permanently and totally disabled or are age 65 and older. Veterans may be eligible for monetary support if they have 90 days or more of active military service, at least one day of which was during a period or war. Payments are made to qualified veterans to bring their total income, including other retirement or Social Security income, to a level set by Congress annually. Veterans of a period of war who are age 65 or older and meet service and income requirements are also eligible to receive a pension, regardless of current physical condition. • Veterans with 0 percent service-connected conditions but receiving VA Conditions Associated with Ionizing Radiation compensation, • Veterans seeking care only for disorders relating to Ionizing Radiation and Project 112/SHAD (see next page), • Veterans seeking care for Agent Orange Exposure during service in Vietnam, or • Veterans seeking care for Gulf War Illness or for conditions related to exposure to environmental contaminants during service in the Persian Gulf.

ENROLLMENT PRIORITY GROUPS	
Priority	**Description**
Priority 6	• Veterans of World War I or the Mexican Border War, or • Veterans who served in combat in a war after the Gulf War or during a period of hostility after November 11, 1998 for two years following discharge or release from the military.

Ionizing Radiation: Atomic-era veterans may have been exposed to ionizing radiation in a variety of ways at various locations. Veterans exposed at a nuclear device-testing site (the Pacific Islands, such as Bikini; NM; or NV) or in Hiroshima and/or Nagasaki, Japan, may be included. Atomic veterans with exposure to ionizing radiation are eligible to receive treatment for conditions related to this exposure. VA has recognized the following conditions by statute or regulation as being associated with radiation exposure:

- Leukemia
- Thyroid cancer
- Breast cancer
- Lung cancer
- Bone cancer
- Primary liver cancer
- Skin cancer
- Esophageal cancer
- Stomach cancer
- Colon cancer
- Salivary gland cancer
- Multiple myeloma
- Parathyroid adenoma
- Ovarian cancer
- Cancer of the rectum
- Cancer of the prostate
- Cancer of the bile duct
- Cancer of the pharynx
- Cancer of the small intestine
- Cancer of the gall bladder
- Kidney cancer
- Urinary bladder cancer
- Pancreatic cancer
- Posterior subcapsular cataracts
- Nonmalignant thyroid nodular disease
- Tumors of the brain and central nervous system
- Lymphomas other than Hodgkin's disease

ENROLLMENT PRIORITY GROUPS

Priority	Description
Priority 6 cont.	• Cancer of the renal pelvis, ureters, and urethra • All other cancers Project 112/SHAD: Project SHAD, an acronym for Shipboard Hazard and Defense, was part of a larger effort called Project 112, which was conducted during the 1960s. Project SHAD encompassed tests designed to identify U.S. warships' vulnerabilities to attacks with chemical or biological warfare agents and to develop procedures to respond to such attacks while maintaining a war-fighting capability. Agent Orange (AO) is a herbicide that was used in Vietnam between 1962 and 1971 to remove unwanted plant life that provided cover for enemy forces. The VA has recognized the following conditions as associated with but not necessarily caused by exposure to Agent Orange: • Diabetes (type 2) • Chloracne or other acneform disease consistent with chloracne (must occur within one year of exposure to AO) • Porphyria cutanea tarda (must occur within one year of exposure to AO) • Acute and subacute peripheral neuropathy (for purposes of this section, the term acute and subacute peripheral neuropathy means temporary peripheral neuropathy that appears within weeks or months of exposure to an herbicide agent and resolves within two years of the date of onset) • Numerous cancers • Prostate cancer • Hodgkin's disease • Multiple myeloma • Non-Hodgkin's lymphoma • Respiratory cancers (cancer of the lung, bronchus, larynx, or trachea, must occur within 30 years of exposure to Agent Orange)

ENROLLMENT PRIORITY GROUPS

Priority	Description
Priority 6 cont.	• Soft-tissue sarcoma (other than osteosarcoma, chondrosarcoma, Kaposi's sarcoma, or mesothelioma)

Environmental Contaminants/Gulf War Illness: Gulf War veterans were exposed to a wide variety of environmental hazards and potentially harmful substances during their service in Southwest Asia. These include depleted uranium, pesticides, the anti-nerve gas pill pyridostigmine bromide, infectious diseases, chemical and biological warfare agents, vaccinations (including anthrax and botulinum toxoid), and oil-well free smoke and petroleum products. VA recognizes that there are other health risk factors encountered by Gulf War veterans. Veterans with service during the Gulf War are eligible to receive treatment for conditions related to this service.

If the treatment provided is for an illness or symptom that may possibly be associated with environmental contamination, copay for medical care and medication copay will not be charged.

Conditions associated with environmental contaminants:

- Persistent fatigue
- Skin rash
- Headache
- Arthralgias/myalgias
- Sleep disturbance
- Forgetfulness
- Joint pain
- Shortness of breath/chest pain
- Feverishness
- Amyotrophic Lateral Sclerosis

- Veterans who agree to pay specified copay with income and/or net worth above VA Income Threshold and income below the Geographic Means Test Threshold (**www.va.gov/healtheligibility/Library/pubs/GMTIncomeThresholds**),

- Subpriority a: Noncompensable 0 percent service-connected disability veterans who were enrolled in VA Healthcare System on a specified date and who have remained enrolled since that date,

- Subpriority c: Nonservice disability-connected veterans who were enrolled in the VA Healthcare System on a specified date and who have remained enrolled since that date.

ENROLLMENT PRIORITY GROUPS

Priority	Description
Priority 7	• Subpriority e: Noncompensable 0 percent service-connected veterans not included in Subpriority a above (V*A is not currently using Subpriority e)* • Subpriority g: Nonservice-connected veterans not included in Subpriority c as described above (*VA is not currently using Subpriority g)* • Veterans who agree to pay specified copay with income and/or net worth above VA Means Test threshold and the Geographic Means Test Threshold (**www.va.gov/healtheligibility/Library/ pubs/GMTIncomeThresholds**). • Subpriority a: Noncompensable 0 percent disabled/ service-connected veterans enrolled as of January 16, 2003, and who have remained enrolled since that date. • Subpriority c: Nonservice-connected disabled veterans enrolled as of January 16, 2003, and who have remained enrolled since that date. • Subpriority e*: Noncompensable 0 percent disabled/ service-connected veterans applying for enrollment after January 16, 2003. • Subpriority g*: Nonservice-connected disabled veterans applying for enrollment after January 16, 2003. * Enrollment Restriction: Effective January 17, 2003, VA suspended new enrollment of veterans assigned to Priority Group 8e and 8g (VA's lowest priority group consisting of higher-income veterans). Veterans assigned to Priority Group 8e and 8g are veterans who are enrolling for the first time on or after January 17, 2003, and whose income exceeds the current year income threshold. They have no other special eligibilities such as a compensable service-connected condition or recent combat service. Those who refuse to provide income information are not eligible for enrollment at this time. Veterans enrolled in Priority Group 8a and 8c on or before January 16, 2003, will remain enrolled and continue to be eligible for the full range of VA healthcare benefits.

ENROLLMENT PRIORITY GROUPS	
Priority	**Description**
Priority 8	New enrollees assigned to subpriority groups e and g are not eligible for enrollment at this time. A fact sheet is available from the VA at: **www.va.gov/healtheligibility/Library/pubs/EPG/EnrollmentPriorityGroups.pdf**.

You may be eligible for more than one Enrollment Priority Group. In that case, VA will always place you in the highest priority group for which you are eligible. Under the medical benefits package, the same services may be available to all enrolled veterans.

The priority groups are complicated, and some reference financial thresholds.

The character of discharge you received from the military can be a factor. It is not an issue if you received:

- An honorable discharge

- A general discharge

- A discharge under honorable conditions

The length of your service may also matter. It depends on when you served. There is no length of service requirement for:

- Former enlisted persons who first started active duty before September 8, 1980

- Former officers who first entered active duty before October 17, 1981

- All other veterans must have 24 months of continuous active duty military service (or meet one of the following exceptions)

If you have a different character of discharge, you may still be eligible for care. Contact an enrollment coordinator at a local VA healthcare facility.

Reservists and National Guard members activated for federal service can qualify for VA healthcare but must be enrolled to receive services.

Reservists and National Guard members who served on active duty in a theater of combat operations during a period of war after the Gulf War or in combat against a hostile force after November 11, 1998, are eligible for enrollment in Priority Group 6 unless otherwise eligible for enrollment in a higher priority group and free healthcare services for conditions potentially related to combat service for two years following separation from active duty. For information, call 1-877-222-VETS (8387).

Minimum Service Requirement

You do not have to meet the 24 continuous months of active duty service requirement if you:

- Were a reservist who was called to active duty and who completed the term for which you were called and who was granted an other than dishonorable discharge

- Were a National Guard member who was called to active duty by federal executive order, who completed the term, and who was granted an other than dishonorable discharge

- Only request a benefit for or in connection with:

  - A service-connected condition or disability

  - Treatment and/or counseling of sexual trauma that occurred while on active military service

  - Treatment of conditions related to ionizing radiation

  - Head or neck cancer related to nose or throat radium treatment while in the military

- Were discharged or released from active duty for a hardship

- Were discharged with an "early out"

- Were discharged or released from active duty for a disability that began in the service or got worse because of the service

- Have been determined by VA to have compensable service-connected conditions

- Were discharged for a reason other than disability, but had a medical condition at the time that was disabling and, in the opinion of a doctor, would have justified a discharge for disability (in this last case, the disability must be documented in service records)

ENROLLMENT IN VA HEALTHCARE SYSTEM

You must be enrolled in the VA healthcare system to receive benefits offered in the medical benefits package. Certain veterans do not need to be enrolled to receive medical care benefits but are urged to do so to permit better planning of health resources:

You do not have to be enrolled if you:

- Have been determined by the VA to be 50 percent or more disabled from service-connected conditions

- Are seeking care for a VA-rated service-connected disability only

- Were discharged for a disability that the military determined was incurred or aggravated by your service but that VA has not yet rated less than one year ago

For most veterans, entry into the VA healthcare system begins by applying for enrollment. To apply, complete VA Form 10-10EZ, Application for Health Benefits, which may be obtained from any VA healthcare facility or regional benefits office, online at **www.va.gov/1010ez.htm**, or by calling

1-877-222-VETS (8387). Once enrolled, veterans can receive healthcare at VA healthcare facilities anywhere in the country.

Veterans enrolled in the VA healthcare system are afforded privacy rights under federal law. VA's Notice of Privacy Practices, which describes how VA may use and disclose veterans' medical information, is also available online at **www.va.gov/vhapublications/ViewPublication.asp?pub_ID=1089**.

Copays and Charges

There is no monthly premium required to use VA care. You may, however, have to agree to pay copays. If you have insurance, it may cover the cost of the copays.

Although many veterans qualify for cost-free healthcare services based on a compensable service-connected condition or other qualifying factor, most veterans are required to complete an annual financial assessment or Means Test to determine if they qualify for cost-free services. Veterans whose gross household income and net worth exceed the established threshold and those who choose not to complete the financial assessment must agree to pay the required copays to become eligible for VA healthcare services. (New veterans who apply for enrollment after January 16, 2003, and who decline to provide income information are not eligible for enrollment.) Along with their enrollment confirmation and priority group assignment, enrollees will receive information regarding their copay requirements, if applicable.

Will I be charged copays?

Many veterans qualify for cost-free healthcare and/or medications based on one of the following:

- Receiving a Purple Heart Medal

- Former Prisoner of War status

- Compensable service-connected disabilities

- Low income

- Other qualifying factors including treatment related to their military service experience

Reduce or Eliminate VA Medical Care Copays

If you are now receiving VA compensation for a service-connected disability or VA pension benefits, your VA medical care and/or prescription copays may be reduced or eliminated. You may also be eligible for a refund of copay charges you have previously paid based on this decision. Call the Health Benefits Service Center at 1-877-222-VETS (8387) or contact the Enrollment Coordinator at your local VA medical center for more information.

If I have private health insurance, will VA bill my insurance company?

VA is required to bill private health insurance providers for medical care, supplies, and prescriptions provided for care veterans receive for conditions that are not service-connected. Often, VA cannot bill Medicare but can bill Medicare supplemental health insurance for covered services.

All veterans applying for VA medical care are required to provide information on their health insurance coverage, including coverage provided under policies of their spouses. Veterans are not responsible for paying any remaining balance of VA's insurance claim not paid or covered by their health insurance, and any payment received by VA may be used to offset a veteran's VA copay responsibility.

Some of the services exempt from inpatient and outpatient copays:

- Special registry examinations offered by VA to evaluate possible health risks associated with military service

- Counseling and care for military sexual trauma

- Compensation and pension examination requested by VBA

- Care that is part of a VA-approved research project

- Care related to a VA-rated service connected disability

- Readjustment counseling and related mental health services for posttraumatic stress disorder (PTSD);

- Emergency treatment at other than VA facilities

- Care for cancer of the head or neck caused from nose or throat radium treatments given while in the military

- Publicly announced VA public health initiatives such as health fairs

- Care related to service for veterans who served in combat or against a hostile force during a period of hostilities after November 11, 1998

- Laboratory services such as flat film radiology services and electrocardiograms

- Preventive screenings (hypertension, hepatitis C, tobacco, alcohol, and colorectal cancer)

- Immunizations (such as influenza and pneumococcal)

What should I do if I cannot afford to pay copays?

There are three options:

(1) Request a waiver of the copays you currently owe. To request a waiver, you must submit proof that you cannot financially afford to make payments to the VA. Contact the revenue coordinator at the VA healthcare facility where you receive care for more information.

(2) Request a hardship determination so you will not be charged in the future. If you request a hardship, you are asking VA to

change your Priority Group assignment. You will need to submit current financial information, and a decision will be made based on the information you provide. You may contact the enrollment coordinator at your local VA for more information.

(3) Request a compromise. A compromise is an offer and acceptance of a partial payment in settlement and full satisfaction of the debt as it exists at the time the offer is made. Most compromise offers that are accepted must be for a lump sum payment payable in full 30 days from the date of acceptance of the offer. You may contact the enrollment coordinator at your local VA for more information.

Who is subject to provide a financial assessment (Means Test)?

Certain nonservice-connected disabled veterans and 0 percent noncompensable service-connected disabled veterans are asked to report gross household income and net worth from the previous calendar year.

In determining your VA healthcare benefit it may be to your advantage to provide your income information if your gross household income (less allowable deductions) is equal to or less than the amount listed below. From the amounts you report on the financial worksheet, VA will calculate and inform you of your income-based benefits.

Current year income and net worth can be considered when there is a hardship. If you decline to give your financial information, the VA will place you in Priority Group 8 and require you to agree to pay the copay fees for Group 8 before treatment can be given.

Note that veterans who are applying for enrollment on or after January 17, 2003, who are assigned to Priority Group 8, are not eligible for enrollment or care of their nonservice-connected conditions.

The financial information the VA gathers from your Financial Assessment (Means Test) will determine your enrollment priority group assignment and if you will or will not be required to pay copays.

VA determines your priority group and copay requirements based on set income and net worth limits. These limits are referred to as the VA National Income Thresholds for VA Healthcare Benefits.

INCOME VERIFICATION

VA is required to verify the gross household income (spouse and dependents, if any) of most nonservice-connected or noncompensable 0 percent service-connected disabled veterans to confirm the accuracy of their:

- Eligibility for VA healthcare

- Copay status

- Enrollment priority group assignment

VA verifies your gross household income (spouse and dependents, if any) by matching the financial data you provided with financial records maintained by the IRS and Social Security Administration. If the matching process reveals that your gross household income is higher than the threshold, you will be provided an opportunity to review the IRS and SSA data and provide additional information regarding the difference. Veterans subject to this process are individually notified by mail and provided with all related information.

At the end of the income verification process, if it is determined that your gross household income is higher than the threshold:

- Your priority group assignment will be changed.

- You will be required to pay copay.

- The facilities that provided you care will be notified to bill you for services provided during the period covered by your income assessment.

- You will be provided with your due-process/appeal rights.

VETERANS CLAIMS ACT OF 2000 AND DUTY TO ASSIST

A recent law requires that the VA obtain any records in the VA's possession or within any other Federal agency. The law also mandates the VA tell the claimant what evidence is needed to support the claim. The VA now must make several efforts to obtain any evidence identified by the claimant.

Evidence to Support a Claim

By law, the burden of proof falls on the veteran or dependent. Even though the VA is now required to look for evidence, this may take many months. You can help your claim and speed up the process if you can obtain supporting evidence.

Evidence can be any number of items:

- Veteran's statements, especially those of combat veterans claiming a combat-related injury or illness

- Statements from friends, relatives, or anyone who has knowledge of your disability and its relationship to service

- Medical evidence

Any lay statements must fit certain criteria and are not always helpful. Some can be harmful to your claim. You should discuss any statements with your representative before submitting it to the VA. If you need assistance completing the form, contact:

- The Enrollment Coordinator at your local VA healthcare facility

- VA's Health Benefits Service Center at 877-222-VETS (8387)

- A state or county veterans service officer

- A service officer with a veterans service organization

Who can sign the form? You or the person acting as your power of attorney must sign and date the form. If your power of attorney signs and dates the form you must submit a copy of the power of attorney with the form. If you sign with an "X," then two people you know should witness as you sign. They must also sign and print their names on the form.

Where do I send my completed application? Mail the original application with a copy of your supporting materials to your local VA healthcare facility.

When will I receive a decision on my application? Once your application for enrollment in the VA healthcare system is processed, VA's Health Eligibility Center will send you a letter informing you of your enrollment priority group assignment and whether you were enrolled. The letter will also give you instructions on how to appeal the decision if you do not agree with it.

Do I need to reapply annually? Veterans who are enrolled will remain enrolled without having to reapply for benefits annually. However, some veterans will need to update their financial information yearly to keep their enrollment priority current. VA will contact these veterans when it is time to update their financial information.

APPLYING FOR LONG-TERM CARE

Long-term care benefits provide for a range of long-term care services, including nursing home care, domiciliary care, adult day healthcare, geriatric evaluation, and respite care.

Nonservice-connected and 0 percent service-connected disability enrolled veterans with income over the single pension rate will need to complete VA Form 10-10EC, Application for Extended Care Services in addition to a VA Form 10-10EZ.

Form 10-10EC is used to measure your family's current income and assets to determine if you will be charged copays for long-term care.

Veterans with a compensable service-connected disability are exempt from long-term care copays.

What Evidence Is Needed to Apply?

To reduce processing time, you may submit any one of the following paperwork for evidence:

- A copy of your discharge papers (DD-214 or "WD" form) if you are not currently receiving benefits from the VA

- Military service records indicating that you received a Purple Heart

- Evidence that you received hostile fire or imminent danger pay or a combat medal after this date if you indicated that you were in combat after November 11, 1998

Domiciliary Residential Care and Treatment

The mission of Domiciliary Residential Rehabilitation and Treatment is to provide coordinated, integrated rehabilitative and restorative clinical care in a bed-based program, with the goal of helping eligible veterans achieve and maintain the highest level of functioning and independence possible. Domiciliary care, as an integral component of VHA's continuum of healthcare services, is committed to providing the highest quality of clinical care in a coordinated, integrated fashion within that continuum.

Domiciliary Residential Rehabilitation and Treatment is defined by the following characteristics:

- It provides clinical care to patients who suffer from a wide range of problems, illnesses, or areas of dysfunction, which can be medical, psychiatric, vocational, educational, or social.

- It provides bed-based care in a safe, secure, semi-structured, homelike environment.

◌ It provides clinical care, which emphasizes a positive therapeutic milieu, functional independence, and patient mutual support, specifically using the therapeutic community model. As used here, this implies the use of the community as method. The peer community is used in a conscious, purposeful manner to facilitate social, psychological, and behavioral change in individuals. Multiple therapeutic and rehabilitative activities are used, all being designed to produce therapeutic and educational changes, and all participants (patients and staff) are considered mediators of these changes.

◌ It uses a broad range of resources.

◌ It provides care by Domiciliary interdisciplinary clinical teams that develop, integrate, and coordinate comprehensive and individualized plans of treatment, rehabilitation, or health maintenance, which include all resources involved in the patient's care, both within and outside the Domiciliary.

◌ It provides optimal opportunities for community interaction, vocational involvement, and graduated independence.

◌ It offers the potential for treatment or rehabilitation of patients with relatively narrowly defined problems if the general definition of Domiciliary Rehabilitation and Treatment is met, in each instance attending to whether a different type of care or treatment program would be more appropriate.

◌ It offers preadmission outreach and post-discharge followup.

◌ It differs from hospital or nursing home care in that Domiciliary Residential Rehabilitation and Treatment patients do not require bedside nursing care and are capable of daily self-care (activities of daily living).

Patient and Nursing Home Resident Rights and Responsibilities

◌ You will be given information about the health benefits you can receive. The information will be provided in a way you can understand.

§ You will receive information about the costs of your care, if any, before you are treated. You are responsible for paying your portion of any costs associated with your care.

§ Your medical record will be kept confidential. Information about you will not be released without your consent unless authorized by law (an example of this is state public health reporting). You have the right to information in your medical records and may request a copy of your medical records. This will be provided except in rare situations when your VA physician feels the information will be harmful to you. In that case, you have the right to have this discussed with you by your VA provider.

§ You will be informed of all outcomes of care, including any potential injuries. You will be informed about how to request compensation for any injuries.

§ You are encouraged and expected to seek help from your treatment team or a patient advocate if you have problems or complaints. You will be given understandable information about the complaint process. You may complain verbally or in writing, without fear of retaliation.

§ You will be treated with dignity, compassion, and respect as an individual. Your privacy will be protected. You will receive care in a safe environment. We will seek to honor your personal and religious values.

§ You or someone you choose has the right to keep and spend your money. You have the right to receive an accounting of any VA-held funds.

§ Treatment will respect your personal freedoms. In rare cases, the use of medication and physical restraints may be used if all other efforts to keep you or others free from harm have not worked and are necessary.

§ As an inpatient or nursing home resident, you may wear your own clothes. You may keep personal items. This will depend on your medical condition.

§ As an inpatient or nursing home resident, you have the right to social interaction and regular exercise. You will have the opportunity for religious worship and spiritual support. You may decide whether to participate in these activities. You may decide whether to perform tasks in or for the Medical Center.

§ As an inpatient or nursing home resident, you have the right to communicate freely and privately. You may have or refuse visitors. You will have access to public telephones. You may participate in civic rights, such as voting and free speech.

§ As a nursing home resident, you can organize and take part in resident groups in the facility. Your family also can meet with the families of other residents.

§ To provide a safe treatment environment for all patients or residents and staff, you are expected to respect other patients, residents, and staff and to follow the facility's rules. Avoid unsafe acts that place others at risk for accidents or injuries. Please immediately report any condition you believe to be unsafe.

§ You, and any persons you choose, will be involved in all decisions about your care. You will be given information you can understand about the benefits and risks of treatment. You will be given other options. You can agree to or refuse treatment. You will be told what is likely to happen to you if you refuse treatment. Refusing treatment will not affect your rights to future care, but you take responsibility for the possible results to your health.

§ Tell your provider about your current condition, medicines (including over-the-counter and herbals), and medical history.

Also, share any other information that affects your health. You should ask questions when you do not understand something about your care. Being involved is important for you to get the best possible results.

§ You will be given, in writing, the name and title of the provider in charge of your care. As our partner in healthcare, you have the right to be involved in choosing your provider. You also have the right to know the names and titles of those who provide you care. This includes students, residents, and trainees. Providers will properly introduce themselves to you when they take part in your care.

§ You will be educated about your role and responsibilities as a patient or resident. This includes your participation in decision making and care at the end of life.

§ If you believe you cannot follow the treatment plan, you have a responsibility to notify your provider or treatment team.

§ You have the right to have your pain assessed and to receive treatment to manage your pain. You and your treatment team will develop a pain-management plan together. You are expected to help the treatment team by telling them if you have pain and if the treatment is working.

§ As an inpatient or nursing home resident, you will be provided any transportation necessary for your treatment plan.

§ You have the right to choose whether you will participate in any research project. Any research will be clearly identified. Potential risks of the research will be identified, and there will be no pressure on you to participate.

§ You will be included in resolving any ethical issues about your care. You may consult with the Medical Center's Ethics Consultation Service and/or other staff knowledgeable about healthcare ethics.

- If you or the Medical Center believes that you have been neglected, abused, or exploited, you will receive help.

HOW TO FIND THE VETERANS ADMINISTRATION FACILITY NEAR YOU

The Veterans Administration makes it easy to find a facility or hospital near you. Visit **www1.va.gov/directory/guide/home.asp** and you will find all facilities in your local area.

MyHealthEVet

The VA established a new Web site for veterans called "MyHealthEVet," located at **www.myhealth.va.gov**.

My HealthEVet (MHV) is the gateway to veteran health benefits and services. It provides access to:

- Trusted health information

- Links to federal and VA benefits and resources

- The Personal Health Journal

- Online VA prescription refills

In the future, MHV registrants will be able to view appointments, copay balances, and key portions of their VA medical records online. My HealthEVet is a powerful tool to help you better understand and manage your health.

The Personal Health Journal provides all these valuable features for managing and tracking your personal health information such as:

- Contact information

- Emergency contacts

- Healthcare providers

- Treatment locations

- Health insurance information

- Wallet ID Card: Print your personal information on a handy, preformatted wallet card for convenient reference. It also has open spaces for you to list allergies and other critical medical conditions.

- Military health history: Record important events from your military service, exposures you think you may have experienced, and assignments related to your health history.

- Medications, over-the-counter drugs, herbals, and supplements: Record the name, starting and ending date, prescription number, and dosage.

- Allergies: Keep track of your allergies by date, severity, reaction, diagnosis, and comments.

- Tests: Keep track of your tests by test name, date of test, location test was performed, provider's name, results, and any comments.

- Medical events: Keep track of illnesses, accidents, or other events by logging their date, treatment prescribed, or comments regarding the event.

- Immunizations: Record the immunization, date received, method used, and any reactions you might have.

- Health eLogs: Track your readings for these many health aspects:

  - Blood pressure

  - Blood sugar

- Cholesterol

- Body temperature

- Body weight

- Heart rate

- Pain

VA BENEFITS AND HEALTHCARE USE

Number of veterans receiving VA disability compensation (as of 06/30/07): 2.8 M

Number of veterans rated 100% disabled (as of 06/30/07):   246,520

Number of veterans receiving VA pension (as of 06/30/07):   323,771

Number of spouses receiving DIC (as of 06/30/07):   316,012

Number of total enrollees in VA healthcare system (FY 06):   7.9 M[1]

Number of total unique patients treated (FY 06):   5.5 M[1]

Number of veterans compensated for posttraumatic stress   292,260

    disorder (as of 06/30/07):

Number of veterans in receipt of IU benefits (as of 06/30/07):   235,316

Number of VA education beneficiaries (FY 06):   498,123

Number of VA veteran life insurance beneficiaries (as of 09/30/06):   1,777 m

Number of VA VOC rehab (chapter 31) trainees (as of FY 06):   53,431

Number of home loans guaranteed by the VA (cumulative as of 06/30/07): 2.2M

Number of healthcare professionals rotating through the VA (FY 06):   100,893

Number of OEF/OIF amputees (as of 07/03/07):   636[2]

* Source: DVA Information Technology Center, Health Services Training Report[1], VBA Education Service, VHA (10A5): [2] Department Of Defense

DISABILITY BENEFITS & COMPENSATION

Military retirement comes with unique benefits, such as a retirement pension, commissary and exchange privileges, and access to VA medical facilities and prescription programs. Disabled veterans can be either retired, medically retired, or discharged, and still be entitled to the same access to veterans' healthcare and other unique programs to assist veterans with the transition from military life to the civilian sector and coping with often traumatic injuries as a result of service-related duties. The war in Iraq and Afghanistan has placed a spotlight on the treatment of our honored servicemen and servicewomen who have paid a severe price for their sacrifice and service. We, as Americans, owe these heroes the quality care and benefits they deserve and are entitled to. This chapter outlines benefits and entitlements as a disabled American veteran. In previous chapters, I outlined the process for determining disability and how the disability percentages are computed. In this chapter, I am simply outlining the benefits and entitlements you will receive as a disabled American veteran. This chapter is specifically geared toward the medical, vocational, and other benefits you are entitled to because of your status as a disabled veteran and is not inclusive of all benefits that are contained in other chapters, such as education, home loans, and other benefits.

VETERANS WITH SERVICE-CONNECTED DISABILITIES

Disability compensation is a monetary benefit paid to veterans who are disabled by an injury or disease that was incurred or aggravated during active military service. These disabilities are considered to be service-connected. Disability compensation varies with the degree of disability and the number of a veteran's dependents and is paid monthly. Veterans with certain severe disabilities may be eligible for additional special monthly compensation. The benefits are not subject to federal or state income tax.

The payment of military retirement pay, disability severance pay and separation incentive payments known as SSB (Special Separation Benefits) and VSI (Voluntary Separation Incentives) affects the amount of VA compensation paid to disabled veterans. To be eligible, the service of the veteran must have been terminated through separation or discharge under conditions other than dishonorable. For additional details, visit the Web site at **www.vba.va.gov/bln/21**.

2007 VA DISABILITY COMPENSATION RATES FOR VETERANS	
Disability Rating	**Monthly Rate Paid**
10 percent	$115
20 percent	$225
30 percent*	$348
40 percent*	$501
50 percent*	$712
60 percent*	$901
70 percent*	$1,135
80 percent*	$1,319
90 percent*	$1,483
100 percent*	$2,471

*Veterans with disability ratings of at least 30 percent are eligible for additional allowances for dependents, including spouses, minor children, children between the ages of 18 and 23 who are attending school, children who are permanently incapable of self-support because of a disability arising before age 18, and dependent parents. The additional amount depends on the disability rating.

The VA offers three payment options to veterans eligible to receive benefit payments. Most veterans receive their payments by direct deposit to a bank, savings and loan, or credit union account. In some areas, veterans who do not have a bank account can open a federally insured Electronic Transfer Account, which costs about $3 a month, provides a monthly statement and allows cash withdrawals. Other veterans may choose to receive benefits by check. To choose a payment method, call toll-free 1-877-838-2778, Monday through Friday, 7:30 a.m. - 4 p.m., CST.

Presumptive Conditions Considered for Awarding Disability Compensation

Certain veterans are eligible for disability compensation based on the presumption that their disability is service connected:

Prisoners of War: For former POWs who were imprisoned for any length of time, the following disabilities are presumed to be service-connected if they are rated at least 10 percent disabling anytime after military service: psychosis, any of the anxiety states, dysthymic disorder, organic residuals of frostbite, posttraumatic osteoarthritis, heart disease or hypertensive vascular disease and their complications, stroke, and residuals of stroke.

For former POWs who were imprisoned for at least 30 days, the following conditions are also presumed to be service-connected: avitaminosis, beriberi, chronic dysentery, helminthiasis, malnutrition (including optic atrophy), pellagra and/or other nutritional deficiencies, irritable bowel syndrome, peptic ulcer disease, peripheral neuropathy, and cirrhosis of the liver.

Veterans exposed to Agent Orange and other herbicides: A veteran who served in the Republic of Vietnam between January 9, 1962, and May 7, 1975, is presumed to have been exposed to Agent Orange and other herbicides used in support of military operations. Eleven diseases are presumed by the VA to be service-connected for such veterans: chloracne or other acneform disease similar to chloracne, porphyria cutanea tarda, soft-tissue sarcoma (other than osteosarcoma, chondrosarcoma, Kaposi's sarcoma or mesothelioma), Hodgkin's disease, multiple myeloma, respiratory cancers (lung, bronchus, larynx, trachea), non-Hodgkin's lymphoma, prostate cancer, acute and subacute peripheral neuropathy, diabetes mellitus (type 2), and chronic lymphocytic leukemia.

Veterans exposed to radiation: For veterans who participated in "radiation risk activities" as defined in VA regulations while on active duty, the following conditions are presumed to be service-connected: all forms of leukemia (except for chronic lymphocytic leukemia); cancer of the thyroid, breast, pharynx, esophagus, stomach, small intestine, pancreas, bile ducts, gall bladder, salivary gland, urinary tract (renal pelvis, ureter, urinary bladder and urethra), brain, bone, lung, colon, and ovary, bronchiolo-alveolar carcinoma, multiple myeloma, lymphomas (other than Hodgkin's disease), and primary liver cancer (except if cirrhosis or hepatitis B is indicated).

To determine service-connection for other conditions or exposures not eligible as presumptive service-connection status, VA considers factors such as the amount of radiation exposure, duration of exposure, elapsed time between exposure and onset of the disease, gender and family history, age at time of exposure, the extent to which a nonservice-related exposure could contribute to disease, and the relative sensitivity of exposed tissue.

Gulf War veterans may receive disability compensation for chronic disabilities resulting from undiagnosed illnesses and medically unexplained chronic multi-symptom illnesses defined by a cluster of signs or symptoms. A disability is considered chronic if it has existed for at least six months. The undiagnosed illnesses must have appeared either during a active service in the Southwest Asia Theater of Operations during the Gulf War or to a degree of at least 10 percent at any time since then through December 31, 2011.

The following are examples of symptoms of an undiagnosed illness: chronic fatigue syndrome, fibromyalgia, skin disorders, headache, muscle pain, joint pain, neurological symptoms, neuropsychological symptoms, symptoms involving the respiratory system, sleep disturbances, gastrointestinal symptoms, cardiovascular symptoms, abnormal weight loss, and menstrual disorders. Amyotrophic Lateral Sclerosis (ALS), also known as Lou Gehrig's Disease, may be determined to be service-connected if the veteran served in the Southwest Asia Theater of Operations anytime during the period of August 2, 1990, to July 31, 1991. The Southwest Asia Theater of

Operations includes Iraq, Kuwait, Saudi Arabia, the neutral zone between Iraq and Saudi Arabia, Bahrain, Qatar, the United Arab Emirates, Oman, the Gulf of Aden, the Gulf of Oman, the Persian Gulf, the Arabian Sea, the Red Sea, and the air space above these locations.

VOCATIONAL REHABILITATION AND EMPLOYMENT

The Vocational Rehabilitation and Employment Program assists veterans who have service-connected disabilities with obtaining and maintaining suitable employment. Independent living services are also available for severely disabled veterans who are not currently ready to seek employment. Additional information is available at **www.vba.va.gov/bln/vre**.

Eligibility: A veteran must have a VA service-connected disability rated at least 20 percent with an employment handicap or be rated 10 percent with a serious employment handicap and be discharged or released from military service under other than dishonorable conditions.

Service members pending medical separation from active duty may also apply if their disabilities are reasonably expected to be rated at least 20 percent following their discharge.

VA pays the cost of all approved training programs. Subsistence allowance may also be provided. Depending on an individual's needs, services provided by the VA may include:

- An evaluation of interests, aptitudes, and abilities

- Assistance with writing a résumé and other job seeking skills

- Assistance with obtaining and maintaining suitable employment

- Vocational counseling and planning

- On-the-job training and work-experience programs

- Training, such as a certificate, two, or four-year college or technical programs

- Supportive rehabilitation services and counseling

Veterans must complete a program within 12 years from their separation from military service or within 12 years from the date VA notifies them that they have a compensable service-connected disability. Depending on the length of program needed, veterans may be provided up to 48 months of full-time services or their part-time equivalent. These limitations may be extended in certain circumstances.

Work-study: Veterans training at the three-quarter or full-time rate may participate in VA's work-study program. Participants may provide VA outreach services, prepare and process VA paperwork, and work at a VA medical facility or perform other VA-approved activities. A portion of the work-study allowance equal to 40 percent of the total may be paid in advance.

FISCAL YEAR 2007 VA VOCATIONAL REHABILITATION MONTHLY PAYMENT RATE SCHEDULES				
Training time	Veterans with no dependents	Veterans with one dependent	Veterans with two dependents	Each additional dependent
Full time	$508.04	$630.19	$742.61	$54.14
3/4 time	$381.73	$473.32	$555.21	$41.63
1/2 time	$255.42	$316.47	$372	$27.78

For unpaid on-the-job training in a federal, state, or local agency or an agency of a federally recognized Indian tribe; training in a home; vocational course in a rehabilitation facility or sheltered workshop; independent instructor; institutional non-farm cooperative, the rates are:

Training time	Veterans with no dependents	Veterans with one dependent	Veterans with two dependents	Each additional dependent
Full time	$508.04	$630.19	$742.61	$54.14

For farm cooperative, apprenticeship, on-the-job training, or on-the-job non-farm cooperative, VA payments are variable, based on the wages received. The maximum VA rates are:

Training time	Veterans with no dependents	Veterans with one dependent	Veterans with two dependents	Each additional dependent
Full time	$444.19	$537.16	$619.07	$40.27

For extended evaluation, the rates are:

FISCAL YEAR 2007 VA VOCATIONAL REHABILITATION MONTHLY PAYMENT RATE SCHEDULES				
Training time	Veterans with no dependents	Veterans with one dependent	Veterans with two dependents	Each additional dependent
Full time	$508.04	$630.19	$742.61	$54.14
3/4 time	$381.73	$473.32	$555.21	$41.63
1/2 time	$255.42	$316.47	$372	$27.78
1/4 time	$127.70	$158.24	$185.99	$13.85

SPECIALLY ADAPTED HOUSING GRANTS

Certain veterans and service members with service-connected disabilities may be entitled to a Specially Adapted Housing (SAH) grant from the VA to help build a new specially adapted house or buy a house and modify it to meet their disability-related requirements. Eligible veterans or service members may now receive up to three grants, with the total dollar amount of the grants not to exceed the maximum allowable amount. Previous grant recipients who had received assistance of less than the current maximum allowable may be eligible for an additional SAH grant.

Eligible veterans who are temporarily residing in a home owned by a family member may also receive assistance in the form of a grant to assist the veteran in adapting the family member's home to meet his or her special needs. Those eligible for a $50,000 total grant would be permitted to use up to $14,000, and those eligible for a $10,000 total grant would be permitted to use up to $2,000. However, the VA is not authorized to make such grants available to assist active duty personnel.

The VA may approve a grant of not more than 50 percent of the cost of building, buying, or adapting existing homes or paying to reduce indebtedness on a previously owned home that is being adapted, up to a maximum of $50,000. In certain instances, the full grant amount may be applied toward remodeling costs. Veterans and service members must be determined eligible to receive compensation for permanent and total service-connected disability due to one of the following:

- Loss or loss of use of both lower extremities, such as to preclude locomotion without the aid of braces, crutches, canes, or a wheelchair

- Loss or loss of use of both upper extremities at or above the elbow

- Blindness in both eyes, having only light perception, plus loss or loss of use of one lower extremity

- Loss or loss of use of one lower extremity together with (a) residuals of organic disease or injury, or (b) the loss or loss of use of one upper extremity that so affects the functions of balance or propulsion as to preclude locomotion without the use of braces, canes, crutches or a wheelchair

The VA may approve a grant for the cost, up to a maximum of $10,000, for necessary adaptations to a veteran's or service member's residence or to help veterans and service members acquire a residence already adapted with special features for their disability. To be eligible for this grant, veterans and service members must be entitled to compensation for permanent and total service-connected disability due to one of the following:

- Blindness in both eyes with 5/200 visual acuity or less.

- Anatomical loss or loss of use of both hands.

Veterans and service members with available loan guaranty entitlement may also obtain a guaranteed loan or a direct loan from the VA to supplement the grant to acquire a specially adapted home. Amounts with a guaranteed loan from a private lender will vary, but the maximum direct loan from the VA is $33,000.

ADAPTING AN AUTOMOBILE TO MEET DISABILITY NEEDS

Veterans and service members may be eligible for a one-time payment of not more than $11,000 toward the purchase of an automobile or other conveyance if they have service-connected loss or permanent loss of use of one or both hands or feet, permanent impairment of vision of both eyes to a certain degree, or ankylosis (immobility) of one or both knees or one or both hips.

They may also be eligible for adaptive equipment and for repair, replacement, or reinstallation required because of disability or for the safe operation of a vehicle purchased with VA assistance. To apply, contact a VA regional office at 1-800-827-1000 or the nearest VA medical center.

ANNUAL CLOTHING ALLOWANCE FOR VETERANS WITH SERVICE-CONNECTED DISABILITIES

Any veteran who has a service-connected disability for which he or she uses prosthetic or orthopedic appliances may receive an annual clothing allowance.

The clothing allowance also is available to any veteran whose service-connected skin condition requires prescribed medication that irreparably damages his or her outer garments. To apply, contact the prosthetic representative at the nearest VA medical center.

VETERANS REQUIRING AID AND ATTENDANCE OR HOUSEBOUND VETERANS

A veteran who is determined by the VA to be in need of the regular aid and attendance of another person, or a veteran who is permanently housebound, may be entitled to additional disability compensation or pension payments. A veteran evaluated at 30 percent or more disabled is entitled to receive an additional payment for a spouse who is in need of the aid and attendance of another person.

CONCURRENT RETIREMENT AND DISABILITY PAYMENTS (CRDP) FOR DISABLED VETERANS

Concurrent Retirement and Disability Payments (CRDP) restores retired pay on a graduated 10-year schedule for retirees with a 50 to 90 percent VA-rated disability. Concurrent retirement payments increase 10 percent per year through 2013. Veterans rated 100-percent disabled by the VA are entitled to full CRDP without being phased in. Veterans receiving benefits at the 100 percent rate due to individual unemployability are entitled to full CRDP in 2009.

To qualify, veterans must also meet all three of the following criteria:

- Have 20 or more years on active duty, or be a reservist age 60 or older with 20 or more creditable years

- Be in a retired status

- Be receiving retired pay (must be offset by VA payments)

Retirees do not need to apply for this benefit.

COMBAT-RELATED SPECIAL COMPENSATION (CRSC) FOR RETIRED VETERANS

Combat-Related Special Compensation (CRSC) provides tax-free monthly payments to eligible retired veterans with combat-related injuries. With CRSC, veterans can receive both their full military retirement pay and their VA disability compensation, if the injury is combat related.

Retired veterans with combat-related injuries must meet all the following criteria to apply for CRSC:

- Active, Reserve, or medically retired with 20 years of creditable service

- Receiving military retired pay

- Have a 10 percent or greater VA-rated injury

- Military retired pay is reduced by VA disability payments (VA waiver)

In addition, veterans must be able to provide documentary evidence that their injuries were a result of one of the following:

- Training that simulates war (such as exercises or field training)

- Hazardous duty (such as flight, diving, or parachute duty)

- An instrumentality of war (such as combat vehicles, weapons, or Agent Orange)

- Armed conflict (such as gunshot wounds [Purple Heart], punji stick injuries)

For more information, visit **www.dod.mil/prhome/mppcrsc.html**, or call the toll-free phone number for the veteran's branch of service: Army, 1-866-281-3254; Air Force, 1-800-616-3775; Navy, 1-877-366-2772; or Coast Guard, 1-866-307-1336.

ELIGIBILITY FOR VA DISABILITY PENSION

Veterans with low incomes who are permanently and totally disabled or who are age 65 and older may be eligible for monetary support if they have 90 days or more of active military service, at least one day of which was during a period of war. (Veterans who entered active duty on or after September 8, 1980, or officers who entered active duty on or after Oct. 16, 1981, may have to meet a longer minimum period of active duty.) The veteran's discharge must have been under conditions other than dishonorable, and the disability must be for reasons other than the veteran's own willful misconduct.

Payments are made to bring the veteran's total income, including other retirement or Social Security income, to a level set by Congress. Unreimbursed medical expenses may reduce countable income for VA purposes.

Improved Disability Pension

Congress establishes the maximum annual improved disability pension rates. Payments are reduced by the amount of countable income of the veteran, spouse, or dependent children. When a veteran without a spouse or a child is furnished nursing home or domiciliary care by the VA, the pension is reduced to an amount not to exceed $90 per month after three calendar months of care. The reduction may be delayed if nursing-home care is being continued to provide the veteran with rehabilitation services.

2007 VA IMPROVED DISABILITY PENSION RATES	
Status of Veteran's Family Situation and Caretaking Needs	Maximum Annual Rate
Veteran without dependents	$10,929
Veteran with one dependent	$14,313
Veteran permanently housebound, no dependents	$13,356
Veteran needing regular aid and attendance, no dependents	$18,243
Veteran needing regular aid and attendance, one dependent	$21,615
Two veterans married to each other	$14,313
Increase for each additional dependent child	$1,866

Additional information can be found in the Compensation and Pension Benefits section of VA's Web site at **www. vba.va.gov/bln/21/index.htm**.

Protected Pension Programs

Pension beneficiaries who were receiving a VA pension on December 31, 1978, and who do not wish to elect the Improved Pension will continue to receive the pension rate they were receiving on that date. This rate continues as long as the beneficiary's income remains within the established limits, his or her net worth does not bar payment, and the beneficiary does not lose any dependents.

These beneficiaries must continue to meet basic eligibility factors, such as permanent and total disability for veterans or status as a surviving spouse or child. The VA must adjust rates for other reasons, such as a veteran's hospitalization in a VA facility.

Medal of Honor Pension

The VA administers pensions to recipients of the Medal of Honor. Congress set the monthly pension at $1,104 effective December 1, 2006.

In addition to the Veterans Administration Web site, the best source of information regarding Disabled Veterans' benefits may be the Disabled American Veterans Organization, which can be found at **www.dav.org**. Later in this book, a large list of veterans' organizations is provided.

DISABLED TRANSITION ASSISTANCE PROGRAM (DTAP)

The Disabled Transition Assistance Program (DTAP) is an integral component of transition assistance that involves intervention on behalf of service members who may be released because of a disability or who believe they have a disability qualifying them for VA's Vocational Rehabilitation and Employment Program. The goal of DTAP is to encourage and assist potentially eligible service members in making an informed decision about VA's Vocational Rehabilitation and Employment Program. It is also intended to facilitate the expeditious delivery of vocational rehabilitation services to eligible persons by assisting them in filing an application for vocational rehabilitation benefits.

DTAP presentations may be group sessions that include a comprehensive discussion of VA's Vocational Rehabilitation and Employment Program and educational/vocational counseling available to separating service members and veterans. Often, the VA regional office VR&E Officer will coordinate DTAP sessions for those service members who are hospitalized, convalescing, or receiving outpatient treatment for a disability and who are unable to attend a DTAP group session. DTAP sessions may include a review of a service member's medical records. A brief overview of the VR&E program can be viewed online at **vetsuccess.gov/dtap/dtap.html**.

LIFE INSURANCE BENEFITS FOR SERVICE — DISABLED VETERANS

If you are a service-disabled veteran, you may be eligible for life insurance benefits, which are covered in depth in Chapter 10. There are four basic types of insurance you may be eligible for as a disabled veteran:

Service-Disabled Veterans Insurance (S-DVI)

The Service-Disabled Veterans Insurance (S-DVI) program was established in 1951 to meet the insurance needs of certain veterans with service connected disabilities. S-DVI is available in a variety of permanent plans and term insurance. Policies are issued for a maximum face amount of $10,000.

Who Can Apply for S-DVI?

You can apply for S-DVI if you meet the following four criteria:

- You were released from active duty under other than dishonorable conditions on or after April 25, 1951.

- You were rated for a service-connected disability (even if only rated 0 percent).

- You are in good health except for any service-connected conditions.

○ You apply within two years from the date VA grants your new service-connected disability.

(Note: An increase in an existing service-connected disability or the granting of individual unemployability of a previous rated condition does not entitle a veteran to this insurance.)

You can also apply online at the **www.va.gov**, or download VA form 29-4364, Application for Service-Disabled Veterans Life Insurance, from the VA Web site. Be sure to also download VA Pamphlet 29-9 from this site for premium rates and a description of the plans available.

Waiver of Premiums for Totally Disabled Veterans

Under certain conditions, the basic S-DVI policy provides for a waiver of premiums in case of total disability. Policyholders who carry the basic S-DVI coverage and who become eligible for a waiver of premiums due to total disability can apply for and be granted additional Supplemental S-DVI of up to $20,000.

Supplemental S-DVI

The Veterans' Benefits Act of 1992 provided for $20,000 of supplemental coverage to S-DVI policyholders. Premiums may not be waived on this supplemental coverage. S-DVI policyholders are eligible for this supplemental coverage if:

○ They are eligible for a waiver of premiums.

○ They apply for the coverage within one year from notice of the grant of waiver.

○ They are under age 65.

Veterans' Mortgage Life Insurance (VMLI)

The Veterans' Mortgage Life Insurance (VMLI) program provides mortgage life insurance to severely disabled veterans. It is designed to pay off home mortgages of disabled veterans in the event of their death.

Who is eligible for VMLI?

Only veterans who have received a Specially Adapted Housing Grant from VA are eligible for VMLI. This is a grant to help a disabled veteran build or modify a home to accommodate his or her disabilities.

What does VMLI provide?

VMLI provides up to $90,000 of mortgage life insurance payable to the mortgage holder (such as a bank or mortgage lender), in the event of the veteran's death. The amount of coverage will equal the amount of the mortgage still owed, but the maximum can never exceed $90,000. VMLI is decreasing term insurance, which reduces as the amount of the mortgage reduced. VMLI has no loan or cash value and pays no dividends.

How much does VMLI cost?

The VA has a premium calculator available to help you determine your VMLI premium amount, available at **https://insurance.va.gov/inForceGliSite/VMLICalc/VMLICalc.asp**.

How are eligible veterans notified about VMLI?

Veterans who receive a grant for the purchase of specially adapted housing are advised by loan guaranty personnel at their interview of their eligibility for life insurance to cover the unpaid mortgage on their home. The Specially Adapted Housing agent will help the veteran complete VA Form 29-8636, Application for Veterans' Mortgage Life Insurance. If a veteran does not apply for VMLI coverage at that time, a letter will be sent by the VA to the veteran again about eligibility for such coverage. In addition to completing the form, evidence must be provided of the current mortgage balance.

Where can I get more information about VMLI?

You can get more information about VMLI by downloading and viewing the VMLI brochure from **www.va.gov**. The application for VMLI, VA

Form 29-8636, Application for Veterans' Mortgage Life Insurance, is also available for download from this site.

SGLI Disability Extension

The SGLI Disability Extension allows service members who are totally disabled at time of discharge to retain the service members' Group Life Insurance (SGLI) coverage they had in the service at no cost for up to two years.

Is the SGLI disability extension for you?

The SGLI Disability Extension is available to you if you are totally disabled at the time of discharge. To be considered totally disabled, you must have a disability that prevents you from being gainfully employed or have one of the following conditions, regardless of your employment status:

- Permanent loss of use of both hands

- Permanent loss of use of both feet

- Permanent loss of use of both eyes

- Permanent loss of use of one hand and one foot

- Permanent loss of use of one foot and one eye

- Permanent loss of use of one hand and one eye;

- Total loss of hearing in both ears

- Organic loss of speech (lost ability to express oneself, both by voice and whisper, through normal organs for speech — being able to speak with an artificial appliance is disregarded in determination of total disability)

Download VA form 8715, Application for SGLI Disability Extension, to apply for this insurance. This form is available at **www.insurance.va.gov/ sgliSite/forms/8715(04-2007).pdf**.

VETERANS' GROUP LIFE INSURANCE (VGLI)

VGLI is a program of post-separation insurance that allows service members to convert their SGLI coverage to renewable term insurance. Members with full-time SGLI coverage are eligible for VGLI upon release from service. See Chapter 10 for more on this coverage.

How much life insurance do I need?

The VA can help your figure out how much insurance you need. To assess your life insurance needs, follow this link to the VA Insurance Needs Calculator: **www.insurance.va.gov/sgliSite/calcuator/LifeIns101.htm**.

TRAUMATIC INJURY PROTECTION UNDER SERVICE MEMBERS' GROUP LIFE INSURANCE (TSGLI)

Every member who has SGLI also has Traumatic Injury Protection (TSGLI) effective December 1, 2005. It applies to active duty members, reservists, National Guard members, funeral honors duty, and one-day muster duty.

This benefit is also provided retroactively for members who incurred severe losses as a result of traumatic a injury between October 7, 2001, and December 1, 2005 if the loss was the direct result of injuries incurred in Operations Enduring Freedom or Iraqi Freedom.

TSGLI coverage will pay a benefit of between $25,000 and $100,000, depending on the loss directly resulting from the traumatic injury.

Every member who has SGLI also has TSGLI effective December 1, 2005. TSGLI coverage is automatic for those insured under basic SGLI and cannot be declined. The only way to decline TSGLI is to decline basic SGLI coverage.

TSGLI is not available to spouses and children under Family SGLI. It is available only to service members insured under SGLI. TSGLI coverage is not available to VGLI policyholders. More is covered in Chapter 10.

CHAPTER 8

TRICARE BENEFITS FOR RETIRED & DISABLED VETERANS

There are a variety of TRICARE, dental, and other medical insurance options when you are retired or disabled. TRICARE and dental options are entitlements, but they are not free. You must weigh your insurance options to determine if it is worth participating in either program.

TRICARE VERSUS CHAMPVA

The Civilian Health and Medical Program of the Department of Veterans Affairs (CHAMPVA) is a comprehensive healthcare program in which the VA shares the cost of covered healthcare services and supplies with eligible beneficiaries. The program is administered by the Health Administration Center, with offices located in Denver, Colorado.

Due to the similarity between CHAMPVA and the Department of Defense TRICARE program (sometimes referred to by its old name, CHAMPUS) the two are often mistaken for each other. CHAMPVA is a Department of Veterans Affairs program, whereas TRICARE is a regionally managed healthcare program for active duty and retired members of the uniformed services, their families, and survivors. In some cases, a veterans may appear on paper to be eligible for both/either program. However, if you are a military retiree or the spouse of a veteran who was killed in action, you are and will always be a TRICARE beneficiary. You cannot choose between the two.

CHAMPVA OVERVIEW

To be eligible for CHAMPVA, you cannot be eligible for TRICARE/ CHAMPUS and you must be in one of these categories:

- The spouse or child of a veteran who has been rated permanently and totally disabled for a service-connected disability by a VA regional office

- The surviving spouse or child of a veteran who died from a VA-rated service-connected disability

- The surviving spouse or child of a veteran who was at the time of death rated permanently and totally disabled from a service-connected disability

- The surviving spouse or child of a military member who died in the line of duty, not due to misconduct (in most of these cases, these family members are eligible for TRICARE, not CHAMPVA)

An eligible CHAMPVA sponsor may be entitled to receive medical care through the VA healthcare system based on his or her own veteran status. Additionally, as the result of a recent policy change, if the eligible CHAMPVA sponsor is the spouse of another eligible CHAMPVA sponsor, both may now be eligible for CHAMPVA benefits. In each instance where the eligible spouse requires medical attention, he or she may choose the VA healthcare system or coverage under CHAMPVA for healthcare needs. If you have been previously denied CHAMPVA benefits and you believe you would now be qualified, please submit an application following the guidelines as listed on the "How to Apply" section.

CHAMPVA Benefits

The CHAMPVA program covers most healthcare services and supplies that are medically and psychologically necessary. Upon confirmation of eligibility, you will receive a CHAMPVA handbook specifically addressing covered and non-covered services and supplies.

General exclusions: Like all health programs, there are certain services and supplies that are not covered by the program:

- Services and supplies obtained as part of a grant, study, or research program

- Services and supplies not provided in accordance with accepted professional medical standards or related to experimental/ investigational or unproven procedures or treatment regimens

- Care for which you are not obligated to pay, such as services obtained at a health fair

- Care provided outside the scope of the provider's license or certification

- Services or supplies above the appropriate level required to provide the necessary medical care

- Services by providers suspended or sanctioned federally

- Services provided by a member of your immediate family or person living in your household

For a complete listing of non-covered services and supplies, consult the CHAMVPA handbook, available on the VA Web site at **www.va.gov**.

Medicare Impact

CHAMPVA is always the secondary payer to Medicare. If you are eligible for CHAMPVA, under age 65, and enrolled in both Medicare Parts A and B, SSA documentation of enrollment in both Parts A and B is required.

For your benefits to be extended past age 65, you must meet the following conditions:

- ☬ If the beneficiary was 65 or older before June 5, 2001, was otherwise eligible for CHAMPVA, and was entitled to Medicare Part A coverage, then the beneficiary will be eligible for CHAMPVA without having to have Medicare Part B coverage.

- ☬ If you turned 65 on/or before June 5, 2001, and have Medicare Parts A and B, you must keep both Parts to be eligible.

- ☬ If you turned 65 on or after June 5, 2001, you must be enrolled in Medicare Parts A and B to be eligible.

- ☬ You are not required to enroll in Medicare Part D to become or remain CHAMPVA eligible.

New & Expectant Parents

If you are expecting and you need to establish CHAMPVA eligibility for your new child, the following must be accomplished before you can submit an application:

- ☬ Obtain a Social Security Number for the newborn by applying to the nearest Social Security Administration office.

- ☬ Establish dependency of the newborn to the veteran sponsor by contacting the local VA regional office.

Since the payment of claims for this child is contingent upon his or her eligibility status, as new parents you are encouraged to take the above action as early as possible.

CHAMPVA Eligibility Definitions

- ☬ **Beneficiary**: Defined as a CHAMPVA-eligible spouse, widow(er), or child

- **Child**: Includes birth, adopted, stepchild, or helpless child as determined by a VA regional office

- **Dependents**: A child, spouse, or widow(er) of a qualifying sponsor

- **Qualifying sponsor:** A veteran who is permanently and totally disabled from a service-connected condition, died as a result of a service-connected condition, was rated permanently and totally disabled from a service-connected condition at the time of death, or died on active duty and whose dependents are not otherwise entitled to DOD TRICARE benefits

- **Service-connected:** A VA regional office determination that a veteran's illness or injury is related to military service

- **Spouse:** The wife or husband of a qualifying sponsor

- **Widow(er):** The surviving spouse of a qualifying sponsor

(Note: The eligibility of a child is not affected by the divorce or remarriage of the spouse except in the case of a stepchild. When a stepchild leaves the sponsor's household, the child is no longer eligible for CHAMPVA.)

Remarried Widows/Widowers

Eligibility for CHAMPVA ends at midnight on the date of your remarriage if you remarry before age 55. If you remarry on or after your 55th birthday, The Veterans Benefit Act of 2002, Public Law 107-330, allows you to keep your CHAMPVA benefits.

If you are a widow(er) of a qualifying sponsor who remarries and the remarriage is later terminated by death, divorce, or annulment, you may re-establish CHAMPVA eligibility. The beginning date of your reeligibility is the first day of the month after termination of the re-marriage, or December 1, 1999, whichever date is later. To reestablish CHAMPVA eligibility, copies of the marriage certificate and death, divorce, or annulment documents (as appropriate) must be provided.

You can read more about CHAMPVA by visiting the fact sheets and the CHAMPVA handbook. You are highly encouraged to carefully read the handbook before using CHAMPVA benefits. You can download it at **www.va.gov/hac/forbeneficiaries/champva/handbook.aspCHAMPVA**.

Communicating with CHAMPVA

CHAMPVA is managed by the VA's Health Administration Center. You can call it at 800-733-8387, Monday through Friday, from 8:05 a.m. to 7:30 p.m. ET. For general questions, contact it via the Inquiry Routing & Information System (IRIS). IRIS is a tool that allows the VA to communicate in a secure format and is used instead of the traditional e-mail links. You can also fax the VA at 1-303-331-7804. Online Chat is available Monday, Wednesday, and Friday, from 10 a.m. to 6:30 p.m. ET. The VA also has an automated Web service available 24 hours a day, 7 days a week at **www.mychampva.com**.

How to Locate a CHAMPVA Provider

The VA does not maintain a provider listing. Most Medicare and TRICARE providers will also accept CHAMPVA (but be sure you ask the provider). If you are having difficulty finding a provider, visit the Medicare Web site at **www.medicare.gov** and use the "Search Tools" at the bottom of that page. You may also visit the TRICARE Web site at **www.tricare.mil/standardprovider** to locate a provider in your area. If you choose to see a provider who does not accept CHAMPVA, you will likely have to pay the entire bill and then submit a claim for reimbursement of our cost share. Remember that CHAMPVA cost shares are based on the CHAMPVA allowable amount.

CHAMPVA Assistance and Claims Address

If you have a general question, need information on payment, or need to reprocess a denied claim, send your request to:

VA Health Administration Center
CHAMPVA
P.O. Box 65023
Denver, CO 80206-9023

For submitting new healthcare claims only, use:

VA Health Administration Center
CHAMPVA Claims
P.O. Box 65024
Denver, CO 80206-9024

Medicare Exclusion List

The Department of Health and Human Services, Office of Inspector General (HHS OIG) maintains and publishes a monthly list of individual medical providers that are not allowed to provide medical services and supplies to federal healthcare program participants. Medical providers on this list have been convicted in state or federal court of certain felonies, criminal offenses, or have had other offenses toward federal agencies related to the delivery of healthcare. Mandatory exclusions include, but are not limited to, convictions related to patient abuse or neglect, felony convictions related to healthcare fraud, and controlled substances.

Excluded individual medical providers and medical institutions cannot, by law, receive payments for healthcare services or supplies from any federal healthcare program. That exclusion includes programs funded by the Department of Veterans Affairs such as CHAMPVA, Foreign Medical Program (FMP), spina bifida, and the Children of Women Vietnam Veterans Healthcare Programs. To access the list, use the following link: **http://exclusions.oig.hhs.gov/search.html**.

Denied CHAMPVA Claims

If you have the Explanation of Benefits (EOB) form available, you can use the denial code on the form to get detailed instruction about how to respond to the claim denial. The VA also offers an e-mail address to submit questions on its less common claims denial codes. Detailed information on how to reprocess rejected claims can be found at **www.va.gov/hac/forbeneficiaries/champva/rejected_claims.asp**.

CHAMPVA Inhouse Treatment Initiative (CITI)

The CHAMPVA Inhouse Treatment Initiative (CITI) (pronounced "city") is a voluntary program that allows for you, the CHAMPVA beneficiary, to be treated at participating VA medical centers with no out-of-pocket cost. Each VA medical center that participates in the CITI program offers different services based on unused capacity. Once you locate a CITI facility that you want to use, contact the CITI coordinator to find out what services are offered at that specific medical center. Unfortunately, if you are a CHAMPVA beneficiary who is also covered by Medicare, you cannot participate in the CITI program because Medicare does not pay for services provided by a VA medical center. A brochure is available at **www.va.gov/hac/forbeneficiaries/champva/brochure/CITI_Brochure.pdf**.

CHAMPVA Pharmacy Benefits

The CHAMPVA program offers a robust pharmacy benefit, paying 75 percent of the allowable charge at any pharmacy for prescription medication. CHAMPVA also offers a medication-by-mail program.

Pharmacies That Accept CHAMPVA

Pharmacies that accept the CHAMPVA card agree to collect your cost share and send a claim to CHAMPVA for the remaining amount. However, not all pharmacies accept the CHAMPVA card. In those cases, you may have to pay the entire amount and submit a claim to CHAMPVA. A good way to find a pharmacy that accepts the CHAMPVA card is to use the Medical Matrix network.

Medications by Mail

The Meds By Mail program offers prescription medication delivered to your home. The best part of Meds By Mail is that there is no cost share or copay. The medication is free. Detailed information on Meds By Mail can be found at **www.va.gov/hac/forbeneficiaries/meds/meds.asp**.

Other Health Insurance (OHI) & CHAMPVA

If you have other health insurance, you must notify the Health Administration Center of any changes (dropped insurance and changes in health plans) immediately upon those changes taking effect so that proper payment of your claims can be made.

If you obtain a major medical policy, you must also notify the Health Administration Center that you have a new policy and when it takes effect. You can make this notification by using an Other Health Insurance (OHI) form and sending it to CHAMPVA, P.O. Box 65023, Denver, CO 80206-9023 or by calling 1-800-733-8387, Monday-Friday, 8:05 a.m. to 6:45 p.m. Eastern Time and talking with a customer service.

(Note: To ensure proper formatting of the CHAMPVA Other Health Insurance (OHI) Certification, use VA Form 10-7959c or Certification CHAMPVA de Otros Seguros de Salud (OSS), VA Forma 10-7959c.)

WHAT IS TRICARE?

TRICARE is the healthcare program serving active duty service members, retirees, their families, survivors, and certain former spouses worldwide. As a major component of the Military Health System, TRICARE brings together the healthcare resources of the uniformed services and supplements them with networks of civilian healthcare professionals, institutions, pharmacies, and suppliers to provide access to high-quality healthcare services while maintaining the capability to support military operations.

To be eligible for TRICARE benefits, you must be registered in the Defense Enrollment Eligibility Reporting System (DEERS). TRICARE offers several health plan options to meet the needs of its beneficiary population. Additionally, TRICARE offers two dental plans and several additional special programs.

TRICARE Eligibility

TRICARE is available to active duty service members and retirees of the seven uniformed services, their family members, survivors, and others who are registered in the Defense Enrollment Eligibility Reporting System. The uniformed services include the:

- U.S. Army
- U.S. Air Force
- U.S. Navy
- U.S. Marine Corps
- U.S. Coast Guard
- Commissioned Corps of the Public Health Service
- Commissioned Corps of the National Oceanic and Atmospheric Association

You must be registered in DEERS and have a valid uniformed services identification card showing you are eligible for TRICARE.

TRICARE Regions

TRICARE is available worldwide and is managed in four separate regions, three in the United States and one overseas region that is divided into three main areas.

The three regions in the United States include:

- TRICARE North
- TRICARE South
- TRICARE West

The overseas regions include:

- TRICARE Europe

- TRICARE Latin America and Canada

- TRICARE Pacific

TRICARE PRIME

TRICARE Prime is a managed care option offering the most affordable and comprehensive coverage. TRICARE Prime is available in areas near military treatment facilities and where regional contractors have established TRICARE Prime networks.

Key features of TRICARE Prime include:

- Enrollment is required to participate, but there are no enrollment fees for active duty service members and their families

- Flexible enrollment options

  - Online via the Beneficiary Web Enrollment Web site

  - Submit a TRICARE Prime Enrollment and PCM Change Form through the mail

  - Submit a TRICARE Prime Enrollment and PCM Change Form at a TRICARE Service Center or contact your regional contractor for details

- Fewer out-of-pocket costs than other TRICARE options

- Enhanced coverage for vision and clinical preventive services

- Priority access for care at military treatment facilities

- Most care is received from an assigned primary care manager (PCM), who refers you to specialists when necessary

- Point-of-service option available (to all but active duty service members) to receive care without requesting a referral from your PCM (resulting in higher out-of-pocket costs)

- No claims to file (in most cases)

- Easy to transfer enrollment when moving to another location in your TRICARE region or to a new TRICARE region

- Time and distance access standards for care, including wait times for urgent, routine, and specialty care

TRICARE Prime Eligibility

TRICARE Prime is available to the following beneficiaries as long as they are not entitled to Medicare Part A and Part B due to age (65):

- Active duty service members and their families

- Retired service members and their families

- Eligible former spouses

- Survivors

- National Guard and Reserve members and their families when the National Guard or Reserve member is activated for more than 30 consecutive days

- Retired National Guard and Reserve members and their families

- Medal of Honor recipients and their families

All eligible beneficiaries must reside in a Prime Service Area (PSA). A PSA is a geographic area where TRICARE Prime benefits are offered. It may be a geographic area around a military treatment facility or specific areas with a significant concentration of uniformed services personnel and retirees and their families. A PSA must also have a substantial medical community to support TRICARE Prime beneficiaries. If you do not live in a PSA, you may be eligible for TRICARE Prime Remote, or you may use TRICARE Standard and Extra.

It is important to note that currently, discharged veterans have entitlements under CHAMPVA if disabled, or possibly through other programs if they serviced in the Gulf War, Iraq, or Afghanistan, as outlined earlier in this book; however, the Bush administration is proposing numerous changes to entitlements that may afford some discharge veterans TRICARE benefits. Described next is summary information from the most recent White House fact sheet.

ENSURING OUR WOUNDED WARRIORS GET THE BEST POSSIBLE CARE

President Bush discussed legislation Congress should pass and actions the administration is taking to implement recommendations of the President's Commission on Care for America's Returning Wounded Warriors. In March, President Bush signed an executive order creating this bipartisan commission to conduct a comprehensive review of the services America is providing our returning wounded warriors. The Commission released its findings on July 25, 2007, and the president immediately instructed the secretaries of defense and Veterans Affairs to implement its recommendations.

The administration is working with Congress and taking action to implement the Commission's six recommendations to improve care for America's returning wounded warriors. The President discussed progress on these goals in a meeting with Commission co-chairs Bob Dole and Donna Shalala, Defense Secretary Robert Gates, acting Veterans Affairs Secretary Gordon Mansfield, and wounded service members and their families:

- Modernizing and improving the disability and compensation systems

- Aggressively preventing and treating posttraumatic stress disorder and traumatic brain injury

- Significantly strengthening support for families

- Immediately creating comprehensive recovery plans to provide the right care and support at the right time in the right place

- Rapidly transferring patient information between the Departments of Defense (DOD) and Veterans Affairs

- Strongly supporting Walter Reed by recruiting and retaining first-rate professionals through 2011

Commission Recommendations

- Change DOD disability entitlement for those deemed unfit for duty for combat-related reasons by providing an annuity based solely on rank and service, rather than percent disability.

- Expand TRICARE coverage to those unfit for duty for combat-related reasons, not just those who are at least 30 percent disabled or with 20 years of service, as in the current system.

- Restructure VA disability entitlement such that, for new entrants retired from service for fitness, VA benefits would include transition payments to cover living expenses equal to either three months of base pay (if no rehabilitation is needed) or family living expenses for longer-term rehab patients. The new VA disability benefits would also include "earnings-loss payments" and "quality-of-life payments."

- Reassess all disability rating schedules to ensure they reflect modern medicine and modern concepts of the impact of disability. The VA would reassess disability status every three years and adjust compensation accordingly.

- Increase vocational rehabilitation benefits such that VA would pay a bonus equal to 10 percent of transition pay after year one, 5 percent after year two, and 10 percent after year three of training completion.

Legislative Proposals (Requiring Congressional Approval)

- ⚲ DOD disability payments should be replaced by DOD annuity payment for all eligible service members separated or retired after the implementation date of this provision. Those separated or retired since the beginning of the Operation Enduring Freedom/ Operation Iraqi Freedom will be able to choose between the existing system and the new system.

- ⚲ TRICARE benefits should be extended for those seriously injured in combat or combat-related activities.

- ⚲ The VA disability system should be strengthened and improved to provide for an immediate transition payment, loss of earnings, and quality of life payment.

- ⚲ Individuals and their conditions will be reassessed every three years.

- ⚲ The disability rating schedule should be updated to reflect modern concepts of medicine and disability.

- ⚲ The disability system restructure will take effect upon conclusion of the seven-month disability compensation study, legislation implementing VA disability payment rates, and regulations updating VA's disability rating schedules.

Administrative Actions

- ⚲ Beginning in November 2007, DOD and VA attempted a replacement to the cumbersome previous system of two entirely separate disability determinations by each department with a single, comprehensive medical exam to be administered by the DOD.

- ⚲ Rule-making is underway to update the VA Schedule for Rating Disabilities include traumatic brain injury (TBI) and severe burns.

The complete report of the commission is available online at **www.pccww. gov/docs/Kit/Main_Book_CC%5BJULY26%5D.pdf**, and the complete subcommittee report is available at **www.pccww.gov/docs/TOC%20 Subcommittee%20Reports.pdf**.

Aggressively Preventing and Treating Posttraumatic Stress Disorder and Traumatic Brain Injury

Commission Recommendations

- Expand VA health coverage to ensure that all veterans of Operation Enduring Freedom and Operation Iraqi Freedom with posttraumatic stress disorder (PTSD) receive care related to this condition.

- Address DOD shortage of mental health clinicians.

- Conduct awareness training and provide clinical guidelines for PTSD and traumatic brain injury.

Legislative Proposals (Requiring Congressional Approval)

- All Operation Enduring Freedom and Operation Iraqi Freedom veterans should be allowed to receive PTSD care from the VA without first showing service connection.

Administrative Actions

- Secretaries of the military departments have begun using existing authorities such as incentive pay and bonuses to recruit and retain sufficient experts in mental health fields.

- DOD and the Department of Health and Human Services are working on an Memorandum of Understanding to provide additional mental health professionals to meet short-term needs.

- By November 30, 2007, DOD and VA expected to establish a National Center of Excellence to conduct training and research, deliver care, and disseminate clinical best practices about TBI, PTSD, and other mental health conditions.

⚕ DOD has expanded mental health and TBI training programs for deploying service members.

⚕ VA is working to screen all patients for PTSD as part of their initial treatment.

Significantly Strengthening Support for Families

Commission Recommendations

⚕ Expand TRICARE respite care and aide and personal attendant benefits to service members seriously injured in combat.

⚕ Provide training and counseling to family members to support them as caregivers. The DOD and the VA should standardize and assure universal access to family services early in the treatment process. This package should include education about the service member's injuries and expected progress, caregiver training and counseling, and psychological services.

⚕ Amend the Family Medical Leave Act (FMLA) to allow up to six months of unpaid leave for family members of combat-injured service members and allow combinations of unpaid and paid leave, when available.

Legislative Proposals (Requiring Congressional Approval)

⚕ TRICARE respite care and aide and personal attendant benefits should be provided to service members seriously wounded in combat under Extended Care Health Option (ECHO).

⚕ Family members of service members with combat-related serious injuries should be eligible to receive 26 weeks of unpaid leave within the first 24 months following the injury or its diagnosis.

Administrative Actions

- The DOD and VA have implemented family caregiver training.

- The DOD and VA are developing a package of employment options and healthcare options for caregivers of seriously injured service members.

- The Bush administration is acting now to implement recommendations that do not require legislative action by immediately creating comprehensive recovery plans to provide the right care and support at the right time in the right place.

Commission Recommendations

- Those seriously injured in combat will receive an individual recovery plan that leads them back to duty or public life seamlessly, guiding and supporting them through medical, rehabilitation, and disability programs.

- A recovery coordinator will be assigned to service members seriously injured in combat to serve as their ultimate resource in the recovery process. The Public Health Service (PHS) Commissioned Corps will help develop this cadre of well-trained and highly skilled advocates.

Administrative Actions

- On September 19, 2007, the DOD, VA, and the Department of Health and Human Services signed a joint Memorandum of Understanding for the creation of a joint recovery coordinator program for service members seriously injured in combat or combat-related activity.

- By December 1, 2007, the DOD and VA were to develop the Recovery "Life" Plan to be used by the federal recovery coordinators for seriously injured service members with combat-related injuries.

◊ The VA will take the lead on creating the organizational structure for the federal recovery coordinators. The PHS Commissioned Corps will serve as consultants for program development and care management.

Rapidly Transferring Patient Information Between the Departments of Defense and Veterans Affairs

Commission Recommendations

◊ The DOD and VA must continue the work underway toward a fully interoperable IT system that will meet long-term administrative and clinical needs.

◊ The DOD and VA must, within the next 12 months, have all patient information viewable by any clinician, health professional, or administrator who needs it within either department.

◊ The DOD and VA must develop a plan for a user-friendly health and benefits portal for service members, veterans, and family members.

Administration Actions

◊ No later than October 31, 2008, the DOD and VA were to make available and viewable all essential health and administrative data.

◊ By March 31, 2008, the DOD and VA were to have the ability to share all essential health images.

◊ The DOD and VA were creating a single Web portal to provide for the care and support needs of veterans and their families.

STRONGLY SUPPORTING WALTER REED BY RECRUITING AND RETAINING FIRST-RATE PROFESSIONALS THROUGH CLOSURE IN 2011

Commission Recommendations

- The DOD must ensure that Walter Reed (WRAMC) has the resources it needs in outpatient and inpatient care.

- The DOD must implement tailored incentive packages to encourage civilian personnel to continue working at Walter Reed and enable recruitment of new professionals as needed.

TRICARE PRIME AND TRICARE STANDARD FOR RETIREES

As a military retiree, you are eligible for either TRICARE Prime or TRICARE Standard or Extra. The choice of which plan is up to you. Annual enrollment fees for TRICARE Prime may be deducted from your retirement pay. Once you are Medicare eligible, you must convert to TRICARE For Life. Use the following table to compare TRICARE Prime to TRICARE Standard or Extra.

COMPARISON OF TRICARE PRIME AND TRICARE STANDARD & EXTRA
What is It?
TRICARE Prime is a managed care option offering the most affordable and comprehensive coverage.
TRICARE Standard & Extra is a fee-for-service option, which allows you the most flexibility in whom you see for care but will cost you more out-of-pocket than a managed care plan such as TRICARE Prime. With TRICARE Standard & Extra, you can seek care from any TRICARE authorized provider. If you see a network provider, you will be using the TRICARE Extra option and will pay less than if you see a nonnetwork provider.

COMPARISON OF TRICARE PRIME AND TRICARE STANDARD & EXTRA

(Note: Eligibility can only be determined by uniformed services, and eligibility information is reflected in the Defense Enrollment Eligibility Reporting System (DEERS). The information provided here is general.)

The following are eligible for TRICARE Prime if it is offered in their location:
- Active duty service members
- Active duty family members
- Retirees and their family members under age 65
- Survivors under age 65
- Certain former spouses under age 65
- Medal of Honor recipients and their family members under age 65
- Members of the National Guard and Reserves and their families if the sponsor is activated for more than 30 consecutive days

The following are eligible for TRICARE Standard & Extra:
- Active duty family members
- Retirees and their family members under age 65*
- Survivors under age 65*
- Certain former spouses under age 65*
- Medal of Honor recipients and their families under age 65*
- Family members of National Guard or Reserve members who are activated for more than 30 consecutive days

* If under age 65 and entitled to Medicare Part A, you must have Medicare Part B to remain eligible for TRICARE. When you have Medicare Part A and Part B, you are automatically covered by TRICARE for Life.

TRICARE Prime's main features include:
- Enrollment required
- Easy to transfer enrollment when you move
- Enhanced vision coverage and clinical preventive series
- Assigned primary care manager (PCM) provides most of your care and gives you referrals for speciality care*
- Time and distance access standards
- First priority for military treatment facility appointments
- Fewer out-of-pocket costs
- No claims to file (in most cases)

* Point of service (POS) option available to receive care without a PCM referral, resulting in higher out-of-pocket costs. POS not available for active duty service members.

TRICARE Standard & Extra's main features include:
- Enrollment not required:
  — No enrollment forms to fill out
  — No annual enrollment fees

COMPARISON OF TRICARE PRIME AND TRICARE STANDARD & EXTRA

- Freedom to choose from any TRICARE authorized provider, network, or non-network provider
- Care in a military treatment facility on a space-available basis only
- Referrals are not required, but some care may require prior authorization
- Highest out-of-pocket costs
  - Tip: Save time and money with the TRICARE Extra option. When you visit a TRICARE network provider, you will pay less out-of-pocket, and providers will file claims for you
- You may have to pay for services when they are received or file your own claims for reimbursement
- TRICARE Standard is available worldwide, but TRICARE Extra is not available overseas

How Do I Get Care?

With TRICARE Prime:

When you enroll, you must select a PCM, or one is assigned to you. Your PCM may be a Military Treatment Facility (MTF) provider or a civilian TRICARE network provider. Your PCM:

- Provides routine healthcare
- Coordinates referrals for speciality care that he or she cannot provide
- Assists with prior authorizations, when needed
- Maintains your patient health records

You have the first priority for appointments at MTFs, and when MTF care is not available, you will be referred to a TRICARE network provider. The POS option allows you to seek care from any provider without a referral from your PCM but at a higher out-of-pocket cost.

With TRICARE Standard and Extra:

You have the freedom to seek care from any TRICARE authorized provider. To save on out-of-pocket costs, you can use the TRICARE Extra option by visiting a TRICARE network provider.

Referrals are not required, but prior authorization is required for certain services, such as adjunctive dental care and inpatient mental healthcare. You may receive care at a military treatment facility but only on a space-available basis.

COMPARISON OF TRICARE PRIME AND TRICARE STANDARD & EXTRA

Will I have to file my own claims?

With TRICARE Prime: Your provider will file claim for you (in most cases).

With TRICARE Standard & Extra: If you receive care from a TRICARE network provider, your provider will submit claims on your behalf. If you receive care from a non-network provider, you may be required to submit your own healthcare claims.

Do I have to enroll? If so, is there an annual enrollment fee?

TRICARE Prime: Yes, to participate in TRICARE Prime, you must enroll by submitting a TRICARE Prime Enrollment and PCM Change Form to your regional contractor.

Active duty service members and activated National Guard and Reserve members are required to enroll in TRICARE Prime (or another Prime option depending on where they live/work). All others may choose to enroll. Eligible beneficiaries who do not enroll in TRICARE Prime are covered by TRICARE Standard and Extra.

Active duty service members and their families, activated National Guard and Reserve members and their families and transitional survivors are not required to pay an annual enrollment fee.

Retirees, their families, and all others must pay an annual enrollment fee:
• $230//Individual
• $460/Family

TRICARE Standard & Extra: You do not have to enroll in TRICARE Standard & Extra to participate. Coverage is automatic, as long as you remain eligible in the Defense Enrollment Eligibility Reporting System.

What is the annual deductible?

TRICARE Prime: There is no annual deductible unless you are using the POS option, which allows you to see any provider without a referral from your primary care manager.

POS outpatient annual deductible:
• $300/Individual
• $600/Family

(Note: Active duty service members and activated National Guard or Reserve members may not use the POS option.)

COMPARISON OF TRICARE PRIME AND TRICARE STANDARD & EXTRA

TRICARE Standard and Extra: The annual outpatient deductible varies depending on the sponsor's military status and rank:

Active duty family members (sponsor rank E-4 and below):
• $50/Individual
• $100/Family

Active duty family members (sponsor rank E-5 and above):
• $150/Individual
• $300/Family

All others:
• $150/Individual
• $300/Family
• Family members of National Guard or Reserve Members activated in support of a contingency operation (OEF, OIF, Noble Eagle): $0; deductibles waived as part of the Reserve Family Demonstration Project.

(Note: There is no annual deductible for care received in military treatment facilities.)

How much do I pay for an outpatient visit?

TRICARE Prime

Military Treatment Facility: No charge

TRICARE Network Provider:
• Active duty service members (including activated National Guard and Reserve members) and their families: $0*
• All others: $12 per visit*

Non-network Provider
• With PCM referral: Same as network provider costs
• Without PCM referral: POS fees apply

* POS Option: 50 percent of the TRICARE allowable charge, after the POS annual deductible is met. Active duty service members and activated National Guard and Reserve members may not use the POS option.

TRICARE Standard & Extra:

Military Treatment Facility: No charge

TRICARE Network Provider (Extra option):

COMPARISON OF TRICARE PRIME AND TRICARE STANDARD & EXTRA

- Active duty family members (including family members of activated National Guard and Reserve members): 20 percent of allowable charges after the annual deductible is met
- All others: 25 percent allowable charges after the annual deductible is met

How much do I pay for clinical preventive services?

TRICARE Prime:

Military Treatment Facility: No charge

TRICARE Network Provider: No charge

Nonnetwork Provider:
- With PCM referral: No charge
- Without PCM referral: POS fees apply

* POS Option: 50 percent of the TRICARE allowable charge, after the POS annual deductible is met. Active duty service members and activated National Guard and Reserve members may not use the POS option.

TRICARE Standard & Extra:

Military Treatment Facility: No charge

TRICARE Network Provider (Extra option):
- Active duty family members (including family members of activated National Guard and Reserve members): 15 percent of negotiated fee after annual deductible is met
- All others: 20 percent of negotiated fee after the annual deductible is met

Nonnetwork Provider (Standard option):
- Active duty family members (including family members of activated National Guard and Reserve members): 20 percent of allowable charges after the annual deductible is met
- All others: 25 percent allowable charges after the annual deductible is met

How much do I pay for hospitalization?

TRICARE Prime:

- Nominal charges may apply. Check with your local facility for details.

TRICARE Network Provider

COMPARISON OF TRICARE PRIME AND TRICARE STANDARD & EXTRA

- Active duty service members (including activated National Guard and Reserve members) and their families: $0*
- All others: $11 per day ($25 minimum)

   * No additional cost for separately billed professional charges.

Non-network Provider:
- With PCM referral: Same as network provider costs
- Without PCM referral: POS fees apply

* POS Option: 50 percent of members and activated National Guard and Reserve members may not use the POS option.

TRICARE Standard & Extra:

Military Treatment Facility:
- Nominal charges may apply. Check with your local facility for details.

TRICARE Network Provider (Extra option)
- Active duty family members (including family members of activated National Guard and Reserve members): $15.15/day ($25 minimum charge)
- All others: $250 or 25 percent for institutional services, whichever is less, plus 20 percent for separately billed professional charges

Non-network Provider (Standard option):
- Active duty family members (including family members of activated National Guard and Reserve members): $15.15/day ($25 minimum charge)
- All others: $535 per day or 25 percent for institutional services, whichever is less, plus 25 percent for separately billed professional charges

How much do I pay for emergency services?

TRICARE Prime:

Military Treatment Facility:
- No charge
- Nominal charges if admitted. Check with your local facility for details.

TRICARE Network Provider
- Active duty service members (including activated National Guard and Reserve members) and their families: $0
- All others: $30 per visit

COMPARISON OF TRICARE PRIME AND TRICARE STANDARD & EXTRA

Non-network Provider:

- Active duty service members (including activated National Guard and Reserve members) and their families: $0
- All others: $30 per visit

TRICARE Standard and Extra:

Military Treatment Facility:
- No charge
- Nominal charges may apply if admitted. Check with your local facility for details.

TRICARE network Provider (Extra option):

- Active duty family members (including family members of activated National Guard and Reserve members): 15 percent of negotiated fee after the annual deductible is met
- All others: 20 percent of negotiated fee after the annual deductible is met

Non-network Provider (Standard option):
- Active duty family members (including family members of activated National Guard and Reserve members): 20 percent of allowable charges after the annual deductible is met
- All others: 25 percent allowable charges after the annual deductible is met

How much do I pay for outpatient behavioral healthcare?

TRICARE Prime:

Military Treatment Facility: No charge

TRICARE Network Provider:
- Active duty service members (including activated National Guard and Reserve members) and their families: $0*
- All others
  - $25 (individual visit)
  - $17 (group visit)

Non-network Provider
- With PCM referral: Same as network provider costs
- Without PCM referral: POS fees apply

COMPARISON OF TRICARE PRIME AND TRICARE STANDARD & EXTRA

* POS Option: 60 percent of the TRICARE allowable charge, after the POS annual deductible is met. Active duty service members and activated National Guard and Reserve members may not use the POS option.

TRICARE Standard & Extra

Military Treatment Facility: No charge

TRICARE Network Provider (Extra option)

- Active duty family members (including family members of activated National Guard and Reserve members): 15 percent of negotiated fee after the annual deductible is met

- All others: 20 percent of negotiated fee after the annual deductible is met

Nonnetwork Provider (Standard option):

- Active duty family members (including family members of activated National Guard and Reserve members): 20 percent of allowable charges after the annual deductible is met

- All others: 25 percent allowable charges after the annual deductible is met

How much do I pay for inpatient behavioral healthcare?

TRICARE Prime:

Military Treatment Facility:

- Nominal charges may apply. Check with your local facility for details.

TRICARE Network Provider

- Active duty service members (including activated National Guard and Reserve members) and their families: $0*

- All others: $40 per day ($25 minimum)

* No additional cost for separately billed professional charges.

Nonnetwork provider:

- With PCM referral: Same as network

- Without PCM referral: POS fees apply

* POS Option: 50 percent of the TRICARE allowable charge, after the POS annual deductible is met. Active duty service members and activated National Guard and Reserve members may not use the POS option.

TRICARE Standard & Extra:

Military Treatment Facility:

- Nominal charges may apply. Check with your local facility for details.

COMPARISON OF TRICARE PRIME AND TRICARE STANDARD & EXTRA

TRICARE Network Provider (Extra option):

- Active duty family members (including family members of activated National Guard and Reserve members): $20/day ($25 minimum charge)
- All others: 20 percent for institutional services, plus 20 percent for separately billed professional services

Nonnetwork Provider (Standard option)
- Active duty family members (including family members of activated National Guard and Reserve members): $20/day ($25 minimum charge)
- All others:
  - High-volume hospitals: 25 percent hospital specific per diem, plus 25 percent for separately billed professional services
  - Low-volume hospitals $187 per day or 25 percent of the billed charges, whichever is less, plus 25 percent for separately billed services
  - Residential Treatment Center 25 percent of the allowed amount
  - Partial hospitalization 25 percent of the allowed amount, plus 25 percent of the allowable charge for separately billed professional services

How much do I pay for inpatient skilled nursing care?

TRICARE Prime:

Military Treatment Facility:
- Nominal charges may apply. Check with your local facility for details.

TRICARE Network Provider:
- Active duty service members (including activated National Guard and Reserve members) and their families: $0*
- All others: $11 per day ($25 minimum)

* No additional cost for separately billed professional charges.

Nonnetwork Provider:
- With PCM referral: Same as network provider costs
- Without PCM referral: POS fees apply

* POS Option: 50 percent of the TRICARE allowable charge. Active duty service members and activated National Guard and Reserve members may not use the POS option.

TRICARE Standard & Extra:

Military Treatment Facility:
- Nominal charges may apply. Check with your local facility for details.

COMPARISON OF TRICARE PRIME AND TRICARE STANDARD & EXTRA

TRICARE Network Provider (Extra Option):

- Active duty family members (including family members of activated National Guard and Reserve members): $15.15/day ($25 minimum charge)
- All others: $250 or 25 percent for institutional services, whichever is less, plus 20 percent for separately billed professional charges

Nonnetwork Provider (Standard Option):

- Active duty family members (including family members of activated National Guard and Reserve members): $15.15/day ($25 minimum charge)
- All others: 25 percent for institutional services, plus 25 percent for separately billed professional charges

What is the maximum I'll pay out-of-pocket? (Catastrophic Cap)

TRICARE Prime:

Your catastrophic cap varies depending on the sponsor's military status:
- Active duty families: $1,000 per family per fiscal year
- National Guard and Reserve families: $1,000 per family per fiscal year
- Retired families (and all others): $3,000 per family, per fiscal year
(Note: POS fees do not apply toward meeting your catastrophic cap.)

TRICARE Standard & Extra:

Your catastrophic cap varies depending on the sponsor's military status:
- Active duty families: $1,000 per family per fiscal year
- National Guard and Reserve families: $1,000 per family per fiscal year
- Retired families (and all others): $3,000 per family per fiscal year

Where is the program available?

TRICARE Prime:

TRICARE Prime is available throughout the continental United States in areas known as Prime service areas.

TRICARE Standard & Extra:

Anywhere in the continental United States. TRICARE Standard is available in the U.S. territories and overseas through the TRICARE Standard Overseas program. The TRICARE Extra option is not available overseas.

How can I learn more?

To learn about how either plan works for you, enter your profile using either TRICARE

COMPARISON OF TRICARE PRIME AND TRICARE STANDARD & EXTRA

Prime or TRICARE Standard & Extra as your plan, and then go to and browse through the Web site at **www.tricare.mil**.
If you have already entered a plan, then click through the site to learn more.

TRAVEL REIMBURSEMENT

Nonactive duty TRICARE Prime beneficiaries and TRICARE Prime Remote family members may qualify to have reasonable travel expenses reimbursed by TRICARE when they are referred by their primary care manager for medically necessary, nonemergency specialty care at a location more than 100 miles (one way) from their PCM's office. Reasonable travel expenses are the actual costs incurred while traveling, including meals, gas, tolls, parking, and tickets for public transportation (such as airplane, train, or bus).

Beneficiaries who may qualify for this travel reimbursement include:

- TRICARE Prime-enrolled active duty family members, including family members of activated National Guard or Reserve members

- TRICARE Prime-enrolled retired service members and their family members

- TRICARE Prime-enrolled transitional survivors, survivors, and former spouses

- Others enrolled in TRICARE Prime except for active duty service members

- TRICARE Prime Remote-enrolled active duty family members, including family members of activated National Guard or Reserve members

- TRICARE Prime Remote-enrolled transitional survivors

TRICARE PRIME OVERSEAS

Retirees and retiree family members are not eligible for TRICARE Prime Overseas program.

TRICARE FOR LIFE

TRICARE For Life (TFL) is TRICARE's Medicare-wraparound coverage available to all Medicare-eligible TRICARE beneficiaries, regardless of age, provided they have Medicare Parts A and B.

Although Medicare is your primary insurance, TRICARE acts as your secondary payer, thereby minimizing your out-of-pocket medical expenses. TRICARE benefits include covering both Medicare's coinsurance and deductible.

Key Features of TRICARE For Life Include:

- Minimal out-of-pocket costs (aside from Medicare Part B premium).

- No enrollment fees for TFL (but, you must purchase Medicare Part B and pay monthly premiums to be eligible for TFL).

- Coordination of benefits between Medicare and TRICARE.

- TRICARE is the secondary payer for all services covered by both TRICARE and Medicare.

- TRICARE is the primary payer for those services covered only by TRICARE.

- Additional steps may be required to coordinate benefits if you have other health insurance in addition to TRICARE and Medicare.

- Freedom to manage your own healthcare.

- No assigned primary care manager.

- Visit any Medicare provider.

- Receive care at a military treatment facility on a space-available basis.

- No claims to file (in most cases).

- Your provider files your claim with Medicare.

- Medicare processes the claims.

- Medicare forwards it electronically to TRICARE.

- TRICARE for Life pays similarly to TRICARE Standard in those overseas locations where Medicare is not available.

TRICARE For Life Eligibility

TFL is available to all Medicare-eligible TRICARE beneficiaries, regardless of age, including retired members of the National Guard and Reserve who are in receipt of retired pay, family members, widows and widowers, and certain former spouses. Dependent parents and parents-in-law are not eligible for TFL.

(Note: If you are under age 65, have Medicare Part B, and live in a TRICARE Prime service area, you have the option to enroll in TRICARE Prime; TRICARE waives your TRICARE Prime enrollment fee.)

You should confirm that your Medicare status is current in the Defense Enrollment Eligibility Reporting System. Your uniformed services ID card and your Medicare card, which must reflect enrollment in Medicare Part B, are evidence of your TFL eligibility.

TFL and Other Health Insurance

If you have other health insurance, such as a Medicare supplement or an employer-sponsored health plan, you may use TFL as long as you are eligible for Medicare Part A and have Medicare Part B coverage. By law, TRICARE pays claims only after all other health insurances pay. After Medicare processes the claim it automatically forwards it to your other health insurance. Once your other health insurance processes the claim, you must file a paper claim with the TFL contractor. The contractor will process the claim and pay TRICARE's portion of the claim directly to you.

You must submit your paper claims to the TFL contractor along with a copy of your provider's itemized bill, the Medicare summary notice, and explanation of benefits from all other health insurances. You must file TFL claims within one year from the date of care.

If you wish to cancel your other health insurance, you must contact your other health insurance administrator. After canceling your other health insurance, you must mail a copy of the termination notice to the TFL contractor.

TFL and Military Treatment Facilities

When using TFL, you may continue to get care in Military Treatment Facilities on a space-available basis.

For access to primary care at MTFs, you may enroll in TRICARE Plus. The option to enroll in TRICARE Plus is based on availability and capacity at each individual MTF. Contact your local MTF for more information about TRICARE Plus.

TFL and Veterans Affairs Facilities

If you are eligible for benefits under both TRICARE and Veterans Affairs programs, you may choose to use your TRICARE benefit at a VA Medical Facility as long as:

　　8 The service is covered under TRICARE and is not for a service-connected condition.

⅄ The VA facility is in the TRICARE network.

Since the VA can bill TRICARE but cannot bill Medicare, you will be responsible for TRICARE cost shares and the deductible.

Tricare For Life Overseas

TRICARE beneficiaries who live overseas must meet the same requirements as TRICARE beneficiaries who live in the United States to use TRICARE For Life. TRICARE beneficiaries who live overseas and become eligible for Medicare must enroll in Medicare Part A and Part B to use TFL. Medicare does not often provide healthcare coverage overseas; therefore, TFL pays first, and you pay TRICARE's deductible and cost shares.

If you seek reimbursement for care received in overseas locations not covered by Medicare, you must submit a paper claim to the TRICARE Overseas claims processor along with a copy of your provider's itemized bill and, if applicable, your other health insurance's explanation of benefits. You do not have to submit a Medicare summary notice. You are responsible for TRICARE's deductible and cost shares.

Medicare pays first for healthcare received in U.S. territories including:

   ⅄ Guam

   ⅄ Puerto Rico

   ⅄ U.S. Virgin Islands

   ⅄ American Samoa

   ⅄ Northern Mariana Islands

Providers who accept Medicare in one of the U.S. territories file the claim with Medicare. Medicare then processes the claim and forwards it to TRICARE for payment. TRICARE pays the provider directly for TRICARE-covered services. If you receive services on a ship (cruise) in territorial waters adjoining the land areas of the United States, Medicare also pays first.

WHAT IS MEDICARE/MEDICAID?

The Centers for Medicare & Medicaid Services manages Medicare. Medicare is a health insurance program for:

- People age 65 or older

- People under age 65 with certain disabilities

- People with end-stage renal disease (ESRD)

Medicare Part A is hospital insurance. Medicare Part B is medical insurance.

Under federal law, if you are a TRICARE beneficiary eligible for premium-free Medicare Part A because of a disability or end-stage renal disease or are eligible based on turning age 65, you must have Medicare Part B coverage to remain TRICARE eligible. The only exceptions are:

- **You have a sponsor on active duty**: If you are an active duty veteran's family member eligible for or entitled to premium-free Medicare Part A, to keep your TRICARE benefits, you do not have to have Medicare Part B until your sponsor retires. You may enroll in Part B during a special enrollment period. The special enrollment period is available to you anytime your sponsor is on active duty or within the first eight months of your sponsor's retirement. If you enroll in Part B after your sponsor's retirement date, you will have a break in TRICARE coverage. To avoid this break, you should enroll in Part B before your sponsor's retirement date.

  If you do not enroll during the special enrollment period, your next opportunity to enroll in Part B is during the general enrollment period, which occurs each year January 1 through

March 31. Your Part B coverage will start on July 1; meaning your TRICARE coverage will not be effective until July 1. You may also be required to pay the 10 percent Medicare surcharge for each 12-month period you were eligible to enroll in Part B but did not.

You are enrolled in the U.S. Family Health Plan: If you are eligible for or entitled to premium-free Medicare Part A and enrolled in the U.S. Family Health Plan (available in six locations) you do not have to have Medicare Part B for U.S. Family Health Plan coverage. The Department of Defense strongly encourages enrollment in Part B when you are first eligible. If you withdraw your enrollment from the U.S. Family Health Plan or move to a non-U.S. Family Health Plan area, you will not be eligible for other TRICARE programs if you do not have Part B. If you do not enroll in Part B when first eligible, you may be required to pay the 10 percent Medicare surcharge for each 12-month period you were eligible to enroll in Part B but did not.

TRICARE Reserve Select members: If you are eligible for or entitled to premium-free Medicare Part A and enrolled in TRICARE Reserve Select (TRS) you do not have to have Medicare Part B, but the DOD strongly encourages enrollment in Part B when first eligible. Although TRICARE treats you as an active duty veteran's family member while in TRS, Medicare does not consider your sponsor to be actively employed by the military. If you do not enroll in Part B when you are first eligible, you may be required to pay the 10 percent Medicare surcharge for each 12-month period you were eligible to enroll in Part B but did not.

If you are required to have Medicare Part B coverage but do not have it, you are not eligible for any TRICARE benefits. If you refused Medicare Part B coverage when you first became eligible, you may be responsible for paying a Medicare Part B premium surcharge, which is 10 percent for each 12-month period that you were eligible to enroll in Part B but did not.

- **Medicare entitlement based on disability**: You are eligible for Medicare Part A (premium-free) and Part B (with a monthly premium) beginning the 25th month of receiving Social Security disability payments. The Social Security Administration notifies you of your Medicare entitlement start date. If your disability claim and Medicare entitlement are awarded retroactively, it is important to make sure your Medicare Part A and Part B effective dates match. If your Medicare effective dates do not match, TRICARE will recoup payments made for claims paid when you had Part A coverage and no Part B.

  Your Medicare entitlement continues up to 4½ years after your disability payments end. During this period, you are still required to have Part B to remain TRICARE-eligible.

- **Medicare entitlement based on End Stage Renal Disease**: Medicare coverage is not automatic for people with ESRD. You need to file an application to receive Medicare benefits. Failure to file for Medicare benefits will result in a loss of TRICARE coverage. Your Medicare coverage begins:

  - The fourth month you are on renal dialysis

  - The month you are admitted to a Medicare-approved hospital for kidney transplant or in the following two months

  - Two months before your transplant if your transplant is delayed more than two months after admission to the hospital.

- **Medicare entitlement based on age**: The age for full Social Security payments is gradually increasing from age 65 to age 67. The age for Medicare eligibility is not changing; it continues to be age 65.

- You become eligible for premium-free Medicare Part A at age 65 if you or your spouse paid into Social Security for at least 40 quarters (at least 10 years of work). Failure to file for Medicare benefits results in loss of TRICARE coverage.

8 If you already receive benefits from Social Security, the Railroad Retirement Board (RRB), or Office of Personnel Management, you automatically receive Medicare Part A and are enrolled in Medicare Part B starting the first day of the month you turn 65. (If your birthday is on the first of the month, Part A is effective on the first day of the previous month.)

8 If you have not filed for Social Security benefits, RRB benefits, or a federal annuity from the Office of Personnel Management, you must file an application for Part A and Part B. To avoid the Medicare surcharge for late enrollment, you must enroll in Part B during your Medicare Initial Enrollment Period (IEP) (seven-month period that begins three months before you turn 65 or four months if your birthday is on the first of the month). To avoid a break in TRICARE coverage, be sure to enroll during the three to four months before you turn 65. If you wait until you are 65 or enroll during the last three months of your IEP, your Part B effective date and TRICARE coverage will be delayed.

TRICARE RESERVE SELECT

TRICARE Reserve Select (TRS) is a premium-based health plan that qualified National Guard and Reserve members may purchase. TRS, which requires a monthly premium, offers coverage similar to TRICARE Standard and Extra.

Key features of TRS include:

8 Available worldwide to most Selected Reserve members (and families) when not on active duty orders or covered under the Transitional Assistance Management Program.

8 Must qualify for and purchase TRS to participate.

8 Must pay monthly premiums. Failure to pay monthly premiums on time may result in disenrollment and an enrollment lockout.

- 8 Freedom to manage your own healthcare; no assigned primary care manager.

- 8 Visit any TRICARE-authorized provider or qualified host nation provider if located overseas. (Network providers not available overseas).

- 8 Pay fewer out-of-pocket costs when choosing a provider in the TRICARE network.

- 8 No referrals are required, but some care may require prior authorization.

- 8 May have to pay for services when they are received and then seek reimbursement.

- 8 May have to submit healthcare claims.

- 8 May receive care in a military treatment facility (MTF) on a space-available basis only.

- 8 Comprehensive healthcare coverage including TRICARE's prescription drug coverage.

TRICARE RETIREE DENTAL PROGRAM

The TRICARE Retiree Dental Program (TRDP) is the first and only dental benefits plan created by Congress especially for uniformed services retirees and their family members (administered by Delta Dental of California).

Under contract with the U.S. Department of Defense, the Federal Services Division of Delta Dental of California administers the TRDP with the same level of quality, service, and dependability for which Delta Dental is known nationwide. This unique program offers:

- 8 Comprehensive coverage for the most commonly needed and sought-after dental services with the full scope of benefits available after only 12 months

- The choice to visit any licensed dentist in the service area, or for more cost savings, to choose from more than 90,000 network dentist locations

- Affordable monthly premiums deducted automatically from uniformed services retired pay

TRICARE Retiree Dental Program Eligibility

You are eligible to enroll in the TRDP if you are:

- A member of the uniformed services who is entitled to uniformed services retired pay, even if you are 65 or older

- A member of the retired Reserve/National Guard, including those in the gray area who are entitled to retired pay but will not begin receiving it until age 60

- A current spouse of an enrolled member

- A child of an enrolled member, up to age 21 (or to age 23 if a full-time student, or older if disabled before losing eligibility)

- An un-remarried surviving spouse or eligible child of a deceased member who died while in retired status or while on active duty

- A Medal of Honor recipient and eligible family members, or an un-remarried surviving spouse/eligible family member of a deceased recipient

- A current spouse and/or eligible child of a nonenrolled member with documented proof the nonenrolled member is: (a) eligible to receive ongoing comprehensive dental care from the Department of Veterans Affairs; (b) enrolled in a dental plan through employment and the plan is not available to family members; or (c) unable to obtain benefits through the TRDP due to a current and enduring medical or dental condition (written documentation supporting any of these three situations must be submitted with your enrollment application)

Former spouses and remarried surviving spouses are not eligible.

TRICARE Retiree Dental Program Benefits

The following chart provides an overview of coverage under the enhanced TRICARE Retiree Dental Program for patients who visit a participating network dentist:

DENTAL BENEFITS	
Benefits available during the first 12 months of enrollment	Delta Dental Pays (Percentage)
Diagnostic services (such as exams)	100
Preventive services (such as cleanings)	100
Basic restorative services (such as fillings)	80
Endodontics (such as root canals)	60
Periodontics (such as gum treatment)	60
Oral surgery (such as extractions)	60
Emergency (such as treatment for minor pain)	80
Dental accident coverage	100
Additional services available after 12 months of continuous enrollment:	
Cast crowns, onlays, and bridges	50
Partial/full dentures	50
Orthodontics	50
Deductibles and maximums	
Annual deductible (per person, $150 cap per family, per benefit year)	$50
Annual maximum (per person, per benefit year)	$1,200
Orthodontic maximum (per person, per lifetime)	$1,200
Dental accident maximum (per person, per benefit year)	$1,000
Benefits year: May 1-April 30	

* The percentage paid by Delta is based on the allowed amount for each procedure. Your out-of-pocket costs may be higher if care is received from a nonparticipating provider. Covered benefits are subject to certain limitations.

TRICARE Retiree Dental Program Cost

The TRDP has been designed to provide you and your family with comprehensive dental benefits at an affordable cost. Monthly premium amounts will vary depending on where you live and the number of family members you elect to enroll.

Premium rates will change slightly on May 1 of each benefit year. To find out the current premium rate for your region, use the premium search available on the TRICARE Web site.

Federal law mandates that monthly premiums for the TRDP be deducted automatically from uniformed services retired pay. If it is determined that uniformed services retired pay is not available or is insufficient to allow the automatic deduction, Delta Dental will notify you of your premium payment options by mail.

TRICARE Retiree Dental Program Dentist Network

As an enrolled member of the TRDP, you may visit any licensed dentist within the service area for treatment. To save you even more out-of-pocket expenses, Delta Dental offers a dentist network with more than 90,000 locations nationwide. These network dentists have agreed to prenegotiated fees and to submit all claims paperwork for you.

If you go to an out-of-network dentist, Delta Dental pays the same percentage of covered services but cannot guarantee the dentist's fees. Out-of-network dentists will bill you for their normal fees, which may be higher than the program-allowed amount for the service. You will be responsible for paying your co-payment plus any difference between the program allowed amount and the dentist's billed charge.

Covered services under the TRDP are offered anywhere in the 50 United States and the District of Columbia, Puerto Rico, Guam, the U.S. Virgin Islands, American Samoa, the Commonwealth of the Northern Mariana Islands, and Canada.

TRICARE Retiree Dental Program Enrollment

Enrollment in the TRDP is voluntary. Each new enrollee must fulfill an initial enrollment period of 12 consecutive months. After the initial 12-month period, you become eligible for the full scope of benefits offered under the TRDP and will continue your enrollment in the TRDP on a month-to-month basis. There is a grace period of 30 days from your coverage effective date during which you may rescind your enrollment agreement without any further obligation, provided you have not used any program services during that time.

If you do not exercise your option to rescind within the 30-day grace period, you must remain enrolled in the program for the duration of the initial 12-month period without further opportunity for voluntary withdrawal.

If you are a new retiree who elects to enroll within 120 days after your retirement from active duty, the National Guard or Reserve, you are eligible for a waiver of the 12-month waiting period for the full scope of benefits. A copy of your retirement orders must be submitted with your enrollment application to verify your eligibility for this waiver. Additionally, if you are retiring soon from the uniformed services and wish to enroll in the TRDP with no gap in coverage, it is recommended that you do so in the month before your retirement date to ensure your coverage under the TRDP begins as soon as your retirement is effective.

A two-month premium prepayment is required at the time of enrollment to ensure that you and all enrolled family members can receive benefits the first day your coverage becomes effective. Once your mandatory allotment is established, any unused portion of the prepayment will be refunded to you.

There are three ways to enroll in the TRDP: online, by telephone, or by mail. Coverage will begin on the first day of the month following the acceptance of your enrollment application and submission of a two-month premium prepayment.

Once your enrollment is processed, you will receive a welcome packet containing your membership identification cards and benefits booklet. Your coverage begins the first day of the month following your enrollment, whether or not you have received your welcome packet. Your eligibility can be verified after the first of the month on the TRDP Web site or by calling customer service. For more information, visit **www.trdp.org**.

TRICARE PHARMACY PROGRAM

TRICARE prescription drug coverage is available to all TRICARE-eligible beneficiaries who are enrolled in the Defense Enrollment Eligibility Reporting System. Prescription drug coverage is the same regardless of which health plan option you are using, and it is available worldwide.

Eligible beneficiaries include:

- Active duty service members and their families

- Activated National Guard and Reserve members and their families (on Title 10 or Title 32 [federal] orders)

- Retired service members and their families

- Retired National Guard and Reserve members and their families (age 60 and above and receiving retired pay)

- Survivors, widows/widowers, and certain former spouses

- Medal of Honor recipients and their families

- Beneficiaries enrolled in TRICARE Reserve Select or the Continued Healthcare Benefit Program

- Other beneficiaries listed in DEERS as eligible for TRICARE, including foreign force members and their families

Filling Prescriptions

TRICARE offers several convenient ways for you to have prescriptions filled, depending on your family's specific needs. You can have prescriptions filled at any of these pharmacies, based on your specific situation, and you can use more than one option at a time.

- Military pharmacy: Least-expensive option with no out-of-pocket costs

- Mail-order pharmacy: Safe, convenient, and the most cost-effective option when a military pharmacy is not available

- Network pharmacy: More than 54,000 network pharmacies in the United States and U.S. territories

- Non-network pharmacy: Most expensive option

Although each option is available worldwide, some may be limited outside the United States.

TRICARE covers most U.S. Food and Drug Administration (FDA)-approved prescription medications. Medications may be available as part of the pharmacy or medical benefit. Often, for a medication to be covered by the TRICARE pharmacy benefit, it must:

- Be a prescription medication approved by the FDA

- Not be part of a procedure covered under the medical benefit

- Be prescribed in accordance with good medical practice and established standards of quality

Pharmacy costs are based on whether the prescription is classified as a formulary generic (Tier 1), formulary brand name (Tier 2) or nonformulary (Tier 3) drug and where you choose to have your prescription filled.

OTHER HEALTH INSURANCE

When you have other health insurance (OHI) with a prescription drug plan, your OHI is the first payer for prescription coverage, and the rules of that insurer will apply.

Medicare Part D

Medicare's prescription drug coverage, Medicare Part D, is available to anyone who is eligible for Medicare (Part A and/or Part B). (Note: Beneficiaries who live in overseas areas (non-U.S. territories) or who are in prison are not eligible for Medicare Part D.)

You do not need to enroll in a Medicare Part D prescription drug plan to keep your TRICARE benefits. If you decide to enroll in a Medicare Part D prescription drug plan outside your initial enrollment period, you will not be required to pay the Medicare Part D late enrollment penalty, because TRICARE prescription drug coverage is creditable coverage.

EYE EXAMS

TRICARE covers one comprehensive ophthalmologic eye exam every two years when enrolled in TRICARE Prime. You can receive these eye exams from a TRICARE-authorized optometrist or ophthalmologist.

If you see a TRICARE network provider, you do not need a referral from your primary care manager. If you see a TRICARE non-network provider, you must have a referral from your primary care manager or the care will be denied.

Through the well-child benefit, children (regardless of plan) are covered for one eye and vision screening (testing for visual acuity, ocular alignment, and red reflex) at birth and 6 months of age by their primary/pediatric provider and two comprehensive eye exams (including screening for amblyopia and strabismus) between the ages of 3 and 6. After age 6, they receive one comprehensive eye exam every two years.

MENTAL HEALTH AND BEHAVIOR

TRICARE covers mental health/behavioral healthcare that is medically or psychologically necessary for treatment of a behavioral health disorder.

IF YOUR SPONSOR DIES

If you die after retiring from active duty, TRICARE continues to provide coverage for your family. Widowed spouses remain eligible for TRICARE unless they remarry. Children (biological or adopted) remain eligible up to the normal age limits. Your surviving family members may remain enrolled in TRICARE Prime but must make arrangements to pay the TRICARE Prime enrollment fee. Family members who decide not to stay enrolled in TRICARE Prime are covered by TRICARE Standard and Extra.

SPECIAL PROGRAMS

TRICARE offers supplemental programs tailored specifically to beneficiary health concerns or conditions. Many of these programs have specific eligibility requirements based on beneficiary category, plan, or status.

These programs include health promotion programs such as alcohol education, smoking cessation, and weight loss. Some are for specific beneficiary populations such as the Foreign Force Member Healthcare Option and the Preactivation Benefit for National Guard and Reserve. Other programs are for specific health conditions such as the Cancer Clinical Trials. Many programs are limited to a certain number of participants or a certain geographic location, such as chiropractic care. Details on these programs is available on the Internet at **www.TRICARE.mil**.

U.S. FAMILY HEALTH PLAN

The U.S. Family Health Plan is an additional TRICARE Prime option available through networks of community-based, not-for-profit healthcare systems in six areas of the United States. You must be enrolled in the Defense Eligibility Reporting System and reside in the one of the designated U.S. Family Health Plan service areas.

Key features of the U.S. Family Health Plan include:

   ꝋ The only TRICARE Prime program that offers benefits to

beneficiaries age 65 and over, regardless of whether you participate in Medicare Part B.

☡ Few out-of-pocket costs (similar to TRICARE Prime).

☡ You do not access Medicare providers, Military Treatment Facilities (MTFs) or TRICARE network providers but instead receive your care from a primary care physician that you select from a network of private physicians affiliated with one of the not-for-profit healthcare systems offering the plan. Your primary care physician assists you in getting appointments with specialists in the area and coordinates your care.

☡ Benefit from the same level of prescription coverage as that available under the TRICARE program and at the same costs. However, you may use only your U.S. Family Health Plan's list of retail or on-site pharmacies and the U.S. Family Health Plan mail-order service instead of TRICARE retail, mail-order, or MTF pharmacies.

☡ If you move or disenroll from the U.S. Family Health Plan, you may choose any TRICARE program that you are eligible for and that is available in your area.

☡ Each U.S. Family Health Plan site offers enhanced benefits and services such as discounts for eyeglasses, hearing aids, and dental care. Enhancements vary by U.S. Family Health Plan site.

☡ There are no claims to file when plan-approved providers are used.

☡ Enrollment is required. You may enroll at any time throughout the year, and enrollment is automatically renewed each year unless you take action to disenroll. Enrollment fees, if applicable, may transfer to another U.S. Family Health Plan location or to TRICARE Prime.

☡ You are encouraged to enroll in the U.S. Family Health Plan as a complete family unit, but you may enroll on an individual basis. When you enroll in the U.S. Family Health Plan, you are committing to the plan for one year unless moving out of the area or disenrolling for another qualified reason.

Eligible beneficiaries include:

- Active duty family members

- Retirees and their eligible family members

- Survivors

- Former spouses

- Medal of Honor recipients and their families

- Family members of activated National Guard or Reserve members

You do not need to have Medicare Part B to enroll in the U.S. Family Health Plan. However, if you do not enroll in Medicare Part B when first eligible and subsequently choose to do so, you will pay (in addition to the normal Medicare Part B monthly premium) an annual 10 percent penalty for each year you were eligible to enroll in Medicare Part B and did not.

In addition, you will be able to in Medicare Part B enroll only during the general enrollment period, January 1-March 31 of each year, and your Part B benefits will not be effective until July 1 of that year. You are encouraged to enroll in Medicare Part B when first eligible.

If you are entitled to Medicare Part A and decide to disenroll from the U.S. Family Health Plan, you will then be able to use the TRICARE For Life benefit, but only if you also are enrolled in Medicare Part B. Additionally, if you subscribe to Medicare Part B, you pay only co-payments for prescription drugs, and your annual enrollment fee is waived. Medicare Part B also adds coverage for End Stage Renal Disease, a condition that often involves kidney failure. Medicare Part B is not required for the U.S. Family Health Plan, but you should carefully consider whether it is in your best interest to enroll.

CHAPTER 9

BENEFITS FOR SURVIVING SPOUSES & FAMILIES OF VETERANS

As the surviving spouse or family member of a military service member, you have certain benefits and entitlements as a result of your spouse or family member's military service. Basically, the single most important factor is whether the death occurred during active duty service or after service. Many of these benefits have been covered in other sections of this book; however, I felt it was important to consolidate key benefits in one chapter as a guide for families of deceased veterans.

The Department of Veterans Affairs offers a wide range of benefits and services for the surviving spouse, dependent children, and dependent parents of deceased veterans and military service members.

DEPENDENCY AND INDEMNITY COMPENSATION (DIC)

Dependency and Indemnity Compensation (DIC) is a tax-free benefit for the surviving spouse and dependent children. A spouse's Survivor Benefit Plan (SBP) annuity is reduced by any DIC amount received.

(Note: A surviving spouse who remarried on or after December 16, 2003, and on or after attaining age 57, is entitled to continue to receive DIC.)

VA also adds a transitional benefit of $250 to the surviving spouse's monthly DIC if there are children under age 18. The amount is based on a family unit, not on individual children. It is paid for two years from the date that entitlement to DIC commences, but it is discontinued earlier when there is no child under age 18 or no child on the surviving spouse's DIC for any reason.

To Apply for DIC

Often an application for DIC benefits is completed by the casualty assistance officer and submitted on behalf of the survivor. VA Form 21-534a, Application for Dependency and Indemnity Compensation by a Surviving Spouse or Child, is used for this purpose. This form needs special processing and should be mailed or faxed along with DD Form 1300, Report of Casualty, to:

Department of Veterans Affairs
Regional Office and Insurance Center
P.O. Box 8079
Philadelphia, PA 19101
Fax: 215-381-3084

PARENTS' DEPENDENCY AND INDEMNITY COMPENSATION (DIC)

Parents' DIC is a monthly benefit amount for the decedent's parents.

SURVIVORS' AND DEPENDENTS' EDUCATIONAL ASSISTANCE (DEA)

Survivors' and Dependents' Educational Assistance provides payment of a monthly education or training allowance to the spouse and children of a veteran who died of a service-connected disability. Eligible persons can receive up to 45 months of benefits. Professional, educational, and vocational counseling will be provided to eligible children and surviving spouses without charge upon request.

WORK-STUDY EMPLOYMENT

Work-study is available to eligible survivors while pursuing a program of education or training under Dependent's Educational Assistance.

HOME LOAN GUARANTY

The surviving spouse of a veteran who died in service, or of a service-connected disability, may be eligible for a guaranteed loan from a private lender. It may be used to purchase, construct, or improve a home; purchase a manufactured home and/or lot; or to refinance existing mortgages or other liens of record on a dwelling owned and occupied by the surviving spouse. There is no time limit to use this benefit.

BURIAL BENEFITS (HEADSTONES, MARKERS, AND PRESIDENTIAL MEMORIAL CERTIFICATES)

Headstones and Grave Markers: The VA provides headstones and grave markers for the graves of veterans anywhere in the world and of eligible dependents who are buried in military post, state veteran, or national cemeteries. Niche markers also are available for identifying cremated remains in columbaria and memorial markers if the remains are not available for burial.

Presidential Memorial Certificate: A certificate bearing the president's signature is issued to recognize the service of deceased veterans who were discharged under honorable conditions. Eligible recipients include next of kin or other loved ones. A certificate can be issued to more than one eligible recipient. VA regional offices can help you in applying for certificates.

LIFE INSURANCE SETTLEMENT

Information on where and how to file for a service member's Group Life Insurance (SGLI) proceeds may be found at VA's Insurance Center Web site. You may also contact the Office of Service Members' Group Life Insurance by phone at 1-800-419-1473, by e-mail at osgli.claims@ prudential.com, or by mail at 290 West Mt. Pleasant Ave., Livingston, NJ 07039-2747. Financial counseling services are available at no cost to SGLI beneficiaries. This service provides a one-on-one counseling session, a detailed step-by-step financial plan, and access to financial counselors for one year. For additional information, call 1-888-243-7351.

VET CENTER BEREAVEMENT COUNSELING

Bereavement counseling is now being offered to parents, spouses, and children of armed forces personnel who died in the service of their country. Also eligible are family members of reservists and National Guardsmen who die while on duty. A new tri-fold brochure is now available for you to read or download. It is in a PowerPoint format but prints out nicely on two standard 8 1/2" by 11" sheets of paper. It is a 972 kb file.

VOCATIONAL REHABILITATION & EMPLOYMENT (VR&E) SERVICES

Vocational Rehabilitation & Employment can provide a wide range of vocational and educational counseling services to survivors and dependents who are eligible for one of VA's educational benefit programs. These services are designed to help an individual choose a vocational direction and determine the course needed to achieve the chosen goal.

EDUCATION PROGRAM REFUNDS

The designated survivor of a deceased service member will be refunded the service member's pay reductions for participation in the Montgomery GI

Bill, less benefits previously paid to the service member contributions to the Veterans Educational Assistance Program (VEAP).

SOCIAL SECURITY ADMINISTRATION BENEFITS

When a person who has worked and paid Social Security taxes dies, certain members of the family may be eligible for survivors' benefits. Up to 10 years of work is needed to be eligible for benefits, depending on the person's age at the time of death.

Who Is Eligible for Survivors' Benefits?

Social Security survivors' benefits can be paid to:

- A widow or widower: full benefits at full retirement age or reduced benefits as early as age 60

- A disabled widow or widower: as early as age 50

- A widow or widower at any age if he or she takes care of the deceased's child who is under age 16 or disabled and receiving Social Security benefits

- Unmarried children under 18, or up to age 19 if they are attending high school full-time (under certain circumstances, benefits can be paid to stepchildren, grandchildren, or adopted children)

- Children at any age who were disabled before age 22 and remain disabled

- Dependent parents age 62 or older

SSA calculators can help you figure how much your benefits will be. They can be found at **www.ssa.gov/planners/calculators.htm**.

How Work Affects Survivors' Benefits

You can receive Social Security survivors' benefits and work at the same time. However, depending on your age, your benefits could be reduced if you earn more than a certain amount. For more information, see the leaflet, "*How Work Affects Your Benefits*" (Publication number 05-10069.

How Divorce Affects Survivors' Benefits

If your divorced spouse dies, you can receive benefits as a widow/widower if the marriage lasted 10 years or longer and you are age 60 or older (or age 50 if you are disabled). Benefits paid to a surviving divorced spouse who is 60 or older (age 50 if disabled) will not affect the benefit rates for other survivors receiving benefits.

How Remarriage Affects Survivors' Benefits

You cannot receive survivors' benefits if you remarry before the age of 60 unless the latter marriage ends, whether by death, divorce, or annulment. If you remarry after age 60 (50 if disabled), you can still collect benefits on your former spouse's record. When you reach age 62 or older, you may get retirement benefits on the record of your new spouse if they are higher.

Your remarriage would have no effect on the benefits being paid to any of your children.

How Retirement Affects Survivors' Benefits

If you are collecting survivors' benefits, you can switch to your own retirement benefits (assuming you are eligible and your retirement rate is higher than the widow/widower's rate) as early as age 62.

In many cases, you can begin receiving retirement benefits either on your own or your spouse's record at age 62 and then switch to the other benefit when you reach full retirement age, if that amount is higher.

DEPARTMENT OF LABOR BENEFITS

The Department of Labor (DOL) has numerous grants and training programs that you may be eligible for. Additionally, DOL manages the veterans' preference programs. The Department of Labor provides many of the same benefits to survivors of deceased veterans ("Eligible persons," 38 U.S.C, Part III, Chapter 41, Sec. 4101 [5]) as to the returning veterans.

More information may be found at the Military Spouse Web site, a collaborative DOL/DOD effort (**www.milspouse.org**). DOL also is working with DOD to add information on military installations and their employment readiness programs to America's Service Locator (ASL), found at **www.servicelocator.org**, which helps individuals to locate One-Stop Career Center services.

The Department of Labor's Employment and Training Administration offers a host of services to military spouses through its extensive network of One-Stop Career Centers and the CareerOneStop Electronic Tools that are broadly available to the general population.

One-Stop Career Centers are the focal point of the workforce investment system, supporting the employment needs of job seekers and the human resource needs of business. The range of services for job seekers includes skill and needs assessments, job counseling, local labor market information on high-growth occupations, job training/retraining and placement, and other services provided through partnerships with community organizations.

On July 11, 2003, Secretary of Defense Donald Rumsfeld and Secretary of Labor Elaine L. Chao signed a Memorandum of Understanding to promote cooperative efforts between the departments to improve the quality of life of service members and their families and to contribute to the quality of the American labor force. A major emphasis of joint efforts targets the employment needs of military spouses, because quality of life for military families plays a major role in retention. The major areas covered include:

> ░ **Expanded employment and training services** for military spouses through DOD Family Centers and DOL One-Stop Career Centers

- Spouse Telework Employment Program (STEP)

- **Web resources:** One of the major joint initiatives between the DOD and the DOL is the Military Spouse Resource Center (**www.MilSpouse.org**), a Web site designed to assist the spouses of military personnel. The MilSpouse Web site provides easy access to information, resources, and opportunities related to education, training, and employment within the United States. The site features more than 2,500 links to employment opportunities and information on education, training, and supportive services, including child care and transportation, and provides online help that directs users to relevant content within the site's Web pages.

- **Greater access to information**: The Labor Department has added information to its telephone help line (1-877-US2-JOBS) to assist military spouses in accessing employment and training services. DOL also is working with DOD to add information on military installations and their employment readiness programs to America's Service Locator (ASL) **www.servicelocator.org**, which helps individuals to locate One-Stop Career Center services. The Department of Defense has added information on the workforce investment system and One-Stop Career Center services to the Standard Installation Topic Exchange Service (SITES) database, the basis for all installation welcome packets.

- **Expanded training opportunities**: The Labor Department has explored opportunities for expanding military spouse participation in existing employment and training programs, such as apprenticeship and the Workforce Investment Act (WIA) Dislocated Worker program.

- **Connections to DOL's National business partners**: The Departments of Labor (DOL) and Defense (DOD) expanded electronic links with DOL's national business partners to promote the hiring of military spouses and transitioning military personnel. DOL has been actively connecting spouses with DOL national business partners by sending information to all business partners about military spouses.

In addition, ETA has championed the following DOD initiatives:

- Career accelerator program

- Adecco

- Military spouse virtual assistant

- Staffcentrix

- Army spouse employment partnership (15 organizations)

Spouse Telework Employment Program (STEP)

The Spouse Telework Employment Program (STEP) is a partnership among six federal agencies (the Departments of State, Defense, Labor, Homeland Security/Coast Guard; National Guard Bureau; and General Services Administration) to improve spouse access to remote training and telework opportunities within the private sector. The Departments finished the STEP Memorandum of Agreement in May 2004.

The STEP partners are developing a pilot program ("Jobs Without Borders") that will connect about 50 military and foreign service spouses with private-sector telework opportunities. Full implementation of a robust telework program under STEP will provide spouses opportunities for career continuity and development no matter where they are located.

DEPARTMENT OF DEFENSE SURVIVOR'S GUIDE

One of the finest publications for survivors is the *Department of Defense Survivor's Guide to Benefits*, which is the most comprehensive publication of its kind. You can download it here: **www.militaryhomefront.dod.mil/dav/lsn/lsn/binary_resource/binary_content/1936651.pdf**.

SURVIVORS AND DEPENDENTS BENEFITS — DEATH AFTER ACTIVE SERVICE

One of the more difficult tasks a survivor faces after the death of a veteran is completing the numerous claims forms for VA survivors' benefits. The anxiety and fear of the unknown — who to call, what to do, or where to go for help — can be an unpleasant experience. Most of the information is contained on the VA Web site at **www.vba.va.gov/bln/dependents/index. htm**. Additionally, the VA provides the following tip of what documents to collect and have ready:

Documents Needed

- The veteran's discharge certificate or DD-214

- The veteran's VA claim's number or Social Security Number

- The veteran's death certificate

- Government life insurance policy

- A copy of all marriage certificates and divorce decrees (if any)

- A copy of each child's birth certificate (or adoption order)

- The veteran's birth certificate to determine parents' benefits

CHAPTER 10

LIFE INSURANCE BENEFITS DURING & AFTER YOUR MILITARY CAREER

Every active duty military service member knows about Service Members' Group Life Insurance (SGLI) coverage. Many do not know about family coverage, and even fewer know about Veterans Group Life Insurance (VGLI), the Survivor Benefit Plan, and other insurance options available to veterans or military retirees. This chapter provides you with an in-depth explanation of costs, benefits, eligibility, and options for each.

SERVICE MEMBERS' GROUP LIFE INSURANCE (SGLI)

SGLI is a program of low cost group life insurance for service members on active duty, ready reservists, National Guard members, Commissioned Corps of the National Oceanic and Atmospheric Administration members and the Public Health Service, cadets and midshipmen of the four service academies, and members of the Reserve Officer Training Corps.

SGLI coverage is available in $50,000 increments up to the maximum of $400,000. SGLI premiums are currently $0.07 per $1,000 of insurance, regardless of the member's age. The monthly premium rate for a member with maximum coverage of $400,000 is $29. (The premium includes an additional $1 per month for Traumatic Injury Protection coverage [TSGLI], which is mandatory and added automatically.)

SGLI Conversion Feature

Service members with SGLI coverage have two options available to them upon release from service. They can convert their full-time SGLI coverage to term insurance under the Veterans' Group Life Insurance program or convert to a permanent plan of insurance with one of the participating commercial insurance companies.

The SGLI Disability Extension

The SGLI Disability Extension allows service members who are totally disabled at time of discharge to retain the Service Members' Group Life Insurance coverage they had in service at no cost for up to two years.

Frequently Asked Questions About SGLI & Deployment

I was recently mobilized, and my SGLI deduction increased. Why?

Under the law, Title 38 of the United States Code, Section 1967, as of the effective date of your orders, your SGLI coverage amount automatically increased to the maximum amount available by law, and your premium increased accordingly.

Why, when, how, and what can I do if I do not want the maximum coverage amount?

Complete Form SGLV 8286 immediately and give it to your personnel clerk.

If I am a reservist/National Guard member who has been mobilized, how will my Family SGLI coverage change?

Your spouse will automatically be insured for the maximum FSGLI as the effective date of your orders. Premiums will be deducted from your pay based on your spouse's date of birth listed in DEERS.

As a reservist/National Guard member, is my SGLI coverage in force 365 days a year, regardless of if I am performing duty on the day of my demise? Or will it pay only if I am killed performing military duty?

If you are a reservist or National Guard member and have been assigned to a unit in which you are scheduled to perform at least 12 periods of inactive duty that is creditable for retirement purposes, full-time SGLI coverage is in effect 365 days of the year. You are also covered for 120 days following separation or release from duty.

Will SGLI pay out the full $400,000 even if I have other life insurance?

Yes. If you have the maximum amount of SGLI, you have the right to retain any other government or private insurance. However, you may not have more than $400,000 (or statutory maximum) of combined SGLI and VGLI coverage.

I need to change the beneficiary on my SGLI coverage. Can a family member do it for me?

No. In order for the change to be valid, you (the service member) must complete Form SGLV 8286 and submit it to your personnel clerk.

Frequently Asked Questions About SGLI & Demobilization

I was recently demobilized and I am returning to my unit in the Army National Guard (or Army Reserve, Air National Guard, Air Reserve, Navy Reserve, Coast Guard Reserve). What happens to my SGLI?

If you are returning to a unit in which you are scheduled to perform at least 12 periods of inactive duty that is creditable for retirement purposes, your SGLI coverage automatically goes to the maximum SGLI coverage of $400,000. This is regardless of your coverage level while on active duty.

Because you are going into a new duty status, you automatically have the maximum SGLI coverage.

What can I do If I do not want the maximum SGLI coverage amount once I am back in my Guard (or Reserve) unit?

You must complete form SGLV 8286 to either select a lesser amount of coverage or to decline having the coverage. You should complete the form upon return to your unit and give it to your personnel clerk.

You say I am eligible for SGLI coverage as a member of the Guard (or Reserve) now that I have been demobilized. Why did I recently receive an application for VGLI?

The SGLI office uses information from the Veterans Assistance Discharge System to mail computer-produced VGLI applications to service members who have recently been discharged from active duty. Regrettably, this information does not allow the office to identify that you will continue to be eligible for SGLI due to your Guard/Reserve duty status.

Should I apply for VGLI while I still have SGLI?

Here are three points that you need to know before deciding on VGLI:

- You can have both SGLI and VGLI, but the combined coverage cannot be more than $400,000.

- Often premiums for the SGLI coverage are less than premiums for the VGLI.

- When you separate from your full-time Guard/Reserve duty, your SGLI entitlement will cease and you will then be eligible to apply for VGLI. You should receive letters about your VGLI eligibility at that time

I have recently been demobilized and I am returning to my former Reserve or National Guard unit. Will my Family SGLI coverage be affected by it?

If you are assigned to a Reserve/National Guard duty and you have full-time SGLI coverage, your Family SGLI coverage on your spouse automatically goes to the maximum coverage of $100,000. This is regardless of your spouse's coverage level while you were on active duty. Because you are going into a new duty status, your spouse is automatically covered at the maximum level.

What can I do if I do not want the maximum amount of Family SGLI coverage?

If you want less than the maximum Family SGLI coverage or no Family SGLI coverage, you must complete form SGLV 8286A and give it to your unit's personnel clerk upon your return to your unit. Your coverage for dependent children ($10,000) is also in effect as long you have full-time SGLI coverage.

I have been demobilized and I am being assigned to the IRR (or ING); how will my SGLI and FSGLI coverage change?

As a member of the IRR, often, you are not entitled to full-time SGLI. The following provisions apply:

- Your SGLI will continue for 120 days from your date of discharge from active duty. Then it will cease.

- You are eligible for part-time SGLI, which provides coverage only for the actual time you are on inactive duty for training.

- Also, you are eligible to apply for VGLI or to apply for permanent insurance with a commercial insurance company participating in the SGLI Conversion Pool.

Your Family SGLI will also cease 120 days from the date your full-time SGLI coverage ends. During this period, your spouse is eligible to apply for permanent insurance with a commercial insurance company participating in the SGLI Conversion Pool. Note that there is no family coverage under the VGLI program.

TRAUMATIC INJURY PROTECTION UNDER SERVICE MEMBERS' GROUP LIFE INSURANCE (TSGLI)

Every member who has SGLI also has TSGLI effective December 1, 2005. This coverage applies to active duty members, reservists, National Guard members, funeral honors duty, and one-day muster duty.

This benefit is also provided retroactively for members who incurred severe losses as a result of traumatic a injury between October 7, 2001, and December 1, 2005, if the loss was the direct result of injuries incurred in Operations Enduring Freedom or Iraqi Freedom.

TSGLI coverage will pay a benefit of between $25,000 and $100,000 depending on the loss directly resulting from the traumatic injury. Every member who has SGLI also has TSGLI effective December 1, 2005.

TSGLI coverage is automatic for those insured under basic SGLI and cannot be declined. The only way to decline TSGLI is to decline basic SGLI coverage.

Are spouses and children covered by TSGLI?

No. TSGLI is not available to spouses and children under Family SGLI. It is available only to service members insured under SGLI.

Are members covered for TSGLI when they are insured under VGLI?

No. TSGLI coverage is not available to VGLI policyholders.

| COVERED LOSSES & PAYMENTS ||
If the loss is	then the payment amount is
Total and permanent loss of sight in both eyes	$100,000
Total and permanent loss of hearing in both ears	$100,000

COVERED LOSSES & PAYMENTS

If the loss is	then the payment amount is
Loss of both hands at or above the wrist	$100,000
Loss of both feet at or above the ankle	$100,000
Quadriplegia	$100,000
Hemiplegia	$100,000
Paraplegia	$100,000
Third-degree or worse burns, covering 30 percent of the body or 30 percent of the face	$100,000
Loss of one hand at or above the wrist and one foot at or above the ankle	$100,000
Loss of one hand at or above the wrist and total and permanent loss of sight in one eye	$100,000
Loss of one foot at or above the ankle and total and permanent loss of sight in one eye	$100,000
Total and permanent loss of speech and total and permanent loss of hearing in one ear	$75,000
Loss of one hand at or above the wrist and total and permanent loss of speech	$100,000
Loss of one hand at or above the wrist and total and permanent loss of hearing in one ear	$75,000
Loss of one hand at or above the wrist and loss of thumb and index finger of other hand	$100,000

COVERED LOSSES & PAYMENTS

If the loss is	then the payment amount is
Loss of one foot at or above the ankle and total and permanent loss of speech	$100,000
Loss of one foot at or above the ankle and total and permanent loss of hearing in one ear	$75,000
Loss of one foot at or above the ankle and loss of thumb and index finger of same hand	$100,000
Total and permanent loss of sight in one eye and total and permanent loss of speech	$100,000
Total and permanent loss of sight in one eye and total and permanent loss of hearing in one ear	$75,000
Total and permanent loss of sight in one eye and loss of thumb and index finger of same hand	$100,000
Total and permanent loss of thumb of both hands, regardless of the loss of any other digits	$100,000
Total and permanent loss of speech and loss of thumb and index finger of same hand	$100,000
Total and permanent loss of hearing in one ear and loss of thumb and index finger of same hand	$75,000
Loss of one hand at or above wrist and coma	$50,000 for loss of hand
Loss of one foot at or above ankle and coma	$50,000 for loss of foot

COVERED LOSSES & PAYMENTS

If the loss is	then the payment amount is
Total and permanent loss of speech and coma	$50,000 for total and permanent loss of speech plus the amount paid for coma, up to a combined maximum of $100,000
Total and permanent loss of sight in one eye and coma	$50,000 for total and permanent loss of sight in one eye plus the amount paid for coma up to a combined maximum of $100,000
Total and permanent loss of hearing in one ear and coma	$25,000 for total and permanent loss of hearing in one ear plus the amount paid for coma up to a combined maximum of $100,000
Loss of thumb and index finger of same hand and coma	$50,000 for loss of thumb and index finger of the same hand plus the amount paid for coma up to a combined maximum of $100,000
Total and permanent loss of sight in one eye and inability to carry out activities of daily living due to traumatic brain injury	$50,000 for loss of sight in one eye plus the amount paid for the inability to carry out activities of daily living due to traumatic brain injury up to a combined maximum of $100,000
Loss of one hand at or above the wrist and inability to carry out activities of daily living due to traumatic brain injury	$50,000 for loss of hand plus the amount paid for the inability to carry out activities of daily living due to traumatic brain injury up to a combined maximum of $100,000
Loss of one foot at or above the ankle and inability to carry out activities of daily living due to traumatic brain injury	$50,000 for loss of foot plus the amount paid for the inability to carry out activities of daily living due to traumatic brain injury up to a combined maximum of $100,000

COVERED LOSSES & PAYMENTS

If the loss is	then the payment amount is
Loss of thumb and index finger of same hand and inability to carry out activities of daily living due to traumatic brain injury	$50,000 for loss of thumb and index finger plus the amount paid for the inability to carry out activities of daily living due to traumatic brain injury up to a combined maximum of $100,000
Total and permanent loss of hearing in one ear and inability to carry out activities of daily living due to traumatic brain injury	$25,000 for total and permanent loss of hearing in one ear plus the amount paid for the inability to carry out activities of daily living due to traumatic brain injury up to a combined maximum of $100,000
Total and permanent loss of speech and inability to carry out activities of daily living due to traumatic brain injury	$50,000 for total and permanent loss of speech plus the amount paid for the inability to carry out activities of daily living due to traumatic brain injury up to a combined maximum of $100,000
Coma from traumatic injury and/or the inability to carry out activities of daily living due to traumatic brain injury Note 1: Benefits will not be paid under this schedule for concurrent conditions of coma and traumatic brain injury. Note 2: Duration of coma includes the day of onset of the coma and the day when the member recovers from coma. Note 3: Duration of the inability to carry out activities of daily living due to traumatic brain injury includes the day of the onset of the inability to carry out activities of daily living and the day the member once again can carry out activities of daily living	$25,000 at 15th consecutive day in a coma, and/or the inability to carry out activities of daily living At 30th consecutive day in a coma, and/or the inability to carry out activities of daily living, additional $25,000 At 60th consecutive day in a coma, and/or the inability to carry out activities of daily living, additional $25,000 (Benefits can be paid for both conditions only if experienced consecutively, not concurrently).

COVERED LOSSES & PAYMENTS	
If the loss is	**then the payment amount is**
Total and permanent loss of speech	$50,000
Loss of one hand at or above the wrist	$50,000
Loss of one foot at or above ankle	$50,000
Total and permanent loss of sight in one eye	$50,000
Loss of thumb and index finger of same hand	$50,000
Total and permanent loss of hearing in one ear.	$25,000
The inability to carry out activities of daily living due to loss directly resulting from a traumatic injury other than an injury to the brain. Note: Duration of the inability to carry out activities of daily living includes the day of onset of the inability to carry out activities of daily living and the day when the member can once again carry out activities of daily living.	$25,000 At 60th consecutive day of the inability to carry out activities of daily living, additional $25,000 At 90th consecutive day of the inability to carry out activities of daily living, additional $25,000 At 120th consecutive day of the inability to carry out activities of daily living, additional $25,000

The table below outlines the rates for various categories of SGLI coverage.

DUTY STATUS	PREMIUM
Active Duty Members	$1 per month
Reservists or National Guard members with full-time coverage	$1 per month
Reservists or National Guard members with part-time coverage	$1 per month
Funeral honors & one-day muster duty	No charge
Note: These rates are determined by the VA and are subject to change based on claims experience	

TSGLI Eligibility and Claims

To be eligible for payment of TSGLI, you must meet all the following requirements:

- You must be insured by SGLI.

- You must incur a scheduled loss, and that loss must be a direct result of a traumatic injury.

- You must have suffered the traumatic injury before midnight of the day that you separate from the uniformed services.

- You must suffer a scheduled loss within two years (730 days) of the traumatic injury.

- You must survive for a period of not less than seven full days from the date of the traumatic injury. (The seven-day period begins on the date and time of the traumatic injury, as measured by Zulu [Greenwich Meridian] time and ends 168 full hours later).

SGLI Disability Extension Increased to Two Years

On June 15, 2006, the President signed P.L. 109- 233, the Veterans' Housing Opportunity & Benefits Improvement Act of 2006. This law extends the free coverage period under the SGLI Disability Extension from one year to two years. As a result of this change, service members who have a SGLI policy and are totally disabled from the time they separate from service can now keep their SGLI coverage for up to two years at no cost to them.

FAMILY SERVICE MEMBERS' GROUP LIFE INSURANCE (FSGLI)

Family Service Members' Group Life Insurance (FSGLI) is a program extended to the spouses and dependent children of members insured under the SGLI program. FSGLI provides up to a maximum of $100,000 of insurance coverage for spouses, not to exceed the amount of SGLI the insured member has in force, and $10,000 for dependent children. Spousal coverage is issued in increments of $10,000.

Family coverage is available for the spouses and children of:

- Active duty service members

- Members of the Ready Reserve or Guard of a uniformed service

(Note: Family coverage is available only for members insured under the SGLI program. It is not available for those insured under the VGLI program.)

Frequently Asked Questions about FSGLI

My father is totally dependent upon me for support. Will he be eligible for SGLI Family coverage?

No. Only spouses and dependent children are eligible for coverage.

I am an active duty member, but my spouse is retired military. Is my spouse eligible to be insured under SGLI Family coverage?

Yes. Eligibility for spousal coverage is based on the status of the member covered under SGLI. All active duty members covered under SGLI are eligible to insure their spouses, regardless of whether their spouse is an active duty member, retired, or a civilian.

I am insured under SGLI and just married. My wife's son is coming to live with us. Will he be covered under FSGLI?

Yes. He will be insured as soon as he becomes a member of your household, provided he has not yet reached age 18. He can be insured between the ages of 18 and 23 if he is pursuing a course of instruction at an approved educational institution.

I am insured under SGLI. My spouse is retired and is now insured under VGLI. Can my spouse be insured under both SGLI and VGLI? Will my spouse be required to pay premiums for both SGLI and VGLI?

Yes. Your spouse can be insured under both SGLI spousal coverage and his or her own VGLI coverage. Unless you decline coverage for your spouse, he or she will automatically be insured under SGLI spousal coverage and will also be able to maintain his or her own VGLI coverage.

Your spouse will not pay premiums for his or her spousal coverage. It is important to understand that family insurance coverage belongs to the SGLI insured member and not to the spouse. Premiums for spousal coverage will be deducted from your pay. If your spouse maintains VGLI coverage, he or she continues to pay VGLI premiums.

I am retired and covered under VGLI. My wife, however, is not covered under any insurance. Is there any coverage for my wife?

No. There is no family or spousal coverage available under the VGLI program at this time.

My spouse and I are both in the military and participate in SGLI. Can we both be covered by both basic and spousal coverage?

Yes, each of you can be insured under both basic SGLI and SGLI family coverage for the maximum coverage amount of $500,000 for each spouse. To ensure that both you and your spouse have spousal coverage, each of you must have the other listed as spouses on your DEERS record.

Are all my children eligible for automatic family coverage?

Any unmarried dependent child under the age of 18 is automatically covered under family insurance, including natural born children, legally adopted children, and stepchildren who are members of the service member's household. Also, unmarried children who, between 18 and 23 years and until completion of education or training, are pursuing a course of instruction at an approved educational institution are covered. And, any unmarried child who became incapable of self-support before the age of 18 is also covered.

What if my spouse or child suffers from a disease that makes it difficult to purchase life insurance? Will he or she be eligible for Family SGLI coverage at the same premium rate?

Yes. Your spouse will be eligible for spousal coverage at the same premium rate, regardless of his or her health. However, if you decline coverage now and later want to insure your spouse, proof of his or her good health will be required.

Your dependent children, as defined above, are covered for free, regardless of their health.

How much coverage is available for my spouse?

You may purchase up to $100,000 of SGLI coverage for your spouse, in increments of $10,000. However, you may not purchase more SGLI coverage for your spouse than you have for yourself. For example, if you have $50,000 of SGLI coverage, you may purchase only $50,000 of SGLI coverage for your spouse.

How much coverage is available for my children?

Each dependent child of every active duty service member, reservist, or National Guard member who is insured under SGLI is automatically insured for $10,000.

My spouse and I are both active duty and insured under SGLI. We have one child. Is the amount of coverage doubled to $20,000?

No. The maximum benefit under family coverage for any one child is $10,000.

If I am covered by family coverage as a spouse or child, can I choose the beneficiary?

No. The beneficiary of the spouse and the child coverage will be the member. If the member were to die before payment could be made, the proceeds of a spouse or child claim would be paid to the member's beneficiary, as designated by the member on the form SGLV 8286.

VETERANS' GROUP LIFE INSURANCE (VGLI)

VGLI is a program of post-separation insurance that allows service members to convert their SGLI coverage to renewable term insurance. Members with full-time SGLI coverage are eligible for VGLI upon release from service.

How much coverage is available? VGLI coverage is issued in multiples of $10,000 up to a maximum of $400,000. However, a service member's VGLI coverage amount cannot exceed the amount of SGLI he or she had in force at the time of separation from service.

How much does VGLI cost? VGLI premiums are based upon the separating member's age.

How do I convert my SGLI to VGLI coverage? To convert SGLI to VGLI, an eligible member must submit an SGLV 8714, Application for Veterans' Group Life Insurance, to the Office of Service Members' Group Life Insurance (OSGLI) with the required premium within one year and 120 days from discharge. However, service members who submit their application within 120 days of discharge do not need to submit evidence of good health. Service members who apply after the 120-day period must submit evidence of good health.

VGLI Commercial Policy Conversion Feature

VGLI policyholders can convert their VGLI to an individual commercial life insurance policy at any time. To convert VGLI coverage, the policyholder must do the following:

- Select a company from the Participating Companies listing.

- Apply to a local sales office of the company selected.

- Obtain a letter from OSGLI verifying coverage (VGLI Conversion Notice).

- Give a copy of that notice to the agent who takes the application.

Policyholders may convert their coverage to a commercial policy at standard premium rates without having to provide proof of good health. The conversion policy must be a permanent policy, such as a whole life policy. A list of participating companies may be found at **www.insurance. va.gov/sgliSite/forms/ParticList.htm.**

Other types of policies, such as term, variable life, or universal life insurance are not allowed as conversion policies. In addition, supplementary policy benefits such as accidental death and dismemberment or waiver of premium for disability are not considered part of the conversion policy.

You may access your VGLI policy online at: **https://giosgli.prudential. com/osgli/web/OSGLIMenu.html**.

SERVICE-DISABLED VETERANS INSURANCE (S-DVI)

The Service-Disabled Veterans Insurance (S-DVI) program was established in 1951 to meet the insurance needs of certain veterans with service-connected disabilities. S-DVI is available in a variety of permanent plans and term insurance. Policies are issued for a maximum face amount of $10,000.

Who Can Apply for S-DVI?

You can apply for S-DVI if you meet the following four criteria:

- You were released from active duty under other than dishonorable conditions on or after April 25, 1951.

- You were rated for a service-connected disability (even if only rated 0 percent).

- You are in good health except for any service-connected conditions.

- You apply within two years from the date VA grants your new service-connected disability.

Waiver of Premiums for Totally Disabled Veterans

Under certain conditions, the basic S-DVI policy provides for a waiver of premiums in the case of total disability. Policyholders who carry the basic S-DVI coverage and who become eligible for a waiver of premiums due to total disability can apply for and be granted additional Supplemental S-DVI of up to $20,000.

Supplemental S-DVI

The Veterans' Benefits Act of 1992 provided for $20,000 of supplemental coverage to S-DVI policyholders. Premiums may not be waived on this supplemental coverage. S-DVI policyholders are eligible for this supplemental coverage if:

- They are eligible for a waiver of premiums.

- They apply for the coverage within one year from notice of the grant of waiver.

- They are under age 65.

THE SURVIVOR BENEFIT PLAN (SBP)

The Survivor Benefit Plan (SBP) is not insurance that pays you a dividend payout upon the death of the service member. Instead it is a program designed to continue partial retirement pay after the retired service member's death.

Overview of the Survivor Benefit Plan

Retired pay stops when you die. The Survivor Benefit Plan helps make up for the loss of part of this income. It pays your eligible survivors an inflation-adjusted monthly income.

You must pay premiums for SBP coverage once you retire. Premiums are taken by reducing retired pay, so they do not count as income. This means less tax and less out-of-pocket cost for SBP. Also, using conservative fiscal assumptions, the plan is partially funded by the government, so the average premiums are well below cost. This subsidy means an attractive plan for most people. The subsidy is an average and does not apply in every case.

Basic SBP for a spouse pays a benefit equal to 55 percent of your retired pay. (Note: This applies only to spouses who were age 62 before April 2008.)

The National Defense Authorization Act for Fiscal Year 2005 provides for increasing the percentage until the benefit becomes 55 percent of base pay by March 2008, regardless of age. Until then, the percentage at age 62 will be:

- 40 percent in October 2005

- 45 percent in April 2006

- 50 percent in April 2007

- 55 percent in April 2008

Eligible children may also be SBP beneficiaries, either alone or added to spouse coverage. In the latter case, the children get benefits only if the spouse dies or remarries before age 55. Eligible children equally divide a benefit equal to 55 percent of your retired pay. Child coverage is relatively inexpensive because children get benefits only while they are still your dependents.

You may choose coverage for a former spouse or, if you have no spouse or children, you may be able to cover an insurable interest (such as a business partner or parent).

SBP as Insurance and Other Estate Planning Information

We buy insurance as a way to cope with major financial risks. We buy it to protect us from the financial hardships of events we cannot foresee, such as car wrecks and house fires. It protects our valuable assets.

Your retired pay is one such valuable asset. Since it stops when you die and you cannot foresee when that will be, it may be useful to insure it.

SBP is a form of life insurance for part of your retired pay. But SBP premiums and benefits differ from those of most other insurance plans.

Like life insurance, SBP protects your survivors against complete loss of financial security when you die. But, SBP does more. It also protects your survivor against the possibility of outliving the benefit. Many insurance plans pay only a fixed benefit that may run out years before the survivor dies.

Besides long life, another unpredictable reason your survivor may outlive the benefits is inflation. SBP protects against this risk through the cost-of-living adjustment (COLA). Inflation may be the biggest financial uncertainty of all. It erodes the value of fixed incomes, making them worth less as time goes by. Few, if any, private insurance plans will fully insure your survivor against the ravages of inflation.

No known insurance company has guaranteed to match SBP benefits at equal cost or less. One reason is SBP premiums have a built-in discount, making the plan a good buy for most people. Plus, a private insurer needs to cover administrative expenses and make a profit, and these are not accounted for in SBP premiums, thus increasing the subsidy.

Also, SBP premiums reduce your taxable income and cut your out-of-pocket cost for coverage. SBP benefits are taxed as income to the survivor, but the tax rate should be less than you now pay. Most insurance plans are the reverse; premiums are paid from after-tax income, while survivors are not taxed on the proceeds.

Still, SBP alone is not a complete estate plan. Other insurance and investments are important in meeting needs outside the scope of SBP. For example, SBP does not have a lump-sum benefit that some survivors may need to meet immediate expenses upon a member's death.

On the other hand, insurance and investments without SBP may be less than adequate. Even if they could duplicate SBP, investments may be much more risky and rely on a degree of financial expertise many do not have. Consider everything carefully. Do not expect SBP to do it all, but give it full credit for what it does.

Is SBP a Good Buy?

Given the expected subsidy, the answer to this question for most retirees is yes! Whether SBP is a good buy for you depends on personal preferences and your age, sex, and health compared to your beneficiary's. Beyond this, the answer lies in three questions you should ask yourself:

- **Is SBP a product I can use?** Personal preferences may control your answer, but a subsidized lifetime inflation-protected income is attractive to most people.

- **How much SBP can I use?** If you know when you will die, how long your survivor will outlive you, and how much inflation will occur, you have the answer. The unknown future is the problem, but SBP meets the need. Even if you die shortly after you retire and your spouse lives for 50 more years and if inflation is higher than expected, SBP will still be paying. It may be paying a lot more than anyone ever expected, because inflation has such a strong impact over a long time. Survivors who began to get SBP benefits in the early 1970s have seen their benefits more than triple through annual COLAs.

- **How much SBP can I afford?** The benefits do carry a price tag, but due to the subsidy and lack of administrative costs and profit, the plan should be attractive for most members. The tax advantage on premiums reduces your out-of-pocket cost.

Caution: Some people think they can join SBP years after they retire, during a so-called open season. In the 25-plus-year history of SBP, only four times have retirees had a second chance at SBP. Each time was after major plan improvements. The second time, premiums were raised for new joiners to help make up for the missed premiums. The third time, new joiners were required to pay all missed premiums with interest, plus an additional amount to protect the solvency of the plan. Open enrollment elections have often required a time (two years) before the election is effective. This prevents too much adverse election (people joining with short life expectancies).

Do not count on an open season. Although an open season may be enacted by special law, it is not part of the regular plan. No more are expected, and it will not give your survivors any peace of mind.

Bottom line: If you want SBP, you need to elect it at the time of retirement.

Survivor Benefit Plan Costs and Benefits

When you retire, you may be able to elect any of several SBP options, which are listed below. SBP elections cannot be canceled or changed after retirement except in specific instances, such as a change in your marital status or after the loss of a beneficiary.

At retirement, full basic SBP for spouse and children will take effect automatically if you make no other valid election. You may not reduce or decline spouse coverage without your spouse's written consent. If you have a former spouse, it may affect your options.

Survivor Benefit Plan Spouse Coverage

The SBP annuity is determined by the base amount you elect. The base amount may range from a minimum of $300 up to a maximum of full retired pay. The annuity is 55 percent of the base amount. Also, the base amount and the payments to the surviving spouse will often increase at the same time and by the same percentage that cost-of-living adjustments are made to retired pay.

Your surviving spouse may remarry after age 55 and continue to receive SBP payments for their lifetime. If they are remarried before age 55, SBP payments will stop but may be resumed if the marriage later ends due to death or divorce.

The SBP premiums for spouse coverage are:

(1) 6.5 percent of your chosen base amount, or if less

(2) 2.5 percent of the first $635 of your elected base amount, plus 10 percent of the remaining base amount

The threshold amount was $635 as of January 1, 2006. The threshold amount will increase at the same time and by the same percentage as future active duty basic pay.

If you became a member of a uniformed service on or after March 1, 1990, and you are retiring for length of service (not for disability), SBP costs will be calculated only under the formula in (1) above.

The following table shows the costs associated with several base amount options and the benefits your spouse will receive based on these options.

SBP BENEFITS BEFORE AGE 62		
Base Amount	SBP Costs*	55% of Base Amount
$300	$7.50	$165
$635	$15.87	$300
$800	$32.37	$440
$1,361	$88.46	$600
$1,400	$91	$770
$1,800	$117	$990
$2,200	$143	$1,210
* The SBP costs used in column two are calculated using the formula that provides the least cost. If the base amount was greater than or equal to $1,091, the formula in (1) was used. For base amounts less than $1,091, the formula in (2) was used.		

The next table shows what can happen after retirement when inflation is a modest 4 percent per year. Retired pay is increased annually to keep pace with inflation. Survivor payments are often increased at the same time, and by the same percentage. These increases are made to the benefits even after the member dies.

YOUR AGE 40	SPOUSE'S AGE	RETIRED PAY	COST OF SBP	BENEFIT*
40	38	$1,000	$65	$550
45	43	$1,214	$78.91	$667
50	48	$1,474	$95.81	$810
55	53	$1,790	$116.35	$984
60	58	$2,175	$141.38	$1,196

YOUR AGE 40	SPOUSE'S AGE	RETIRED PAY	COST OF SBP	BENEFIT*
65	63	$2,644	$171.86	$1,454
70	68	$3,213	$208.85	$1,767
80	78	$4,749	$308.69	$2,611
90	88	$7,024	$456.56	$3,863

In this example, the annuity at age 90 would be nearly four times the covered retired pay at age 40. This demonstrates two favorable features of SBP:

- Payments can never run out.

- Payments keep increasing along with the increased cost of living.

If you die shortly after retirement, your surviving spouse could receive cost-of-living adjusted payments for 50 years or more. Lifetime payments from an original election to cover $1,000 of retired pay could total more than $1 million.

Monthly SBP costs are not included in your taxable federal income. The true cost for SBP is thus less than the amount deducted from retired pay because less federal tax will be paid. This also applies to most state income taxes. SBP payments to survivors are taxable, but spouses often receive benefits when their total income is less and the extra tax exemption for being over age 65 is applicable. The surviving spouse's tax rate should be lower, and a long-run significant tax savings should result.

Loss of Spouse

If your spouse dies first or you get divorced, SBP costs will stop (once you notify the pay center). In divorce cases, spouse coverage may be converted to former spouse coverage.

In some instances of divorce, conversion of the coverage to provide for the former spouse may be required by court order.

SBP Former Spouse Coverage

SBP allows selection of coverage for former spouses. Costs and benefits under this option are identical to those for spouse coverage.

Election of coverage for a former spouse precludes coverage of the current spouse and/or children of the current spouse.

When former spouse coverage is elected, the current spouse must be informed. Only one SBP election may be made. If there is more than one former spouse, the member must specify which one will be covered.

When electing the former spouse option, a member must give the finance center a written statement signed by both the member and the former spouse. It must state:

- Whether the election is made to comply with a court order

- Whether the election is made to comply with a voluntary written agreement related to a divorce action, and if so, whether that voluntary agreement is part of a court order for divorce, dissolution, or annulment

SBP Children Coverage

SBP was designed to give income protection not only to your spouse, but also to your children until they become self-supporting (until they are no longer dependents). Child coverage may be elected with or without spouse/former spouse coverage.

Children are eligible for SBP payments as long as they are unmarried, under age 18, or under age 22 if still in school. A child who is disabled and incapable of self-support remains eligible if the disability occurred before age 18 (or before age 22 if a full-time student). Marriage at any age will terminate a child's eligibility. If you elect former spouse and children coverage, only those eligible children from the marriage between you and your former spouse are covered.

Your children who are under 22 years of age and pursuing a full-time course of study or training in a high school, trade school, technical or vocational institute, junior college, college, university, or comparable recognized educational institute are eligible to receive SBP benefits. While pursuing a full-time course of study or training, a child whose 22nd birthday occurs before July 1 or after August 31 of a calendar year, is considered to be 22 years of age on the first day of July after that birthday.

The payments for children equal 55 percent of your covered retired pay. All eligible children divide in equal shares. If the SBP election was for spouse (or former spouse) and children, the children receive payments only when your spouse loses eligibility because of death or remarriage before age 55. The following is an example of benefit payments for four children and for the remaining children when one child becomes ineligible:

The example is based on the following information:

- Number of children: 4

- Base amount of retired pay: $2,000

- Base amount multiplied by 55 percent: $1,100

- Amount of annuity divided by the number of children: $1,100 / 4 = Amount each child will receive: $275

If the oldest child becomes ineligible because of age, marriage, or is no longer a full time student after the age of 18, only three children will receive payment and the annuity amount per child will be as follows:

- Annuity amount: $1,100

- Amount of annuity divided by the number of children $1,100 / 3 = Amount each child will receive: $366.66

Costs for child coverage are based on your age and the age of your youngest child at the time of election. Costs for child coverage stop when all children are no longer eligible to receive payments. Contact the finance center or your personnel counselor for an exact cost computation. The table below shows the monthly cost for selected cases of child-only coverage per $100 of covered retired pay.

COST PER $100 OF CHILD ONLY COVERAGE				
	Youngest Child's Age			
Your Age	6	10	14	17
35	$0.68	$0.46	$0.29	$0.18
40	$0.52	$0.33	$0.18	$0.11
45	$0.84	$0.53	$0.29	$0.16
50	$1.47	$0.94	$0.53	$0.31

SBP Insurable Interest Coverage

The insurable interest option is available only if you are unmarried with either no dependent children or one dependent child. You may elect insurable interest coverage for that child regardless of the child's age or dependency.

People who can be covered are:

- Any relative more closely related to you than a cousin. This includes relatives such as parents, stepparents, grandparents, grandchildren, aunts, uncles, sisters, brothers, half-sisters, half-brothers, dependent or nondependent children or stepchildren

- A close business associate who would be financially affected by your death; this associate must be a natural person (not a company, organization, or fraternity) with a financial interest in your life)

The monthly cost is 10 percent of retired pay plus 5 percent more for each full five years the person covered is younger than the retiree. The maximum cost is 40 percent of retired pay.

For example, if a retiree is 45 and the person covered is 32, the age difference is 13 years, or two full five-year periods. Therefore, the cost percentage of retired pay would be 20 percent.

If retired pay is $1,000 per month, then the monthly cost will be 20 percent of $1,000, or $200.

The monthly SBP payment to an insurable interest person is equal to 55 percent of the gross retired pay (the base amount is always the gross retired pay) less SBP cost of coverage. Payments are increased by cost-of-living adjustments at the same time and by the same percentage as retired pay is increased.

Continuing our example, the monthly benefit will be 55 percent of the remaining $800 ($1,000 - $200 = $800) of retired pay. Thus, the benefit amount will be $440 (.55 x $800 = $440) per month.

Unlike other coverage categories, you may voluntarily terminate SBP coverage (if the insured is not a former spouse) or change SBP to cover a new spouse or child. See "Stopping SBP" for details.

Note that Public Law 106-65, October 5, 1999, provides that a participant is considered paid-up after completing 30 years (360 payments) in the plan. This applies to a specific category of beneficiary (such as spouse), at a specific base amount (such as full retired pay). Contact your personnel counselor for details on this feature, which went into effect on October 1, 2008.

CHAPTER 11

VETERANS' HOME LOAN GUARANTEE PROGRAM

The VA Home Loan Program is designed to streamline the process for you to get a home loan. Often, VA loans are made without any down payment and may offer lower interest rates than ordinarily available with other types of loans. Aside from the veteran's certificate of eligibility and the VA-assigned appraisal, the application process is identical to any other mortgage loan.

If a lender is approved under VA's Lender Appraisal Processing Program (LAPP), the lender may review the appraisal completed by a VA-assigned appraiser and close the loan on the basis of that review. The process can be quick and efficient.

FIVE STEPS TO A VA LOAN

1. Apply for a certificate of eligibility.

   a. A veteran who does not have a certificate can obtain one easily by completing VA Form 26-1880, Request for a Certificate of Eligibility for VA Home Loan Benefits, and submitting it to one of the VA Eligibility Centers with copies of your most recent discharge or separation papers covering active military duty since September 16, 1940, which show active duty dates and type of discharge.

2. Decide on a home you want to buy and sign a purchase agreement or contract.

3. Order an appraisal from VA.

4. Apply to a mortgage lender for the loan. The VA is not the bank. It does not loan you the money; it simply guarantees a portion of the mortgage to the lender.

5. Close the loan and move in.

WHAT VA DOES FOR THE HOME-BUYING VETERAN

VA guarantees part of your loan, which helps you to get a VA loan featuring:

- No down payment (unless required by the lender or the purchase price exceeds the reasonable value as determined by the VA)

- A competitive interest rate and the flexibility of negotiating interest rates with the lender

- Assurance that you can pay off all or part of the loan in advance without penalty

VA appraises the house to determine its reasonable value in the housing market at the time the appraisal is made. VA requires compliance inspections in most cases on proposed new construction to see that the house:

- Meets accepted standards of good construction

- Conforms to the plans and specifications on which VA's appraisal is based

The VA will try to assist you in getting your builder to correct any defects about which you may have valid complaints.

WHAT THE VA DOES NOT DO

The VA does not have the legal authority to:

- Act as your architect. It does not supervise construction of the house you buy.

- Guarantee that the house is free of defects.

- Act as your attorney. It cannot provide you legal services if you run into trouble in buying or constructing your home.

The VA cannot compel a builder to remedy defects in construction or otherwise compel the builder to live up to a contract with you.

The VA cannot guarantee that you will be completely satisfied with the house or that you can resell it at the price you paid. The VA cannot guarantee that you are making a good investment. That is a decision that only you can make.

The VA does not guarantee the condition of the house that you are buying, whether it is new or previously occupied. The VA guarantees only the loan. You may talk to many people when you are in the process of buying a house. Particularly with a previously occupied house, you may pick up the impression along the way that you need not be overly concerned about any needed repairs or hidden defects because the VA will be sure to find them and require them to be repaired. This is not true. In every case, ultimately, it is your responsibility to be an informed buyer and to assure yourself that what you are buying is satisfactory to you in all respects.

If you have any doubts about the condition of the house that you are buying, it is in your best interests to seek expert advice before you legally commit yourself in a purchase agreement. Particularly with a previously occupied house, most sellers and their real estate agents are willing to permit you, at your expense, to arrange for an inspection by a qualified residential inspection service. Also, most sellers and agents are willing to negotiate with you concerning what repairs are to be included in the purchase agreement. Steps of this kind can prevent many later problems.

VA HOME LOAN ELIGIBILITY

Military Service Requirements for VA Loan Eligibility

(Note: Applications involving other than honorable discharges may require further development by the VA. This is necessary to determine if the service was under other than dishonorable conditions.)

Wartime — Service During:

- World War II: September 16, 1940, to July 25, 1947

- Korea: June 27, 1950, to January 31, 1955

- Vietnam: August 5, 1964, to May 7, 1975

You must have at least 90 days on active duty and been discharged under other than dishonorable conditions. If you served less than 90 days, you may be eligible if discharged for a service-connected disability.

Peacetime — Service during periods:

- July 26, 1947, to June 26,1950

- February 1, 1955, to August 4, 1964

- May 8, 1975, to September 7, 1980 (enlisted)

- May 8, 1975, to October 16, 1981 (officer)

You must have served at least 181 days of continuous active duty and been discharged under other than dishonorable conditions. If you served fewer than 181 days, you may be eligible if discharged for a service-connected disability.

- Service after September 7, 1980 (enlisted) or October 16, 1981 (officer)

If you were separated from service and the separation began after these dates, you must have:

- Completed 24 months of continuous active duty or the full period (at least 181 days) for which you were ordered or called to active duty and been discharged under conditions other than dishonorable

- Completed at least 181 days of active duty and been discharged under the specific authority of 10 USC 1173 (Hardship) or 10 USC 1171 (Early Out)

- Been discharged with less than 181 days of service for a service-connected disability; individuals may also be eligible if they were released from active duty due to an involuntary reduction in force, certain medical conditions, or, in some instances, for the convenience of the government

- Gulf War: Service during period August 2, 1990, to date yet to be determined

If you served on active duty during the Gulf War, you must have:

- Completed 24 months of continuous active duty or the full period (at least 90 days) for which you were called or ordered to active duty and been discharged under conditions other than dishonorable

- Completed at least 90 days of active duty and been discharged under the specific authority of 10 USC 1173 (Hardship) or 10 USC 1173 (Early Out)

- Been discharged with less than 90 days of service for a service-connected disability; individuals may also be eligible if they were released from active duty due to an involuntary reduction in force, certain medical conditions, or, in some instances, for the convenience of the government

Active Duty Service Personnel

If you are now on regular duty (not active duty for training), you are eligible after having served 181 days (90 days during the Gulf War) unless discharged or separated from a previous qualifying period of active duty service.

Selected Reserves or National Guard

You may be eligible if you are not otherwise eligible and you have completed a total of six years in the Selected Reserves or National Guard (member of an active unit, attended required weekend drills and two-week active duty for training), and you:

- Were discharged with an honorable discharge

- Were placed on the retired list

- Were transferred to the Standby Reserve or an element of the Ready Reserve other than the Selected Reserve after service characterized as honorable service

- Continue to serve in the Selected Reserves

Individuals who completed fewer than six years may be eligible if discharged for a service-connected disability.

You may also be determined eligible if you:

- Are an un-remarried spouse of a veteran who died while in service or from a service connected disability

- Are a spouse of a service member missing in action or a prisoner of war

(Note: Also, a surviving spouse who remarries on or after attaining age 57, and on or after December 16, 2003, may be eligible for the home loan benefit. VA must deny applications from surviving spouses who remarried before December 6, 2003, that were received after December 15, 2004.)

Eligibility may also be established for:

- Certain United States citizens who served in the armed forces of a government allied with the United States in World War II.

- Individuals with service as members in certain organizations, such as Public Health Service officers, cadets at the United States Military, Air Force, or Coast Guard Academy, midshipmen at the United States Naval Academy, officers of National Oceanic & Atmospheric Administration, and merchant seamen with World War II service.

VA determines your eligibility, and if qualified, a certificate of eligibility will be issued. Eligibility applications can involve:

- An original determination of eligibility for the home loan benefit

- A request to replace a lost certificate of eligibility

- A request for restoration of the benefit after payment in full of a previous VA home loan

- Issuance of a certificate reflecting a current outstanding loan for refinance purposes

VA Home Loan Eligibility Frequently Asked Questions

How do I apply for a VA-guaranteed loan?

You can apply for a VA loan with any mortgage lender that participates in the VA home loan program. At some point, you will need to get a certificate of eligibility from the VA to prove to the lender that you are eligible for a VA loan.

How do I get a certificate of eligibility?

Complete a VA Form 26-1880, Request for a Certificate of Eligibility. You can apply for a certificate of eligibility by submitting a completed VA Form 26-1880, Request For A Certificate of Eligibility For Home Loan Benefits, to the Winston-Salem Eligibility Center, along with proof of military service. In some cases it may be possible for the VA to establish eligibility without your proof of service. However, to avoid any possible delays, it is best to provide such evidence.

Can my lender get my certificate of eligibility for me?

Yes, it is called ACE (automated certificate of eligibility). Most lenders have access to the ACE (automated certificate of eligibility) system. This Internet-based application can establish eligibility and issue an online certificate of eligibility in a matter of seconds. Not all cases can be processed through ACE — only those for which the VA has sufficient data in its records. However, veterans are encouraged to ask their lenders about this method of obtaining a certificate.

What is acceptable proof of military service?

If you are still serving on regular active duty, you must include an original statement of service signed by, or by direction of, the adjutant, personnel officer, or commander of your unit or higher headquarters which identifies you and your Social Security Number and provides your date of entry on your current active duty period and the duration of any time lost.

If you were discharged from regular active duty after January 1, 1950, a copy of DD Form 214, Certificate of Release or Discharge From Active Duty, should be included with your VA Form 26-1880. If you were discharged after October 1, 1979, DD Form 214 copy 4 should be included. A photocopy of DD-214 will suffice. Do not submit an original document.

If you were discharged from the Selected Reserves or the National Guard, you must include copies of adequate documentation of at least six years of honorable service. If you were discharged from the Army or Air Force National Guard, you may submit NGB Form 22, Report of Separation and Record of Service, or NGB Form 23, Retirement Points Accounting, or its equivalent. If you were discharged from the Selected Reserve, you may submit a copy of your latest annual points statement and evidence of honorable service. Unfortunately, there is no single form used by the Reserves or National Guard similar to the DD Form 214.

If you are still serving in the Selected Reserves or the National Guard, you must include an original statement of service signed by, or by the direction of, the adjutant, personnel officer, or commander of your unit or higher headquarters showing the length of time that you have been a member of the Selected Reserves. Again, at least six years of honorable service must be documented.

How can I obtain proof of military service?

Standard Form 180, Request Pertaining to Military Records, is used to apply for proof of military service regardless of whether you served on regular active duty or in the Selected Reserves. This request form is not processed by the VA. Rather, Standard Form 180 is completed and mailed to the appropriate custodian of military service records. Instructions are provided on the reverse of the form to assist in determining the correct forwarding address.

I have already obtained one VA loan. Can I get another one?

Yes. Your eligibility is reusable depending on the circumstances. Normally, if you have paid off your prior VA loan and disposed of the property, you can have your used eligibility restored for additional use. Also, on a one-time only basis, you may have your eligibility restored if your prior VA loan has been paid in full but you still own the property. In either case, to obtain restoration of eligibility, the veteran must send the VA a completed VA Form 26-1880 to the Winston-Salem Eligibility Center. To prevent delays in processing, it is also advisable to include evidence that the prior loan has been paid in full and, if applicable, the property disposed of. This evidence can be in the form of a paid-in-full statement from the former lender or a copy of the HUD-1 settlement statement completed in connection with a sale of the property or refinance of the prior loan.

I sold the property I obtained with my prior VA loan on an assumption. Can I get my eligibility restored to use for a new loan?

In this case the veteran's eligibility can be restored only if the qualified assumer is also an eligible veteran who is willing to substitute his or her available eligibility for that of the original veteran. Otherwise, the original veteran cannot have eligibility restored until the assumer has paid off the VA loan.

My prior VA loan was assumed, the assumer defaulted on the loan, and VA paid a claim to the lender. The VA said it was not my fault and waived the debt. Now I need a new VA loan, but I am told that my used eligibility cannot be restored. Why?

Or,

My prior loan was foreclosed on, or I gave a deed in lieu of foreclosure, or the VA paid a compromise (partial) claim. Although I was released from liability on the loan and/or the debt was waived, I am told that I cannot have my used eligibility restored. Why?

In either case, although the veteran's debt was waived by VA, the government still suffered a loss on the loan. The law does not permit the used portion of the veteran's eligibility to be restored until the loss has been repaid in full.

Only a portion of my eligibility is available at this time because my prior loan has not been paid in full even though I do not own the property anymore. Can I still obtain a VA guaranteed home loan?

Yes, depending on the circumstances. If a veteran has already used a portion of his or her eligibility and the used portion cannot yet be restored, any partial remaining eligibility would be available for use. The veteran would have to discuss with a lender whether the remaining balance would be sufficient for the loan amount sought and whether any down payment would be required.

Is the surviving spouse of a deceased veteran eligible for the home loan benefit?

The unmarried surviving spouse of a veteran who died on active duty or as the result of a service-connected disability is eligible for the home loan benefit. If you wish to make application for the home loan benefit as a surviving spouse, contact the Winston-Salem Eligibility Center. In addition, a surviving spouse who obtained a VA home loan with the veteran before his or her death (regardless of the cause of death), may obtain a VA guaranteed interest rate reduction refinance loan. For more information, contact the Winston-Salem Eligibility Center.

(Note: Also, a surviving spouse who remarries on or after attaining age 57, and on or after December 16, 2003, may be eligible for the home loan benefit. The VA must deny applications from surviving spouses who remarried before December 16, 2003,and that are received after December 15, 2004.

Are the children of a living or deceased veteran eligible for the home loan benefit?

No. The children of an eligible veteran are not eligible for the home loan benefit.

VA Eligibility Center Address and Telephone Number

Please send your request for determination of eligibility (VA Form 26-1880), along with proof of military service to:

VA Loan Eligibility Center
P.O. Box 20729
Winston-Salem, NC 27120

For overnight delivery:

VA Loan Eligibility Center
251 N. Main Street
Winston-Salem, NC 27155
Toll-free: 1-888-244-6711
E-mail: nceligib@vba.va.gov

The following chart lists the contact information (addresses, telephone numbers, and Web sites) for Regional Loan Centers. The Centers are listed by city and each is assigned specific states in its jurisdiction.

REGIONAL LOAN CENTERS

Regional Loan Center	Jurisdiction	Mailing and Web site	Telephone Number
Atlanta	Georgia North Carolina South Carolina Tennessee	Department of Veterans Affairs Regional Loan Center 1700 Clairmont Road P.O. Box 100023 Decantur, GA 30031 **www.vba.va.gov/ro/atlanta/ric/ index.htm**	1-888-768-2132
Cleveland	Delaware Indiana Michigan New Jersey Ohio Pennsylvania	Department of Veterans Affairs Cleveland Regional Loan Center 1240 East Ninth Street Cleveland, OH 44199 **www.vba.va.gov/ro/central/ cleve/index1.htm**	1-800-729-5772
Denver	Alaska Colorado Idaho Montana Oregon Utah Washington Wyoming	Department of Veterans Affairs VA Regional Loan Center Box 25126 Denver, CO 80225 **www.vba.va.gov/ro/denver/ loan/lgv.htm**	1-888-349-7541
Honolulu	Hawaii	Department of Veterans Affairs Loan Guaranty Division (26) 459 Patterson Road Honolulu, HI 96819 *Although not an RLC, this office is a fully functioning loan guaranty operation for Hawaii.	1-808-433-0481
Houston	Arkansas Louisiana Oklahoma Texas	Department of Veterans Affairs VA Regional Loan Center 6900 Almeda Road Houston, TX 77030 **www.vba.va.gov/houstonric. htm**	1-888-232-2571

REGIONAL LOAN CENTERS

Regional Loan Center	Jurisdiction	Mailing and Web site	Telephone Number
Manchester	Connecticut Massachusetts Maine New Hampshire New York Rhode Island Vermont	Department of Veterans Affairs VA Regional Loan Center 275 Chestnut Street Manchester, NH 03101 www.vba.va.gov/romanchester/ lgmain/loans.htm	1-800-827-6311 1-800-827-0336
Phoenix	Arizona California New Mexico Nevada	Department of Veterans Affairs VA Regional Loan Center 3333 North Central Avenue Phoenix, AZ 85012 www.vba.va.gov/phoenixlgy. htm	1-888-869-0194
Roanoke	District of Columbia Kentucky Maryland Virginia West Virginia	Department of Veterans Affairs Roanoke Regional Loan Center 210 Franklin Road SW Roanoke, VA 24011 www.vba.va.gov/ro/roanoke/ric	1-800-933-5499
St. Paul	Illinois Iowa Kansas Minnesota Missouri Nebraska North Dakota South Dakota Wisconsin	Department of Veterans Affairs VA Regional Loan Center 1 Federal Drive, Fort Snelling St. Paul, MN 55111 www.vba.va.gov/ro/central/ stpau/pages/homeloans.html	1-800-827-0611
St. Petersburg	Alabama Florida Mississippi Puerto Rico U.S. Virgin Islands	Department of Veterans Affairs VA Regional Loan Center P.O. Box 1437 St. Petersburg, FL 33731 www.vba.va.gov/ro/south/ spete/ric/index.htm	1-888-611-5916 (out of state) 1-800-827-1000 (in Florida)

IRRRL FACTS FOR VETERANS

IRRRL stands for Interest Rate Reduction Refinancing Loan. You may see it referred to as a "Streamline" or a "VA to VA." Except when refinancing an existing VA guaranteed adjustable rate mortgage (ARM) to a fixed rate, it must result in a lower interest rate. When refinancing from an existing VA ARM loan to a fixed rate, the interest rate may increase.

No appraisal or credit underwriting package is required by the VA. You should be aware, however, that lenders may require an appraisal and credit report anyway.

A certificate of eligibility is not required. Your lender may use our e-mail confirmation procedure for interest rate reduction refinance in lieu of a certificate of eligibility.

An IRRRL may be done with "no money out of pocket" by including all costs in the new loan or by making the new loan at an interest rate high enough to enable the lender to pay the costs.

No lender is required to make you an IRRRL; however, any lender of your choice may process your application for an IRRRL. Although it might be the best place to start shopping for an IRRRL, you do not have to go to the lender you make your payments to now or to the lender from whom you originally obtained your VA loan.

Veterans are strongly urged to contact several lenders. There may be big differences in the terms offered by the various lenders you contact. Some lenders may contact you suggesting that they are the only lender with authority to make IRRRLs, but this is not true.

Some lenders may say that the VA requires certain closing costs to be charged and included in the loan. The only cost required by the VA is a funding fee of .5 percent of the loan amount, which may be paid in cash or included in the loan.

You must not receive any cash from the loan proceeds.

An IRRRL can be done only if you have already used your eligibility for a VA loan on the property you intend to refinance. It must be a VA to

VA refinance, and it will reuse the entitlement you originally used. You may have used your entitlement by obtaining a VA loan when you bought your house or by substituting your eligibility for that of the seller, if you assumed the loan. If you have your certificate of eligibility, take it to the lender to show the prior use of your entitlement.

The occupancy requirement for an IRRRL is different from other VA loans. When you originally got your VA loan, you certified that you occupied or intended to occupy the home. For an IRRRL you need only certify that you previously occupied it.

The loan may not exceed the sum of the outstanding balance on the existing VA loan, plus allowable fees and closing costs, including funding fee and up to two discount points. You may also add up to $6,000 of energy efficiency improvements into the loan.

(Note: Adding all these items into your loan may result in a situation in which you owe more than the fair market value of the house and will reduce the benefit of refinancing since your payment will not be lowered as much as it could be. Also, you could have difficulty selling the house for enough to pay off your loan balance.)

Some lenders offer IRRRLs as an opportunity to reduce the term of your loan from 30 years to 15 years. Although this can save you money in interest over the life of the loan, if the reduction in the interest rate is not at least 1 percent (2 percent is better) and new loan costs are rolled into the new loan, you may see a large increase in your monthly payment. Beware: It could be a bigger increase than you can afford.

No loan other than the existing VA loan may be paid from the proceeds of an IRRRL. If you have a second mortgage, the holder must agree to subordinate that lien so that your new VA loan will be a first mortgage.

CHAPTER 12

NONPROFIT VETERANS' ORGANIZATIONS

Military service members, and in particular military veterans and their families, enjoy an immense support base. There are dozens of outstanding veterans' organizations whose entire purpose is to support veterans, perform veterans' advocacy work, lobby for veterans' benefits, and provide a wealth of information and support services. I have provided some of the more popular groups here for you. You can find others by using Google or your favorite search engine. Additionally, all states have their own veterans' Web sites that list nonprofit veterans groups that operate within your state.

American Ex-Prisoners of War
3201 East Pioneer Parkway, #40
Arlington, TX 76010
817-649-2979
www.axpow.org

American Red Cross
2025 E. Street NW
Washington, DC 20006
202-303-5834
202-303-0221 fax
www.redcross.org

American Legion
P.O. Box 1055
Indianapolis, IN 46206
317-630-1200
202-861-2786 fax
www.legion.org

AMVETS
4647 Forbes Boulevard
Lanham, MD 20706
301-459-9600
301-459-7924 fax
amvets@amvets.org
www.amvets.org

Blinded Veterans Association
477 H. Street NW
Washington, DC 20001
202-371-8880
202-371-8258 fax
hva@hva.org
www.bva.org

Disabled American Veterans
P.O. Box 14301
Cincinnati, OH 45250
859-441-7300
www.dav.org

Military Chaplains Association of the United States of America
P.O. Box 7056
Arlington, VA 22207
703-533-5890
703-533-5890 fax
chaplains@mca.usa.org
www.mca-usa.org

Military Order of the World Wars
435 North Lee Street
Alexandria, VA 22314
703-683-4911
703-683-4501 fax
www.militaryorder.net

National Association for Black Veterans, Inc.
P.O. Box 11432
Milwaukee, WI 53211
800-842-4597
414-342-1073 fax
nabvets@nnabvets.com
www.nabvets.com

Congressional Medal of Honor Society of the United States of America
40 Patriots Point Road
Mt. Pleasant, SC 29464
843-884-8861
843-884-1471 fax
www.cmohs.org/medal.htm

Fleet Reserve Association
125 N West Street
Alexandria, VA 22314
800-FRA-1924
adminfra@fra.org
www.fra.org

Military Order of the Purple Heart of the U.S.A., Inc.
5413-C Backlick Road
Springfield, VA 22151
703-354-2140
info@purpleheart.org
www.purpleheart.org

National Amputation Foundation, Inc.
40 Church Street
Malverne, NY 11565
516-887-3600
516-887-3667 fax
www.nationalamputation.org

National Association of State Directors of Veterans Affairs (NASDVA)
P.O. Box 2324
Santa Fe, NM 87504
505-827-6334
http://dvs.state.nm.us

Navy Club of the United States of America
6134 South 375 W
Lafayette, IN 47909
800-628-7265
enewman@tctc.com
www.navyclubusa.org

Non Commissioned Offers Association
610 Madison Street
Alexandria, VA 22314
703-548-0311
reschneider@ncoausa.org
www.ncoausa.org

The Retired Enlisted Association
1111 S. Abilene Court
Aurora, CO 80012
800-338-9337
303-752-0835 fax
treahq@trea.org
www.trea.org

Veterans Assistance Foundation, Inc.
P.O. Box 109
Newburg, WI 53060
262-692-6333
262-692-6467 fax
www.veteransassistance.org

Veterans of the Vietnam War, Inc./Vets Coalition
805 South Township Boulevard
Pittston, PA 18640
570-603-9740
570-603-9741 fax
www.vvnw.org

Navy Mutual Aid Association
29 Carpenter Road
Henderson Hall
Arlington, VA 22212
703-614-1638
800-628-6011
703-695-4635 fax

Paralyzed Veterans of America
801 18th Street NW
Washington, DC 20006
202-872-1300
202-416-7643 fax
info@pva.org
www.pva.org

U.S. Submarine Veterans of World War II
6505 Camino de Luna
Rancho Murieta, CA 95683
916-354-2811

Veterans of Foreign Wars of the United States
406 W 34th Street
Kansas City, MO 64111
816-756-3390
202-543-6719 fax
info@vfw.org

Vietnam Veterans of America
8605 Cameron Street
Suite 400
Silver Spring, MD 20910
301-585-4000
301-585-0519 fax
www.vva.org

Women's Army Corps Veterans Association
P.O. Box 5577
Fort McClellan, AL 36205
256-820-6824
www.armywomen.org

A complete directory of veterans service organizations may be downloaded from:

www1.va.gov/vso

Other veterans organizations that may not yet have a congressional charter include:

Iraq War Veterans Organization, Inc.: **www.iraqwarveterans.org**

National Veterans Organization: **www.nvo.org**

American Gulf War Veterans Association: **www.gulfwarvets.com**

Gulf War Veterans Resource: **www.gulfWeb.org**

Iraq and Afghanistan Veterans of America: **www.iava.org**

There are many other organizations that support veterans. This is certainly not intended to be an all-inclusive list but should serve as a reference.

VETERANS' SCHOLARSHIPS, GRANTS, & AID

Veterans enjoy a multitude of benefits in return for their service to our country. An outstanding benefit is eligibility of the veteran and family members to be eligible for a wide variety of scholarships, grants, and other programs to support them. Although there are hundreds of programs sponsored by corporations, organizations, the government, colleges, institutions, and states, I have listed several of them here to get you started. You will find that most scholarships are geared toward high school-age dependents of active duty military, and many others are for dependents of veterans; however, there are many that are for the veteran. This list is certainly not all inclusive, and discovering some of them may take some detective work on your part. My personal experience is that there is a multitude of scholarships and grants available, many you merely have to ask for. You will find that in addition to the wealth of information provided by the VA, each state has significant veterans' benefits available. A search of your state Web site will reveal a wealth of benefits that are either federally or state funded and that you may be entitled to. For example, the State of Florida publishes its veterans' benefits information at **www.floridavets. org/benefits/benefits.asp**.

Although I have included some national scholarships, most of the scholarships (and grants) are at the college or university level, and you will need to visit your specific university Web site for veterans' preference, benefits, scholarships and grants to verify what each school offers to veterans, survivors, and family members of veterans.

SEVERELY INJURED SERVICE MEMBER AND SPOUSE SCHOLARSHIP OPPORTUNITIES

The Department of Defense dedicated the Severely Injured Joint Operations Center in early February 2005. The center was developed to address care, recuperation, health, benefits, and transition issues for military returning from Iraq and Afghanistan who have been severely injured.

Severely injured service members, and their spouses, have expressed an interest in an opportunity to pursue diploma and certification programs or college degrees that will help prepare them for jobs and careers while they are convalescing, when they return home, and after discharge from the military. The Defense Activity for Non-Traditional Education Support (DANTES) Web site hosts a scholarship search page, which is located at **www.dantes.doded.mil/sfd/participantSearch.asp?param=school.** You can e-mail the organization at Scholarships@voled.doded.mil for more information.

THE MG JAMES URSANO SCHOLARSHIP PROGRAM

The MG James Ursano scholarship is for dependent children of soldiers on federal active duty, retired, or deceased while in active or retired status.

Army Emergency Relief (AER) is a private nonprofit organization with the primary mission of providing financial assistance to soldiers and their dependents in time of valid emergency need. The MG James Ursano Scholarship Program was established in 1976 as a secondary mission to help Army families with undergraduate college expenses for their dependent children.

The MG James Ursano Scholarship Program offers scholarships based on financial need, academics, and leadership/achievement.

To be eligible, applicants must:

- ☷ Maintain a cumulative GPA of a 2.0 on a 4.0 scale

- ☷ Be full-time undergraduate students for the entire academic year at a school accredited by the U.S. Department of Education

- ☷ Be dependents of a soldier on federal active duty, a retiree, or a deceased active or retired soldier

To be a dependent you must be:

- ☷ Under the age of 23 for the entire academic year

- ☷ Registered in DEERS

- ☷ Unmarried for the entire academic year

Scholarship Fund Uses

The scholarship funds are split evenly between the fall and spring semesters, terms, or quarters. The funds are to be used for tuition, fees, books, supplies, and school room and board either on or off campus, as requested by the student. Applications are available at **www.aerhq.org**.

For additional information, contact:

Kasey Phillips
703-428-0035
E-mail: Kasey@aerhq.org

Mailing Address:
Army Emergency Relief
MG James Ursano Scholarship Program
200 Stovall Street, Room 5N13
Alexandria, VA 22332-0600

DEPENDENTS OF DECEASED SERVICE MEMBERS SCHOLARSHIP PROGRAMS

The Navy-Marine Corps Relief Society provides educational assistance to the children and un-remarried spouses of deceased service members. Awards are determined by NMCRS Headquarters Education Division:

- If the service member died in retired status

- If the active duty service member died on active duty

- USS STARK Memorial Scholarship Fund (dependent children of those crew members of USS STARK who died or were disabled as a result of the missile attack on the ship in the Persian Gulf on May 17, 1987)

- USS COLE Memorial Fund (dependent children of crew members who perished as a result of the terrorist attack of October 12, 2000)

- Pentagon Assistance Fund (dependent children of deceased military personnel who perished as a result of the terrorist attack on September 11, 2001)

The application package and submission procedures can be found by visiting **www.nmcrs.org/child-dec.html**.

IRAQI/AFGHANISTAN WAR VETERANS SCHOLARSHIP FUND

The AFCEA Northern Virginia (NOVA) Chapter has contributed $100,000 to establish the Iraqi/Afghanistan War Veterans Scholarship Fund. This scholarship fund will award $2,500 annual scholarships to qualified soldiers, sailors, airmen, Marines, and Coast Guardsmen.

The NOVA Chapter sees its $100,000 as the first installment in a campaign to raise $1 million over the next five years that would generate 20 scholarships for veterans every year in perpetuity.

For more information about this co-sponsored scholarship, please contact Norma Corrales, director of scholarships and awards, AFCEA Educational Foundation at scholarship@afcea.org or visit **www.afcea. org/education/scholarships** or **www.afceanova.org**.

Scholarships of $2,500 each are offered to active-duty and honorably discharged U.S. military veterans (to include reservists and National Guard personnel) of the Enduring Freedom (Afghanistan) or Iraqi Freedom operations who are actively pursuing an undergraduate degree in an eligible major at an accredited two- or four-year institutions in the United States. Distance-learning or online programs affiliated with a major U.S. institution are eligible.

Eligibility: Applicants must be currently enrolled and attending either a two- or four-year accredited college or university in the United States. Applications will be accepted from qualified freshman, sophomore, junior, and senior undergraduate students enrolled at the time of application, either part- or full-time in an eligible degree program as stated below.

Candidates must be majoring in the following C4I-related fields of electrical, aerospace, systems, or computer engineering; computer engineering technology; computer network systems; information systems security; computer information systems; information systems management; technology management; electronics engineering technology; computer science; physics; mathematics; or science or mathematics education. Majors directly related to the support of U.S. intelligence or national security enterprises with relevance to the mission of AFCEA will also be eligible.

FEDERAL PELL GRANTS

Federal Pell Grants provide eligible undergraduate students who have not earned a bachelor's degree or a professional degree the opportunity for a grant that does not require repayment. A student enrolled in a post-baccalaureate teacher certification program may also qualify. Information on Pell Grants can be found at **www.ed.gov/programs/fpg/index.html**.

THE FULBRIGHT PROGRAM

The Fulbright Program is the U.S. government's flagship program in international educational exchange and offers a variety of programs. Fulbright Grants are given to U.S. citizens and nationals of other countries for a variety of educational activities, primarily university lecturing, advanced research, graduate study, and teaching in elementary and secondary schools. Find information at **http://fulbright.state.gov**.

FEDERAL CAMPUS-BASED AID

These programs are called campus-based programs because they are administered directly by financial aid offices at participating schools. Not all schools participate in all three of the following programs:

- **Federal Supplemental Educational Opportunity Grants**: These grants are available to undergraduate students with exceptional financial need. Pell Grant recipients with the lowest expected family contributions will be the first to get FSEOGs. The amount may vary from $100 to $4,000 per year, depending on various factors. Like Pell Grants, FSEOGs do not have to be repaid. Visit **www.ed.gov/programs/fseog/index.html**.

- **Federal work-study**: Provides part-time jobs for undergraduate and graduate students with financial need. The program encourages community service work and work related to the recipient's course of study. The work may be performed on- or off-campus, often for the school or for a private nonprofit organization or a public agency. The work must be in the public interest. Visit **www.ed.gov/programs/fws/index.html**.

- **Federal Perkins Loans**: These loans are low-interest (5 percent) loans for both undergraduate and graduate students with exceptional financial need. These loans are made through a school's financial aid office. The school is the lender, and the loan is made with government funds. The student must repay the loan to the school. The maximum loan amount is $4,000 per year for undergraduate and up to $6,000 per year for graduate students. Visit **www.ed.gov/programs/fpl/index.html**.

STAFFORD LOANS

In addition to Perkins Loans, the Department of Education administers the Federal Family Education Loan (FFEL) Program and the William D. Ford Federal Direct Loan (Direct Loan) Program. The FFEL and Direct Loan programs comprise what are known as Stafford Loans for students and PLUS Loans for parents. Schools often participate in either the FFEL program or the Direct Loan Program, but some schools participate in both programs. Under the Direct Loan Program, funds for the loan come directly from the federal government. Under the FFEL Program, funds for the loan come from a bank, credit union, or other lender that participates in the program. The eligibility rules and loan amounts are identical under both programs, but repayment plans differ somewhat. The maximum loan amount depends on the student's year in school and whether the loan is a subsidized or unsubsidized Direct or FFEL Stafford Loan. For more information on Stafford Loans, visit **http://studentaid.ed.gov/students/publications/FYE/2003_2004/english/stafford-loans.htm**.

FEDERAL STUDENT LOAN REPAYMENT PROGRAM

The federal student loan repayment program provides student loan repayment of up to $10,000 per year per employee or a total of $60,000 per employee. The program is limited to loans made under the Higher Education Act of 1965 and the Public Service Health Act, and is limited to employees in the service of an agency for at least three years. To learn more, visit **www.opm.gov/oca/PAY/StudentLoan**.

MILITARY.COM

Military.com provides valuable scholarships and grant information for the military community. This Internet site features a search browser (type of financial aid desired, service affiliation, educational goal), and the search results identify available internships, grants, loans, and scholarships. One example of a searched loan return is:

The 25th Infantry Division Association Educational Memorial Scholarship Award provides financial assistance for college to the children of veterans and current members of the 25th Infantry Division Association. Award amounts of up to $1,500 are available. For more information, go to **www.25thida.com/associat.html#scholarships**.

Other sources of financial aid include the student's state government and educational institution. Often the best source of information and assistance will be the school's financial aid office. Information about financial aid specific to individual states may also be obtained from state grant and guaranty agencies.

(Note: The Department of Education administers about 70 percent of all financial aid for post-secondary education. The Federal Student Aid programs administered by the Department of Education provide more than $60 billion a year in grants, loans, and work-study assistance. Except for some loan programs, student eligibility is based on financial need. Age is not a factor, and aid is available for part- and full-time attendance. The Department of Education Web site (**www.DOE.gov**) provides information including types of aid, eligibility criteria, and application processes.)

VETERANS' EMPLOYMENT AND TRAINING STATE GRANTS

The U.S. Department of Labor, Veterans' Employment and Training Service (VETS) offers employment and training services to eligible veterans through a noncompetitive Jobs for Veterans State Grants program. Under this grant program, funds are allocated to state workforce agencies in direct proportion to the number of veterans seeking employment within each state. The grants support two principal staff positions:

- Disabled Veterans' Outreach Program Specialists

- Local Veterans' Employment Representatives

This grant provides funds to exclusively serve veterans, other eligible persons, transitioning service members, their spouses, and, indirectly, employers. The grant also gives the state the flexibility to determine the most effective and efficient distribution of their staff resources based on the distinct roles and responsibilities of the two positions.

DVOP and LVER staff provide services to all veterans that Title 38 indicates are eligible for their services, but their efforts are concentrated, according to their respective roles and responsibilities, on outreach and the provision and facilitation of direct client services to those who have been identified as most in need of intensive employment and training assistance. Through outreach with employers, DVOP and LVER staff develop increased hiring opportunities within the local work force by raising the awareness of employers of the availability and the benefit of hiring veterans.

Disabled Veterans' Outreach Program Specialists

Disabled Veterans Outreach Program (DVOP) specialists provide intensive services to meet the employment needs of disabled veterans and other eligible veterans, with the maximum emphasis directed toward serving those who are economically or educationally disadvantaged, including homeless veterans and veterans with barriers to employment. DVOP specialists are actively involved in outreach efforts to increase program participation among those with the greatest barriers to employment which may include but should not be limited to: outplacement in Department of Veterans' Affairs (DVA) Vocational Rehabilitation and Employment Program offices; DVA medical centers, routine site visits to Veterans' Service Organization meetings, Native American Trust Territories, military installations, and other areas of known concentrations of veterans or transitioning service members. The case management approach, taught by the National Veterans' Training Institute, may be accepted as the method to use when providing vocational guidance or related services to eligible veterans identified as needing intensive services.

Local Veterans' Employment Representatives

Local Veterans' Employment Representatives conduct outreach to employers and engage in advocacy efforts with hiring executives to increase employment opportunities for veterans, encourage the hiring of disabled veterans, and assist veterans in gaining and retaining employment. LVER staff conduct seminars for employers and job search workshops for veterans seeking employment and facilitate priority of service about employment, training, and placement services furnished to veterans by all staff of the employment service delivery system.

To meet the specific needs of veterans, particularly those veterans with barriers to employment, DVOP and LVER staff are thoroughly familiar with the full range of job development services and training programs available at the State Workforce Agency One-Stop Career Centers and Department of Veterans Affairs Vocational Rehabilitation and Employment Program locations.

Eligible Applicants

Applications for funds under the Jobs for Veterans State Grants Program will be accepted only from the designated administrative entity that operates the employment service delivery system within each state.

CHAPTER 14

EDUCATIONAL BENEFITS & TRAINING PROGRAMS

In addition to a wealth of training and educational benefits while serving on active duty, there all also substantial benefits you are entitled to as a veteran of the armed forces. Additional entitlements may be available if you are disabled.

MONTGOMERY GI BILL — ACTIVE DUTY

The Montgomery GI Bill — Active Duty, called "MGIB" for short, provides up to 36 months of education benefits to eligible veterans for:

- College, business, technical, or vocational school

- Tuition assistance: "top-up"

- On-the-job training and apprenticeship programs

- Correspondence courses

- Remedial, deficiency, and refresher training (in some cases)

- Flight training (in some cases)

- The cost of tests for licenses or certifications needed to get, keep, or advance in a job

- National tests

Benefits are payable for 10 years following your release from active duty. This program is also commonly known as Chapter 30.

Who Is Eligible?

If you are currently in service, you may be eligible after two years of active duty. Please consult with the Education Services Officer at your installation, or call the toll-free number below for information about your eligibility.

If you are separated from service, you may be an eligible veteran if one of the following applies to you:

- Entered active duty for the first time after June 30, 1985

- Received a high-school diploma or equivalent (or, in some cases, 12 hours of college credit) before the end of your first obligated period of service

- Received an honorable discharge

- Continuously served for three years, or two years if that is what you first enlisted for, or two years if you have an obligation to serve four years in the Selected Reserve and entered Selected Reserve within a year of leaving active duty

(Note: Different rules apply if you entered active duty before July 1, 1985, and in certain other cases.)

You should be aware that the following pitfalls could cause you to lose all MGIB benefits:

General Discharge: You must have an honorable discharge to be eligible for education benefits. A "general" or "under honorable conditions" makes you ineligible for education benefits.

Early Discharge: To be eligible with an early discharge, your separation reason must meet certain requirements.

How Much Does the VA Pay?

The monthly benefit paid to you is based on the type of training you take, length of your service, your category, and if the DOD put extra money in your MGIB Fund (called "kickers"). Often, you have 10 years to use your MGIB benefits. The current full-time rate for those with three or more years of service and who are enrolled in an institutional program is $1,075 per month.

How Can You Apply?

You can apply by filling out VA Form 22-1990, Application for Education Benefits. You can also apply online through the VA Web site at **http:// vabenefits.vba.va.gov/vonapp.**

$600 Buy-up Program

Some service members may contribute up to an additional $600 to the GI Bill to receive increased monthly benefits. For an additional $600 contribution, you may receive up to $5,400 in additional GI Bill benefits. The increased benefit is payable only after leaving active duty, and the additional contribution must be made while on active duty. For more information, contact your personnel or payroll office.

MONTGOMERY GI BILL — SELECTED RESERVE — CHAPTER 1606

The Montgomery GI Bill — Selected Reserve is an education program that provides up to 36 months of education benefits to members of the Selected Reserve. This includes the Army, Navy, Air Force, Marine Corps, Coast Guard Reserves, the Army National Guard, and the Air National Guard. It is the first program that does not require a person to serve on active duty in the regular armed forces to qualify.

An eligible reservist may get education benefits while in a program approved for VA training.

Who Is Eligible?

You may be considered an eligible reservist or National Guard member if:

- After June 30, 1985, you signed a six-year obligation to serve in the Selected Reserve.

- You completed your Initial Active Duty for Training (IADT.)

- You got your high school diploma or GED before you completed your IADT.

- You are in good standing in a drilling Selected Reserve unit.

If you stay in the Selected Reserves, benefits end 10 years from the date you became eligible for the program if you became eligible before October 1, 1992. Benefits end 14 years from the date you became eligible if you became eligible on or after October 1, 1992. Your period of eligibility may be extended if you were unable to train because of a service-related disability. Often, your eligibility ends when you leave the Selected Reserves.

One exception to this rule exists if you are mobilized (or recalled to active duty from your reserve status). In this case, your eligibility may be extended for the amount of time you are mobilized, plus four months. For example, if you are mobilized for 12 months, your eligibility period is extended for 16 months (12 months active duty plus four months.) So even if you leave the reserves after mobilization, you may have additional eligibility to the MGIB-SR.

How Much Does VA Pay?

The monthly benefit paid to you is based on the type of training. If you are attending school, your payment is based on your training time (such as full-time, half-time). The current full-time rate for college is $309 per month.

How Can You Apply?

Your unit will give you a Notice of Basic Eligibility (DD Form 2384 or 2384-1) when you become eligible for the Montgomery GI Bill — Selected Reserve. Once you find a program approved for VA training, complete VA Form 22-1990, Application for Education Benefits, and send it to the VA regional office that serves the state where you will study.

You can also apply online through the Web site found at **http://vabenefits. vba.va.gov/vonapp**.

POST-9/11 GI BILL

Summary

By the time this book is published, I anticipate that the Post-9/11 GI bill will be signed into law by the President. This is the most sweeping educational benefit package since World War II. Here are some of the key benefits expected to be incorporated into the Post 9/11 GI Bill:

- Increased educational benefits would be available to members of the military who have served on active duty since September 11, 2001;

- Tuition up to the highest established charges for full-time undergraduate students charged by the public institution of higher education in the State in which you are enrolled. Tuition will be paid directly to the school;

- If enrolled in a traditional college program full time or three-quarter time, you will be paid a monthly housing stipend equal to the monthly amount of the Basic Allowance for Housing for an E-5 with dependents.;

- Lump sum payment to help cover the cost of books, supplies, equipment, and other educational fees up to a $1,000 annual cap;

- Unlike the Montgomery GI Bill, the new GI Bill will allow you to use this benefit for up to 15 years after your last discharge or separation from active duty;

- Provide up to $2,000 to cover the cost of one licensing or certification test. This benefit is not charged against your 36 month entitlement;

- Provide up to a maximum of $1,200 for tutorial assistance. The program will pay up to $100 per month, for a maximum of 12 months. This benefit is not charged against your 36 month entitlement;

- Enable you to transfer a portion of your 36 month benefit entitlement to a designated dependent;

A good source of information on the new Post 9/11 GI Bill can be found at http://www.newgibill.org/.

RESERVE EDUCATIONAL ASSISTANCE PROGRAM (REAP) — CHAPTER 1607

Reserve Educational Assistance Program (REAP, Chapter 1607 of title 10, U.S. Code) is an education program that provides up to 36 months of education benefits to members of the Selected Reserves, Individual Ready Reserve (IRR), and National Guard who are called or ordered to active service in response to a war or national emergency, as declared by the President or Congress.

Who Is Eligible?

Eligibility will be determined by the Department of Defense or Department of Homeland Security (DHS), as appropriate. A member of a Reserve component who serves on active duty on or after September 11, 2001, under title 10, U.S. Code, for at least 90 consecutive days under a contingency operation is eligible for REAP. There is no specific time to use REAP; however, your eligibility ends when you leave the Selected Reserves.

National Guard members are eligible if their active service extends for 90 consecutive days or more and their service is:

- Authorized under section 502(f), title 32, U.S. Code

- Authorized as a national emergency

- Supported by federal funds

How Much Does VA Pay?

The educational assistance allowance payable under REAP is a percentage of the Montgomery GI Bill-Active Duty (MGIB) rate based on the number of continuous days served on active duty. Persons released before 90 days due to an injury, illness, or disease incurred or aggravated in the line of duty receive the 40 percent rate. Current rates of payment can be found on our Internet Web site or by calling the toll-free number.

- Members who serve 90 days but less than one year will receive 40 percent of the MGIB three-year rate.

- Members who serve one year but less than two years will receive 60 percent of the MGIB three-year rate.

- Members who serve two or more continuous years will receive 80 percent of the MGIB three-year rate.

The amount VA pays is based on the type of program and time (such as full-time, half-time). If attendance is less than a month or less than full-time, payments are reduced proportionately.

What Programs Are Available?

The following programs are available:

- College or university-degree programs

- Flight training

- Vocational programs

- On-the-job training and apprenticeship programs

- Independent study or distance-learning programs

- Entrepreneurship courses

- Correspondence courses

How Can You Apply?

Once you find a program approved for VA funding, complete VA Form 22-1990, Application for Education Benefits, and send it to the VA regional office that serves the state where you will study. Indicate on the form you are applying for REAP. You can also apply online at **http://vabenefits. vba.va.gov/vonapp**.

POST-VIETNAM VETERANS' EDUCATIONAL ASSISTANCE PROGRAM (VEAP) — CHAPTER 32

The Post-Vietnam Veterans' Educational Assistance Program (VEAP) is an education benefit for veterans who paid into VEAP while they were in the service. Eligible veterans may be entitled to as much as 36 months of training. Eligibility often ends 10 years after getting out of the service, but the time limit can be longer in certain cases. Eligible veterans may pursue any of the following types of training:

- College or university program

- Correspondence courses

- Business, technical, or vocational training

- Flight training (in some cases)

- On-the-job training and apprenticeship programs

- High school diploma or equivalent

- Remedial, deficiency, and refresher training (in some cases)

- The cost of tests for licenses or certifications needed to get, keep, or advance a job

- National tests

Who Is Eligible?

To establish eligibility to VEAP, you must have

- First entered active duty after December 31, 1976, and before July 1, 198

- Contributed to VEAP before April 1, 1987

- Completed your first period of service

- Been discharged under conditions other than dishonorable

What Does VA Pay?

The total dollar amount of your benefits is the sum of:

- Your total contributions, plus

- Matching funds from VA equal to two times your contributions, plus

- Any DOD contributions or "kickers"

The monthly amount you will receive is based on the total (above), the number of months you contributed, the type of training you are pursuing, and your training time (such as full-time or half-time). (Note: Contributions may be refunded.)

How Can You Apply?

When you find a program approved for VA funding, you can apply for VEAP by completing VA Form 22-1990, Application for Education Benefits. You can also apply online at **http://vabenefits.vba.va.gov/vonapp**.

OTHER EDUCATIONAL PROGRAMS

The various GI Bills are available for many different types of education programs. Here is a listing of the programs available.

- IHL (institutes of higher learning)

- NCD (non-college degree programs)

- On-the-job and apprenticeship training

- Flight training

- Independent training, distance learning, and internet training

- Correspondence training

- National testing program

- Licensing and certification

- Entrepreneurship training

- Work-study program

- Co-op training

- Accelerated payment of MGIB-AD

- Tuition assistance top-up

- Tutorial assistance program

IHL (Institutes of Higher Learning)

The GI Bill is available for attendance at IHLs such as:

- Four-year universities

- Community colleges

- For advanced degrees

Payment is based on the number of classes you attend:

- 12 hours or more: full-time

- 9 - 11 hours: ¾ time

- 6 - 8 hours: ½ time

- Fewer than six hours: reimbursed at a rate not to exceed the tuition and fees charged for the course(s)

For graduate level training, training time is determined by the college — for example, if a two-hour class is considered full-time in a graduate program at your school, the VA will pay you the full-time rate.

The GI Bill will allow you to attend more than one college at a time, as long as the classes at both institutions count toward your degree and the school granting your degree accepts the classes at the second school as part of your requirements. However, the GI Bill will not pay you to take the same classes twice unless you receive a failing grade in a class that is a graduation requirement.

The GI Bill can pay you for more than one degree; for example, it will pay you for a degree in business and then for a second degree in computer science or for an AA, BA, or MA in the same field. Once you have a degree, you could pursue another one, provided you have remaining entitlement on your GI Bill.

NCD (Non-College-Degree) Training

The GI Bill is available for training at noncollege degree institutions. Examples of this type of training are diploma vocational schools such as:

- HVAC certification

- Truck driving

- EMT certification

- Barber/beautician school

On-the-Job or Apprenticeship Training

The GI Bill is available for on-the-job or apprenticeship training. Examples of this type of training are:

- Union plumber

- Hotel management

- Firefighter

Effective January 1, 2008, the VA will reimburse you at the following rates:

- 75 percent of the full-time GI Bill rate for the first six months

- 55 percent of the full-time GI Bill rate for the second six months

- 35 percent of the full-time GI Bill rate for the remainder of the training program

You may also receive a salary from your employer during the training.

Flight Training

The GI Bill (except Survivors' and Dependents' Educational Assistance

[DEA]) is available for flight training such as:

- Rotary wing qualification

- B747-400 qualification

- Dual qualification

To qualify, you must have a private pilot's license and valid medical certification before beginning training. VA will reimburse you for 60 percent of the approved charges.

Independent, Distance Learning, or Internet Training

The GI Bill is available for independent, distance or internet training. This type of training may be offered by IHLs, and similar rules and rates apply.

Correspondence Training

The GI Bill (except for children training under DEA) is available for correspondence training. This type of training differs from distance learning by the means of delivery. Often in correspondence training, you receive lessons in the mail and have a certain amount of time to complete and return them for a grade. VA will reimburse you 55 percent of the approved costs for this type of training.

National Testing Program

Section 106 of PL 108-454 allows VA to reimburse claimants for fees for:

- National tests for admission to institutions of higher learning

- National tests providing an opportunity for course credit at institutions of higher learning

Examples of tests covered are SAT, GRE, CLEP, GMAT, and LSAT.

Currently this program is available only for MGIB-AD, VEAP, and DEA.

Licensing and Certification

You can receive reimbursement for licensing and certification tests (MGIB-AD, VEAP, and DEA beneficiaries only). Effective January 6, 2006, MGIB-SR and REAP participants became eligible for this program. These tests must be specifically approved for the GI Bill. VA can pay only for the cost of the tests, up to $2,000, and not other fees connected with obtaining a license or certification. VA will pay for tests even if failed.

Entrepreneurship Training

Available to all GI Bill programs with the exception of DEA: Are you interested in starting your own business? Would you like to learn how to get started? Or are you a current business owner who wants to learn how to boost your small business operation? As a service member or veteran you now have an opportunity to use your education benefits to learn how to start or enhance a small business. VA pays for programs offered only by SBCD or Veterans Corporation.

Work-Study Program Information

Work-study is available to any student receiving VA education benefits who is attending school three-quarter time or more. An individual working under this program may work at the school veterans' office, VA regional office, VA Medical Facilities, or at approved state employment offices. Work-study students are paid at either the state or federal minimum wage, whichever is greater. If you have questions on this program, call toll-free at 1-888-442-4551.

Co-op Training

Co-op training allows you to attend school and gain valuable work experience at the same time. Some schools partner with employers, allowing you to attend classes in your desired field, such as computer programming, and work for an employer in that field as well.

There are several different scenarios:

- You can attend classes in the morning and work in the afternoon.

- You can attend classes at night and work during the day.

- You can attend full-time during one semester and work full-time during another semester.

Accelerated Payment for MGIB-AD

An accelerated payment is a lump sum payment of 60 percent of tuition and fees for certain high cost, high-tech programs. To qualify, you must be enrolled in a high-tech program, and you must certify that you intend to seek employment in a high-tech industry as defined by the VA. Accelerated payment is paid instead of Montgomery GI Bill benefits that you would otherwise receive.

Tuition Assistance "Top-Up"

On October 30, 2000, the president signed into law an amendment to the Montgomery GI Bill — Active Duty education program that permits the VA to pay a tuition assistance top-up benefit. The amount of the benefit can be equal to the difference between the total cost of a college course and the amount of tuition assistance that is paid by the military for the course.

Tutorial Assistance Program

Tutorial assistance is available if you are receiving VA educational assistance at the half-time or more rate and have a deficiency in a subject, making tutoring necessary. If you have questions on this program, please contact VA toll-free at 1-888-442-4551.

EDUCATIONAL ASSISTANCE TEST PROGRAM (SECTION 901 OF PUBLIC LAW 96-342)

Section 901 is an Educational Assistance Test Program created by the

Department of Defense Authorization Act of 1981 (Public Law 96-342) to encourage enlistment and reenlistment in the armed forces. Benefits are available to individuals who entered on active duty after September 30, 1980, and before October 1, 1981 (or before October 1, 1982, if entry was under a delayed enlistment contract signed between September 30, 1980, and October 1, 1981).

(Note: Although Public Law 96-342 established a beginning date for the test program as October 1, 1980, the military service departments did not start offering the test program to new enlistees until December 1, 1980.)

Air Force Eligibility Requirements for Section 901: All three of the following criteria must have been met to establish eligibility for this benefit.

- Must have enlisted between December 1, 1980, and September 30, 1981.

- Enlistment must have been in one of the following Air Force Specialties: 20723, 20731, 20830, 46130, 46230A, B, C, D, E, F, G, H, J, or Z, 46430, 81130.

- Enlistment must have taken place at one of the following locations: Beckley, West Virginia; Buffalo, New York; Dallas, Texas; Fargo, North Dakota; Houston, Texas; Jackson, Mississippi; Louisville, Kentucky; Memphis, Tennessee; Omaha, Nebraska; Philadelphia, Pennsylvania; Seattle, Washington; Sioux Falls, South Dakota; or Syracuse, New York.

SURVIVORS' AND DEPENDENTS' EDUCATIONAL ASSISTANCE PROGRAM (DEA)

Section 301 of Public Law 109-461 in 2006 added a new category to the definition of eligible person for survivors' and dependents' educational benefits. The new category includes the spouse or child of a person who:

- VA determines has a service-connected permanent and total disability

§ At the time of VA's determination is a member of the armed forces who is hospitalized or receiving outpatient medical care, services, or treatment

§ Is likely to be discharged or released from service for this service-connected disability

Persons eligible under this new provision may be eligible for DEA benefits effective December 23, 2006, the effective date of the law.

DEA provides education and training opportunities to eligible dependents of veterans who are permanently and totally disabled due to a service-related condition or who died while on active duty or as a result of a service-related condition. The program offers up to 45 months of education benefits. These benefits may be used for degree and certificate programs, apprenticeship, and on-the-job training. If you are a spouse, you may take a correspondence course. Remedial, deficiency, and refresher courses may be approved under certain circumstances.

Special restorative training is available to persons eligible for DEA benefits. The Department of Veterans Affairs may prescribe special restorative training where needed to overcome or lessen the effects of a physical or mental disability for the purpose of enabling an eligible person to pursue a program of education, special vocational program, or other appropriate goal. Medical care and treatment or psychiatric treatment are not included. Contact your local VA office for more information.

Special vocational training is also available to persons eligible for DEA benefits. This type of program may be approved for an eligible person who is not in need of special restorative training but who requires such a program because of a mental or physical handicap. Contact your local VA office for more information.

NATIONAL TESTING PROGRAMS (CLEP, DSST, EXCELSIOR)

DANTES and CLEP tests are a fast track to a college degree. I am a firm believer in the program and have passed more than 40 DANTES, CLEP, and Excelsior college exams. DANTES is a Department of Defense activity, located at Saufley Field, Pensacola, Florida. Its mission is to support the off-duty, voluntary education programs of the Department of Defense and to conduct special projects and developmental activities in support of education-related functions of the department.

As a veteran, you are entitled to participate in National Testing Program. Currently the approved tests are:

- SAT (Scholastic Assessment Test)

- LSAT (Law School Admission Test)

- GRE (Graduate Record Exam)

- GMAT (Graduate Management Admission Test)

- AP (Advanced Placement Exam)

- CLEP (College-Level Examination Program)

- ACT (American College Testing Program)

- DAT (Dental Admissions Test)

- MAT (Miller Analogies Test)

- MCAT (Medical College Admissions Test)

- OAT (Optometry Admissions Testing)

- PCAT (Pharmacy College Admissions Test)

- TOEFL (Test of English as a Foreign Language)

- DSST (DANTES Subject Standardized Tests)

- ECE (Excelsior College Examinations)

What test fees does VA reimburse?

Although VA reimburses a person for required test fees, VA has no authority to reimburse a person for any optional costs related to the testing process. Test fees that VA will reimburse include:

- Registration fees

- Fees for specialized tests

- Administrative fees.

Fees VA will not reimburse include:

- Fees to take pretests (such as Kaplan tests)

- Fees to receive scores quickly

- Other costs or fees for optional items that are not required to take an approved test

Does every applicant for a national test need to have filed an original claim for benefits?

Yes. Every applicant for reimbursement for a national test must have filed an original application and have been found eligible.

Is there a particular form that I must submit to receive reimbursement for a national test?

No. The best way to claim the benefit to submit the following:

- A copy of your test results

- A signed note or a signed VA Form 21-4138, Statement in Support of Claim, stating that you are requesting reimbursement for the cost of a national test

The following information is required:

- Name of the test

- Name of the organization offering the test

- Date the person took the test

- The cost of taking the test

You do not normally have to submit a receipt or proof of payment for the cost of the test. In certain instances, however, it is necessary to submit this proof. These situations are:

- DSST Tests (DANTES Subject Standardized Tests)

- Certain situations regarding the CLEP, MAT, and PCAT tests

DANTES, CLEP, and Excelsior tests are accepted at most universities and colleges and can earn you three to six semester hours (upper and lower level) college credit per exam. DANTES has vast amounts of information, study guides, and course information on its Web site. It is one of the most valuable resources you will find to further your education. Unfortunately at this time, this benefit has not been extended to dependents or survivors. The DANTES Web site is located at: **www.dantes.doded.mil/Dantes_web/DANTESHOME.asp**.

TROOPS TO TEACHERS

Troops to Teachers provides referral assistance and placement services to military personnel interested in beginning a second career in public education as a teacher. The DANTES Troops to Teachers office will help applicants identify teacher certification requirements, programs leading to certification, and employment opportunities.

Troops to Teachers (TTT) was established in 1994 as a Department of Defense program. The National Defense Authorization Act for FY 2000 transferred the responsibility for program oversight and funding to the U.S. Department of Education but continued operation by the Department of Defense. The No Child Left Behind Act of 2001 provides for the continuation of the TTT Program. TTT is managed by DANTES, Pensacola, Florida.

Reflecting the focus of the No Child Left Behind Act of 2001, the primary objective of TTT is to help recruit quality teachers for schools that serve students from low-income families throughout America. TTT helps relieve teacher shortages, especially in math, science, and special education, and assists military personnel in making successful transitions to second careers in teaching.

Funding has been appropriated to provide financial assistance to eligible participants, provide placement assistance and referral services, and to maintain a network of state offices. Military personnel interested in a second career in public education may submit a registration form to DANTES.

The purpose of TTT is to assist eligible military personnel to transition to a new career as public school teachers in targeted schools. A network of state TTT offices has been established to provide participants with counseling and assistance regarding certification requirements, routes to state certification, and employment leads. The TTT home page provides information and resource links, including a job referral system to allow participants to search for job vacancies and links to state Departments of Education, state certification offices, model résumés, and other job listing sites in public education.

Pending availability of funds, financial assistance may be provided to eligible individuals as stipends up to $5,000 to help pay for teacher certification costs or as bonuses of $10,000 to teach in schools serving a high percentage of students from low-income families. Participants who accept the stipend or bonus must agree to teach for three years in targeted schools in accordance with the authorizing legislation.

Educational and Service eligibility requirements for referral and placement assistance services and financial assistance are outlined on the TTT Home Page at **www.ProudToServeAgain.com**. Also available is a *"Self Determination Guide"* to quickly assess eligibility.

Registration

Register with Troops to Teachers by downloading a registration form from **www.ProudToServeAgain.com**. Eligible active duty and reserve personnel may register with Troops to Teachers at any time. Counseling and information are available to all participants; however, financial assistance may not be provided to active duty personnel until one year before retirement.

The Department of Education establishes the operating rules that govern the schools where Troops to Teachers participants who accept financial assistance may fulfill their three-year teaching obligation. There are revised rules, which determine these eligible schools. These revised rules became effective September 15, 2005.

For more information about Troops to Teachers, write or call:

DANTES Troops to Teachers
6490 Saufley Field Road
Pensacola, FL 32509-5243
Phone: 850-452-1241
Toll-free: 1-800-231-6242
DSN: 922-1241
www.ProudToServeAgain.Com
E-mail: ttt@voled.doded.mil

SERVICEMEMBERS OPPORTUNITY COLLEGES (SOC)

Servicemembers Opportunity Colleges (SOC) Consortium colleges and universities are dedicated to helping service members and their families get college degrees. Military students can take courses in their off-duty hours at or near military installations in the United States, overseas, and on Navy ships. Information on SOC can be found at **www.soc.aascu.org**.

CHAPTER 15

BENEFITS FOR HOMELESS VETERANS

It is amazing how many of our homeless citizens are also military veterans of the armed forces — the statistics are staggering. Many suffer mental and physical ailments caused by their military service. Most do not even realize there are specific programs in place to assist them in this time of need. One-third of adult homeless men and nearly one-quarter of all homeless adults have served in the armed forces. Although there is no true measure of the number of homeless veterans, it has been estimated that fewer than 200,000 veterans may be homeless on any given night and twice as many veterans experience homelessness during a year. Many other veterans are considered at risk because of poverty, lack of support from family and friends, and precarious living conditions in overcrowded or substandard housing. Ninety-seven percent of homeless veterans are male, and the vast majority are single. About half of all homeless veterans suffer from mental illness, and more than two-thirds suffer from alcohol or drug problems. Nearly 40 percent have both psychiatric and substance abuse disorders.

The Department of Veterans Affairs is the only federal agency that provides substantial hands-on assistance directly to homeless people. Last year, the VA provided healthcare services to more than 100,000 homeless veterans and provided services to 70,000 veterans in its specialized homeless programs. More than 40,000 homeless veterans receive compensation or pension benefits annually. Although limited to veterans and their dependents, VA's major homeless programs constitute the largest integrated network

of homeless assistance programs in the country, offering a wide array of services and initiatives to help veterans recover from homelessness and live as self-sufficiently and independently as possible. Nearly three-quarters of homeless veterans we have contacted use VA healthcare services, and 55 percent have used VA homeless services.

The VA, using its own resources or in partnerships with others, has secured more than 15,000 residential rehabilitative, transitional, and permanent beds for homeless veterans throughout the nation. The VA spends more than $1 billion from its healthcare and benefit assistance programs to assist tens of thousands of homeless and at-risk veterans. To increase this assistance, the VA conducts outreach to connect homeless veterans to both mainstream and homeless-specific VA programs and benefits. These programs strive to offer a continuum of services that include:

- Aggressive outreach to veterans living on the streets and in shelters who otherwise would not seek assistance

- Clinical assessment and referral for treatment of physical and psychiatric disorders, including substance abuse

- Long-term transitional residential assistance, case management, and rehabilitation

- Employment assistance and linkage with available income supports and permanent housing

The VA has awarded more than 400 grants to public and nonprofit groups to assist homeless veterans in 50 states and the District of Columbia to provide transitional housing, service centers, and vans to provide transportation to services and employment.

The VA sponsors and supports national, regional, and local homeless conferences and meetings, bringing together thousands of homeless providers and advocates to discuss community planning strategies and to provide technical assistance in such areas as transitional housing, mental health and family services, and education and employment opportunities for the homeless.

HOMELESS PROGRAMS

VA's Healthcare for Homeless Veterans Program (HCHV) operates at 133 sites, where extensive outreach, physical and psychiatric health exams, treatment, referrals, and ongoing case management are provided to homeless veterans with mental health problems, including substance abuse. This program assesses more than 40,000 veterans annually.

The VA's Domiciliary Care for Homeless Veterans (DCHV) Program provides medical care and rehabilitation in a residential setting on VA medical center grounds to eligible ambulatory veterans disabled by medical or psychiatric disorders, injury, or age and who do not need hospitalization or nursing home care. There are more than 1,800 beds available at 34 sites. Residential treatment is provided to more than 5,000 homeless veterans each year. The domiciliaries conduct outreach and referral; admission screening and assessment; medical and psychiatric evaluation; treatment; vocational counseling; rehabilitation; and post-discharge community support.

Veterans' benefits assistance at VA regional offices is provided by designated staff members who serve as coordinators and points of contact for homeless veterans. Homeless coordinators at VA regional offices provide outreach services and help expedite the processing of homeless veterans' claims. The Homeless Eligibility Clarification Act allows eligible veterans without a fixed address to receive VA benefits checks at VA regional offices. VA also has procedures to expedite the processing of homeless veterans' benefits claims. Last year more than 35,000 homeless veterans received assistance, and nearly 4,000 had their claims expedited by Veterans Benefits Administration staff members.

The Acquired Property Sales for Homeless Providers Program makes properties VA obtains through foreclosures on VA-insured mortgages available for sale to homeless providers at a discount of 20 to 50 percent. To date, more than 200 properties have been sold. These properties have been used to provide homeless people, including veterans, with nearly 400,000 sheltered nights in VA-acquired property.

Readjustment Counseling Service's Vet Centers provide outreach, psychological counseling, supportive social services, and referrals to other

VA and community programs. Every Vet Center has a homeless veteran coordinator assigned to make sure services for homeless veterans are tailored to local needs. Annually, the program's 207 Vet Centers see about 130,000 veterans and provide more than 1 million visits to veterans and family members. More than 10,000 homeless veterans are served by the program each year.

VA'S HOMELESS PROVIDERS GRANT AND PER DIEM PROGRAM

The Homeless Providers Grant and Per Diem Program provides grants and per diem payments to help public and nonprofit organizations establish and operate new supportive housing and service centers for homeless veterans. Grant funds may also be used to purchase vans to conduct outreach or provide transportation for homeless veterans. Since the program's inception in fiscal year 1994, the VA has awarded more than 400 grants to faith and community-based service providers, state or local government agencies, and Native American tribal governments in the 50 states and the District of Columbia.

Up to 20,000 homeless veterans are expected to be provided supported housing under this program annually in the more than 10,000 beds.

The Grant and Per Diem Program is offered annually (as funding permits) to fund community-based agencies providing transitional housing or service centers for homeless veterans.

Only programs with supportive housing (up to 24 months) or service centers (offering services such as case management, education, crisis intervention, and counseling) are eligible for these funds. The program has two levels of funding: the Grant component and the Per Diem component.

Grants: Limit is 65 percent of the costs of construction, renovation, or acquisition of a building for use as service centers or transitional housing for homeless vets. Renovation of VA properties is allowed; acquiring VA properties is not. Recipients must obtain the matching 35 percent share from other sources. Grants may not be used for operational costs, including salaries.

Per Diem: Priority in awarding the Per Diem funds goes to the recipients of Grants. Non-Grant programs may apply for Per Diem under a separate announcement, when published in the Federal Register, announcing the funding for "Per Diem Only."

Operational costs, including salaries, may be funded by the Per Diem component. For supportive housing, the maximum amount payable under the Per Diem is $33.01. Veterans in supportive housing may be asked to pay rent if it does not exceed 30 percent of the veteran's monthly-adjusted income. In addition, reasonable fees may be charged for services not paid with Per Diem funds. The maximum hourly Per Diem rate for a service center not connected with supportive housing is one-eighth of the daily cost of care, which is not to exceed the current VA State Home rate for domiciliary care. Payment for a veteran in a service center will not exceed eight hours in any day.

The contact person for the Homeless Providers Grant and Per Diem Program is Roger Casey. Mr. Casey's current address is VA Homeless Providers Grant and Per Diem Program, Mental Health Strategic Healthcare Group (116E), VAHQ, 810 Vermont Avenue, NW, Washington, DC 20420; telephone (toll-free): 1-877-332-0334; e-mail: roger.casey@mail.va.gov.

LOAN GUARANTEE PROGRAM FOR MULTIFAMILY TRANSITIONAL HOUSING

The Loan Guarantee Program for Multifamily Transitional Housing authorizes the VA to guarantee no more than 15 low-interest loans with an aggregate value of $100 million within five years for construction, renovation of existing property, refinancing of existing loans, facility furnishing, or working capital. The amount financed is a maximum of 90 percent of project costs. Legislation allows the secretary to issue a loan guarantee for large-scale, self-sustaining multifamily loans. Eligible transitional projects are those that: (1) Provide supportive services, including job counseling; (2) require veterans to seek and maintain employment; (3) require veterans to pay reasonable rent; (4) require sobriety as a condition of occupancy; and (5) serve other veterans in need of housing on a space available basis. Loans would be originated by the Federal

Financing Bank (FFB), an arm of the U.S. Department of the Treasury. The VA will offer a 100 percent loan guarantee on program funds.

The program objectives are to:

- Increase the number of community beds for homeless veterans nationally by at least 5,000.

- Help homeless veterans transition to permanent housing through supportive services, counseling, and requiring that residents take personal responsibility to remain sober, employed, and to pay monthly rent.

- Promote the development and operation of supportive multifamily transitional housing for homeless veterans in geographic areas of greatest need.

- Determine whether a federal loan guarantee program is an effective tool for facilitating the development of transitional supportive housing for homeless veterans.

VA anticipates that multifamily housing financed under this program will be at least 100 units.

This program does not fund single-family housing.

VA ASSISTANCE TO STAND DOWNS

Stand Downs are one-to three-day events that provide homeless veterans a variety of services and allow VA and community-based service providers to reach more homeless veterans. Stand Downs give homeless veterans a temporary refuge where they can obtain food, shelter, clothing, and a range of community and VA assistance. In many locations, Stand Downs provide health screenings, ID cards, access to VA and Social Security benefits counseling, and referrals to a variety of other necessary services, such as housing, employment, and substance abuse treatment. Stand Downs are collaborative events, coordinated between local VAs, other government agencies, and community agencies who serve the homeless.

In wartime Stand Downs, front line troops are removed to a place of relative safety for rest and needed assistance before returning to combat. Similarly, peacetime Stand Downs give homeless veterans one to three days of safety and security.

VA programs and staff have actively participated in each of the Stand Downs for Homeless Veterans run by local coalitions in various cities each year. Each year, the VA participates in more than 100 Stand Downs coordinated by local entities. Surveys show that more than 23,000 veterans and family members attend these events with more than 13,000 volunteers contributing annually.

The first Stand Down was organized in 1988 by a group of Vietnam veterans in San Diego. Since then, Stand Downs have been used as an effective tool in reaching out to homeless veterans, serving more than 200,000 veterans and their family members between 1994 and 2000.

COMPENSATED WORK THERAPY/ TRANSITIONAL RESIDENCE AND VETERANS' INDUSTRIES

In VA's Compensated Work Therapy/Transitional Residence (CWT/TR) Program, disadvantaged, at-risk, and homeless veterans live in CWT/TR community-based supervised group homes while working for pay in VA's Compensated Work Therapy Program (also known as Veterans Industries). Veterans in the CWT/TR program work about 33 hours per week, with approximate earnings of $732 per month, and pay an average of $186 per month toward maintenance and up-keep of the residence. The average length of stay is about 174 days. The VA contracts with private industry and the public sector for work done by these veterans, who learn new job skills, relearn successful work habits, and regain a sense of self-esteem and self-worth.

Compensated Work Therapy/Veterans Industries (VI/CWT) is a Department of Veterans Affairs vocational rehabilitation program that endeavors to match and support work-ready veterans in competitive jobs and to consult with business and industry regarding their specific employment needs. Using a business model, VI/CWT program staff members specialize in working with facility management, human resources, and/or production personnel to address labor force deficits. Over the years VI/CWT veterans have been successfully employed in various competitive positions including healthcare, information technology, manufacturing, warehousing, construction trades, clerical and office support, retail, and delivery services.

From more than 162 locations throughout the country, VI/CWT programs strive to maintain highly responsive long-term quality relationships with business and industry promoting employment opportunities for veterans with physical and mental disabilities. Professional VI/CWT staff members provide state-of-the-art vocational rehabilitation services, job matching and employment supports, case management, work site and job analysis, consultation regarding assistive technology, accommodation, and guidance in addressing ADA regulations compliance. Many of the individual programs are CARF accredited and are members of usPRA. VI/CWT programs are located within VA medical centers in most large metropolitan areas and many smaller communities.

VA's National Cemetery Administration and Veterans Health Administration have formed partnerships at national cemeteries, where formerly homeless veterans from the CWT program have received therapeutic work opportunities while providing VA cemeteries with a supplemental work force.

VA operates 66 homes with more than 520 beds in transitional residences. Nine sites with 18 houses serve homeless veterans exclusively. Two-thirds of all CWT and TR beds serve homeless veterans. There are more than 110 CWT operations nationwide. About 14,000 veterans participate in CWT programs annually.

CHALENG

The Community Homelessness Assessment, Local Education, and Networking Groups (CHALENG) for veterans is a nationwide initiative in which VA medical center and regional office directors work with other federal, state, and local agencies and nonprofit organizations to assess the needs of homeless veterans, develop action plans to meet identified needs, and develop directories that contain local community resources to be used by homeless veterans.

More than 10,000 representatives from non-VA organizations have participated in Project CHALENG initiatives, which include holding conferences at VA medical centers to raise awareness of the needs of homeless veterans, creating new partnerships in the fight against homelessness, and developing new strategies for future action.

In 1994, the VA launched Project CHALENG for Veterans. The guiding principle behind Project CHALENG is that no single agency can provide the full spectrum of services required to help homeless veterans become productive members of society. Project CHALENG enhances coordinated services by bringing the VA together with community agencies and other federal, state, and local governments who provide services to the homeless to raise awareness of homeless veterans' needs and to plan to meet those needs.

The legislation guiding this initiative is contained in Public Laws 102-405, 103-446, and 105-114. Specific legislative requirements relating to Project CHALENG are that local medical center and regional office directors:

- Assess the needs of homeless veterans living in the area.

- Make the assessment in coordination with representatives from state and local governments, appropriate federal departments and agencies, and nongovernmental community organizations that serve the homeless population.

- Identify the needs of homeless veterans with a focus on healthcare, education and training, employment, shelter, counseling, and outreach.

- Assess the extent to which homeless veterans' needs are being met.

- ☷ Develop a list of all homeless services in the local area.

- ☷ Encourage the development of coordinated services.

- ☷ Take action to meet the needs of homeless veterans.

- ☷ Inform homeless veterans of non-VA resources that are available in the community to meet their needs.

At the local level, VA medical centers and regional offices designate CHALENG Points of Contact (POCs) who are responsible for the above requirements. These CHALENG POCs — often local VA homeless center/ project coordinators — work with local agencies throughout the year to coordinate services for homeless veterans.

For more information, contact John Kuhn, National CHALENG Coordinator at 908-647-0180 ext. 4066; e-mail: John.Kuhn2@med.va. gov. You may also contact Jim McGuire, CHALENG Evaluation Director, at 310-478-3711 ext. 41450; e-mail: James.McGuire@med.va.gov, or John Nakashima, CHALENG program analyst, at 310-478-3711 ext. 41946; e-mail: John.Nakashima@med.va.gov.

THE DOMICILIARY CARE FOR HOMELESS VETERANS (DCHV)

The Domiciliary Care for Homeless Veterans (DCHV) Program provides biopsychosocial treatment and rehabilitation to homeless veterans. The program provides residential treatment to about 5,000 homeless veterans with health problems each year, and the average length of stay in the program is four months. The domiciliaries conduct outreach and referral; vocational counseling and rehabilitation; and post-discharge community support.

HUD-VASH

This joint Supported Housing Program with the Department of Housing and Urban Development provides permanent housing and ongoing treatment services to the harder-to-serve homeless mentally ill veterans and those suffering from substance abuse disorders. HUD's Section 8 Voucher Program has designated 1,780 vouchers worth $44.5 million for homeless, chronically mentally ill veterans. VA staff at 35 sites provide outreach, clinical care, and ongoing case management services. Rigorous evaluation of this program indicates that this approach significantly reduces days of homelessness for veterans plagued by serious mental illness and substance abuse disorders.

SUPPORTED HOUSING

Like the HUD-VASH program, staff members in VA's Supported Housing Program provide ongoing case management services to homeless veterans. Emphasis is placed on helping veterans find permanent housing and providing clinical support needed to keep veterans in permanent housing. VA staff work with private landlords, public housing authorities, and nonprofit organizations to find housing arrangements. Staff in these programs operate without benefit of the specially dedicated Section 8 housing vouchers available in the HUD-VASH program but are often successful in locating transitional or permanent housing through local means, especially by collaborating with veterans' service organizations. VA staff at 22 supported housing program sites helped more than 1,400 homeless veterans find transitional or permanent housing in the community.

DROP-IN CENTERS

Drop-in centers provide a daytime sanctuary where homeless veterans can clean up, wash their clothes, and participate in therapeutic and rehabilitative activities. Linkages with longer-term assistance are also available.

COMPREHENSIVE HOMELESS CENTERS

VA's Comprehensive Homeless Centers (CHCs) place the full range of VA homeless efforts in a single medical center's catchment area and coordinate administration within a centralized framework. With extensive collaboration among non-VA service providers, VA's CHCs in Anchorage, Alaska; Brooklyn, New York; Cleveland, Ohio; Dallas, Texas; Little Rock, Arkansas; Pittsburgh, Pennsylvania; San Francisco, California; and West Los Angeles, California, provide a comprehensive continuum of care that reaches out to homeless veterans and helps them escape homelessness.

VBA-VHA SPECIAL OUTREACH AND BENEFITS ASSISTANCE

VHA has provided specialized funding to support 12 veterans' benefits counselors as members of HCMI and Homeless Domiciliary Programs as authorized by Public Law 102-590. These specially funded staff provide dedicated outreach, benefits counseling, referral, and additional assistance to eligible veterans applying for VA benefits. This specially funded initiative complements VBA's ongoing efforts to target homeless veterans for special attention. To reach more homeless veterans, designated homeless veterans coordinators at VBA's 58 regional offices annually make more than 4,700 visits to homeless facilities and more than 9,000 contacts with non-VA agencies working with the homeless and provide more than 24,000 homeless veterans with benefits counseling and referrals to other VA programs. These special outreach efforts are assumed as part of ongoing duties and responsibilities. VBA has also instituted new procedures to reduce the processing times for homeless veterans' benefits claims.

VA EXCESS PROPERTY FOR HOMELESS VETERANS INITIATIVE

The VA Excess Property for Homeless Veterans Initiative provides for the distribution of federal excess personal property, such as hats, parkas, footwear, socks, sleeping bags, and other items to homeless veterans and homeless veteran programs. A Compensated Work Therapy Program, employing formerly homeless veterans, has been established at the Medical Center in Lyons, New Jersey to receive, warehouse, and ship these goods to VA homeless programs across the country.

PROGRAM MONITORING AND EVALUATION

The VA has built program monitoring and evaluation into all its homeless veterans' treatment initiatives, and it serves as an integral component of each program. Designed, implemented, and maintained by the Northeast Program Evaluation Center (NEPEC) at VAMC West Haven, Connecticut, these evaluation efforts provide important information about the veterans served and the therapeutic value and cost effectiveness of the specialized programs. Information from these evaluations also helps program managers determine new directions to pursue expanding and improving services for homeless veterans.

HOMELESS VETERANS REINTEGRATION PROGRAM

The Homeless Veterans Reintegration Program (HVRP) is the only federal program wholly dedicated to providing employment assistance to homeless veterans. HVRP is funded by DOL-VETS in compliance with the requirements of 38 United States Code, Section 2021, as added by Section 5 of Public Law 107-95, the Homeless Veterans Comprehensive Assistance Act of 2001. Section 2021 requires the secretary of labor to conduct, directly or through grant or contract, such programs as the secretary determines appropriate to expedite the reintegration of homeless veterans into the labor force

HVRP programs fill a special need because they serve veterans who may be shunned by other programs and services because of problems such as severe posttraumatic stress disorder, long histories of substance abuse, serious psychosocial problems, legal issues, and those who are HIV-positive. These veterans require more time consuming, specialized, and intensive assessment, referrals, and counseling than is possible in other programs that work with veterans seeking employment.

The employment focus of HVRP distinguishes it from most other programs for the homeless, which concentrate on more immediate needs such as emergency shelter, food, and substance abuse treatment. Although these are critical components of any homeless program, and grantees are required to demonstrate that their clients' needs in those areas are met, the objective of HVRP programs is to enable homeless veterans to secure and keep jobs that will allow them to re-enter mainstream society as productive citizens.

THE NATIONAL COALITION FOR HOMELESS VETERANS (NCHV)

The National Coalition for Homeless Veterans (NCHV) — a 501(c)(3) nonprofit organization governed by a 13-member board of directors — is the resource and technical assistance center for a national network of community-based service providers and local, state, and federal agencies that provide emergency and supportive housing, food, health services, job training and placement assistance, legal aid, and case management support for hundreds of thousands of homeless veterans each year.

NCHV also serves as the primary liaison between the nation's care providers, Congress, and the executive branch agencies charged with helping them succeed in their work. NCHV's advocacy has strengthened and increased funding for virtually every federal homeless veterans' assistance program in existence today.

Under a technical assistance grant awarded by the Department of Veterans Affairs, NCHV provides guidance and information about program development, administration, governance, and funding to all the nation's homeless veteran service providers.

CHAPTER 16

BURIAL, FUNERAL, & MEMORIAL BENEFITS

As a military veteran, you are entitled to burial, funeral, and memorial benefits to honor you for your significant contributions in service of the United States. This chapter should also be referred to by spouses, surviving family members, and beneficiaries of veterans. Some benefits even extend to spouses of veterans.

BURIAL BENEFITS IN A NATIONAL CEMETERY

Burial benefits available include a grave site in any of the 125 national cemeteries with available space, opening and closing of the grave, perpetual care, a government headstone or marker, a burial flag, and a Presidential Memorial Certificate, at no cost to the family. Some veterans may also be eligible for burial allowances. Cremated remains are buried or inured in national cemeteries in the same manner and with the same honors as casketed remains.

Burial benefits available for spouses and dependents buried in a national cemetery include burial with the veteran, perpetual plot care, and the spouse or dependents' names and dates of birth and death inscribed on the veteran's headstone. These benefits are all available at no cost to the veteran's family.

BURIAL BENEFITS IN A PRIVATE CEMETERY

Burial benefits available for veterans buried in a private cemetery include a government headstone or marker, a burial flag, and a Presidential Memorial Certificate, at no cost to the family. Some veterans may also be eligible for burial allowances. There are no benefits available to spouses and dependents buried in a private cemetery.

HEADSTONES AND MARKERS

The Department of Veterans Affairs furnishes upon request, at no charge to the applicant, a government headstone or marker for the grave of any deceased eligible veteran in any cemetery around the world. For all deaths occurring before September 11, 2001, the VA may provide a headstone or marker only for graves that are not marked with a private headstone.

Spouses and dependents buried in a private cemetery are not eligible for a government-provided headstone or marker.

Flat markers in granite, marble, and bronze and upright headstones in granite and marble are available. The style chosen must be consistent with existing monuments at the place of burial. Niche markers are also available to mark columbaria used for inurnment of cremated remains.

When burial or memorialization is in a national, post, or state veterans' cemetery, a headstone or marker will be ordered by the cemetery officials based on inscription information provided by the next of kin.

Persons Eligible for a Government Headstone or Marker in a Private Cemetery

a. Veterans and members of the armed forces (Army, Navy, Air Force, Marine Corps, Coast Guard)

(1) Any member of the armed forces of the United States who dies on active duty.

(2) Any veteran who was discharged under conditions other than dishonorable. With certain exceptions, service beginning after September 7, 1980, as an enlisted person, and service after

October 16, 1981, as an officer, must be for a minimum of 24 months or the full period for which the person was called to active duty. (Examples include those serving less than 24 months in the Gulf War or reservists who were federalized by Presidential Act.) Any other type of discharge other than honorable may qualify the individual for veterans' benefits, depending upon a determination made by a VA regional office. Cases presenting multiple discharges of varying character are also referred for adjudication to a VA regional office.

b. Members of Reserve components and Reserve Officers' Training Corps

(1) Reservists and National Guard members who, at time of death, were entitled to retired pay under Chapter 1223, title 10, United States Code, or who would have been entitled, but for being under the age of 60. Specific categories of individuals eligible for retired pay are delineated in section 12731 of Chapter 1223, title 10, United States Code.

(2) Members of Reserve components who die while hospitalized or undergoing treatment at the United States' expense for injury or disease contracted or incurred under honorable conditions while performing active duty for training or inactive duty training or undergoing such hospitalization or treatment.

(3) Members of the Reserve Officers' Training Corps of the Army, Navy, or Air Force who die under honorable conditions while attending an authorized training camp or on an authorized cruise, while performing authorized travel to or from that camp or cruise, or while hospitalized or undergoing treatment at the expense of the United States for injury or disease contracted or incurred under honorable conditions while engaged in one of those activities.

(4) Members of Reserve components who, during a period of active duty for training, were disabled or died from a disease or injury incurred or aggravated in the line of duty or, during

a period of inactive duty training, were disabled or died from an injury incurred or aggravated in line of duty.

c. Commissioned Officers, National Oceanic and Atmospheric Administration

(1) A Commissioned Officer of the National Oceanic and Atmospheric Administration (formerly titled the Coast and Geodetic Survey and the Environmental Science Services Administration) with full-time duty on or after July 29, 1945.

(2) A Commissioned Officer who served before July 29, 1945, and for whom one of the following applies:

(a) Was assigned to an area of immediate military hazard while in time of war, or of a presidentially declared national emergency as determined by the secretary of defense.

(b) Served in the Philippine Islands on December 7, 1941, and continuously in such islands thereafter.

(c) Transferred to the Department of the Army or the Department of the Navy under the provisions of the Act of May 22, 1917 (40 Stat. 87; 33 USC. § 855).

d. Public Health Service

(1) A commissioned officer of the Regular or Reserve Corps of the Public Health Service who served on full-time duty on or after July 29, 1945. If the service of the particular Public Health Service Officer falls within the meaning of active duty for training, as defined in section 101(22), title 38, United States Code, he or she must have been disabled or died from a disease or injury incurred or aggravated in the line of duty.

(2) A commissioned officer of the Regular or Reserve Corps of the Public Health Service who performed full-time duty before July 29, 1945:

(a) In time of war

(b) On detail for duty with the Army, Navy, Air Force, Marine Corps, or Coast Guard

(c) While the service was part of the military forces of the United States pursuant to executive order of the president

(3) A commissioned officer serving on inactive duty training as defined in section 101(23), title 38, United States Code, whose death resulted from an injury incurred or aggravated in the line of duty.

e. World War II Merchant Mariners

(1) United States Merchant Mariners with ocean-going service during the period of armed conflict, December 7, 1941, to December 31, 1946. Before the enactment of Public Law 105-368, United States Merchant Mariners with ocean-going service during the period of armed conflict of December 7, 1941, to August 15, 1945, were eligible. With enactment of Public Law 105-368, the service period is extended to December 31, 1946, for those dying on or after November 11, 1998. A DD-214 documenting this service may be obtained by submitting an application to Commandant (G-MVP-6), United States Coast Guard, 2100 2nd Street SW, Washington, DC 20593. Notwithstanding, the Mariner's death must have occurred after the enactment of Public Law 105-368 and the interment not violate the applicable restrictions while meeting the requirements held therein.

(2) United States Merchant Mariners who served on blockships in support of Operation Mulberry during World War II.

Persons Not Eligible for a Headstone or Marker

a. Disqualifying characters of discharge

A person whose only separation from the armed forces was under dishonorable conditions or whose character of service results in a bar to veterans' benefits.

b. Discharge from draft

A person who was ordered to report to an induction station but was not inducted into military service.

c. Person found guilty of a capital crime

Eligibility for a headstone or marker is prohibited if a person is convicted of a federal capital crime and sentenced to death or life imprisonment, or is convicted of a state capital crime and sentenced to death or life imprisonment without parole. Federal officials are authorized to deny requests for headstones or markers to persons who are shown by clear and convincing evidence to have committed a federal or state capital crime but were not convicted of such crime because of flight to avoid prosecution or by death before trial.

d. Subversive activities

Any person convicted of subversive activities after September 1, 1959, shall have no right to burial in a national cemetery from and after the date of commission of such offense, based on periods of active military service commencing before the date of the commission of such offense; neither shall another person be entitled to burial on account of such an individual. Eligibility will be reinstated if the President of the United States grants a pardon for the subversive activities.

e. Active or inactive duty for training

A person whose only service is active duty for training or inactive duty training in the National Guard or Reserve component, unless the individual meets the following criteria:

> (1) Reservists and National Guard members who, at time of death, were entitled to retired pay under Chapter 1223, title 10, United States Code, or would have been entitled but for being under the

age of 60. Specific categories of individuals eligible for retired pay are delineated in section 12731 of Chapter 1223, title 10, United States Code.

(2) Members of Reserve components who die while hospitalized or undergoing treatment at the expense of the United States for injury or disease contracted or incurred under honorable conditions while performing active duty for training or inactive duty training or undergoing such hospitalization or treatment.

(3) Members of the Reserve Officers' Training Corps of the Army, Navy, or Air Force who die under honorable conditions while attending an authorized training camp or on an authorized cruise, while performing authorized travel to or from that camp or cruise, or while hospitalized or undergoing treatment at the expense of the United States for injury or disease contracted or incurred under honorable conditions while engaged in one of those activities.

(4) Members of Reserve components who, during a period of active duty for training, were disabled or died from a disease or injury incurred or aggravated in line of duty or, during a period of inactive duty training, were disabled or died from an injury incurred or aggravated in line of duty.

f. Other groups

Members of groups whose service has been determined by the secretary of the Air Force under the provisions of Public Law 95-202 as not warranting entitlement to benefits administered by the secretary of Veterans Affairs.

Setting Government Headstones and Markers

Cemetery staff in national, military post, and military base cemeteries are responsible for setting the headstone or marker at no cost to the applicant. Some state veterans' cemeteries may charge the applicant a nominal fee for setting a government-furnished headstone or marker.

Arrangements for setting a government-furnished headstone or marker in a private cemetery are the applicant's responsibility, and all placement costs are at private expense.

Replacement Headstones and Markers

Headstones and markers previously furnished by the government may be replaced at government expense if badly deteriorated, illegible, stolen, or vandalized. It may also replace the headstone or marker if the inscription is incorrect, if it was damaged during shipping, or if the material or workmanship does not meet contract specifications.

If a government headstone or marker in a private cemetery is damaged by cemetery personnel, the cemetery should pay all replacement costs.

Marble and granite headstones or markers that are permanently removed from a grave must be destroyed, ensuring that the inscription is no longer legible. Bronze markers must be returned to the contractor.

For guidance on obtaining a replacement headstone or marker, you may call the Memorial Programs Service Applicant Assistance Unit between the hours of 8 a.m. and 5 p.m. (ET), Monday through Friday, at 1-800-697-6947.

BURIAL FLAGS FAQS

Why does VA provide a burial flag?

A United States flag is provided, at no cost, to drape the casket or accompany the urn of a deceased veteran who served honorably in the U.S. armed forces. It is furnished to honor the memory of a veteran's military service to his or her country. VA will furnish a burial flag for commemoration for each (other than dishonorable) discharged:

- Veteran who served during wartime

- Veteran who died on active duty after May 27, 1941

- Veteran who served after January 31, 1955

- Peacetime veteran who was discharged or released from service before June 27, 1950

- Certain persons who served in the organized military forces of the Commonwealth of the Philippines while in service of the U.S. armed forces and who died on or after April 25, 1951

- Certain former members of the Selected Reserves

Who is eligible to receive the burial flag?

The flag is given to the next of kin, as a keepsake, after its use during the funeral service. When there is no next of kin, VA will furnish the flag to a friend making request for it. For VA national cemeteries with an Avenue of Flags, families of veterans buried in these national cemeteries may donate the burial flags of their loved ones to be flown on patriotic holidays.

How can you apply?

You may apply for the flag by completing VA Form 21-2008, Application for United States Flag for Burial Purposes. You may get a flag at any VA regional office or U.S. Post Office. The funeral director will help you obtain the flag.

Can a burial flag be replaced?

The law allows us to issue one flag for a veteran's funeral. We cannot replace it if it is lost, destroyed, or stolen. However, some veterans' organizations or other community groups may be able to help you get another flag.

How should the burial flag be displayed?

The proper way to display the flag depends upon whether the casket is open or closed. VA Form 21-2008 provides the correct method for displaying and folding the flag. The burial flag is not suitable for outside display because of its size and fabric. It is made of cotton and can easily be damaged by weather. For more information call the VA at 1-800-827-1000.

PRESIDENTIAL MEMORIAL CERTIFICATES

A Presidential Memorial Certificate (PMC) is an engraved paper certificate, signed by the current president, to honor the memory of honorably discharged deceased veterans.

History

This program was initiated in March 1962 by President John F. Kennedy and has been continued by all subsequent presidents. Statutory authority for the program is Section 112, Title 38, of the United States Code.

Administration

The Department of Veterans Affairs administers the PMC program by preparing the certificates, which bear the current president's signature expressing the country's grateful recognition of the veteran's service in the United States armed forces.

Eligibility

Eligible recipients include the next of kin and loved ones of honorably discharged deceased veterans. More than one certificate may be provided.

Application

Eligible recipients, or someone acting on their behalf, may apply for a PMC in person at any VA regional office or by U.S. mail or toll-free fax. Requests cannot be sent via e-mail. Please be sure to enclose a copy of the veteran's discharge and death certificate to verify eligibility, along with VA Form 40-0247, Application for Presidential Memorial Certificate.

VA BURIAL ALLOWANCES

VA burial allowances are partial reimbursements of an eligible veteran's burial and funeral costs. When the cause of death is not service-related, the reimbursements may be described as two payments: (1) a burial and funeral expense allowance, and (2) a plot interment allowance.

Who Is Eligible?

You may be eligible for a VA burial allowance if:

8 You paid for a veteran's burial or funeral.

8 You have not been reimbursed by another government agency or some other source, such as the deceased veteran's employer.

8 The veteran was discharged under conditions other than dishonorable.

In addition, at least one of the following conditions must be met:

8 The veteran died because of a service-related disability.

8 The veteran was receiving VA pension or compensation at the time of death.

8 The veteran was entitled to receive VA pension or compensation but decided not to reduce his/her military retirement or disability pay.

8 The veteran died in a VA hospital, in a nursing home under VA contract, or while in an approved state nursing home.

How Much Does VA Pay?

8 **Service-related death:** The VA will pay up to $2,000 toward burial expenses for deaths on or after September 11, 2001. The VA will pay up to $1,500 for deaths before September 10, 2001. If the veteran is buried in a VA national cemetery, some or all the cost of transporting the deceased may be reimbursed.

8 **Nonservice-related death:** VA will pay up to $300 toward burial

and funeral expenses, and a $300 plot-interment allowance for deaths on or after December 1, 2001. If the death happened while the veteran was in a VA hospital or under VA contracted nursing home care, some or all the costs of transporting the deceased's remains may be reimbursed.

You can apply by filling out VA Form 21-530, Application for Burial Benefits. You should attach proof of the veteran's military service (DD-214), a death certificate, and copies of any funeral and burial bills you have paid.

MILITARY FUNERAL HONORS

The Department of Defense is responsible for providing military funeral honors. "Honoring Those Who Served" is the title of the DOD program for providing dignified military funeral honors to veterans who have defended our nation.

Upon the family's request, Public Law 106-65 requires that every eligible veteran receive a military funeral honors ceremony, to include folding and presenting the United States burial flag and the playing of "Taps." The law defines a military funeral honors detail as consisting of two or more uniformed military persons, with at least one being a member of the veteran's parent service of the armed forces. The DOD program calls for funeral home directors to request military funeral honors on behalf of the veterans' family. However, the Department of Veterans Affairs National Cemetery Administration cemetery staff can also assist with arranging military funeral honors at VA national cemeteries. Veterans' organizations may assist in providing military funeral honors. When military funeral honors at a national cemetery are desired, they are arranged before the committal service by the funeral home.

The Department of Defense began the implementation plan for providing military funeral honors for eligible veterans as enacted in Section 578 of Public Law 106-65 of the National Defense Authorization Act for FY 2000 on January 1, 2000.

Questions or comments concerning the DOD military funeral honors program may be sent to the address listed below. The military funeral honors Web site is located at **www.militaryfuneralhonors.osd.mil**.

Department of Defense
Directorate for Public Inquiry and Analysis
Room 3A750, The Pentagon
Washington, DC 20301-1400

To arrange military funeral honors, contact your local funeral home.

DEPARTMENT OF VETERANS AFFAIRS NATIONAL CEMETERIES

The Department of Veterans Affairs' National Cemetery Administration maintains 125 national cemeteries in 39 states (and Puerto Rico) and 33 soldiers' lots and monument sites.

There is not a VA national cemetery in every state. A complete listing of all national cemeteries is available online at **www.cem.va.gov/cem/cems/listcem.asp**. State veterans' cemeteries are listed at **www.cem.va.gov/cem/scg/lsvc.asp**.

STATE CEMETERY GRANTS PROGRAM — GENERAL INFORMATION

The Department of Veterans Affairs State Cemetery Grants Program was established in 1978 to complement the VA's National Cemetery Administration.

The program assists states in providing grave sites for veterans in those areas where VA's national cemeteries cannot fully satisfy their burial needs.

Grants may be used only for the purpose of establishing, expanding, or improving veterans' cemeteries that are owned and operated by a state or U.S. territory. Aid can be granted only to states or U.S. territories. VA cannot provide grants to private organizations, counties, cities, or other government agencies.

VA can now provide up to 100 percent of the development cost for an approved project. For establishment of new cemeteries, VA can provide for operating equipment. VA does not provide for acquisition of land. The value of the land cannot be considered an allowable cost under the grant. States are solely responsible for acquisition of the necessary land. Any state ceasing to own or operate a cemetery established, expanded, or improved through the use of grant funds, or using the funds for any other purpose than for which the grant was made, will be liable for the total refund of all grants disbursed for that cemetery. Federal funds can also be suspended or withdrawn for noncompliance with the terms and conditions of the cemetery grant.

Cemeteries established under the grant program must conform to the standards and guidelines pertaining to site selection, planning, and construction prescribed by the VA. Cemeteries must be operated solely for the burial of service members who die on active duty, veterans, and their eligible spouses and dependent children. Any cemetery assisted by a VA grant must be maintained and operated according to the operational standards and measures of the National Cemetery Administration.

The administration, operation, and maintenance of a VA-supported state cemetery is solely the responsibility of the state. The secretary of Veterans Affairs is authorized to pay a plot or interment allowance (not to exceed $300) to a state for expenses incurred by the state in the burial of eligible veterans in a cemetery owned and operated by the state if the burial is performed at no cost to the veteran's next of kin. This benefit is administered by the Veterans Benefits Administration, and the state must apply to VBA to receive it.

VA's State Cemetery Grant Program is designed to complement VA's 125 national cemeteries across the country. This state cemetery grant program helps states establish new state veterans cemeteries and expand or improve existing state cemeteries. To date, the VA program has helped establish, expand, or improve 67 state veterans cemeteries in 36 states, Northern Mariana Islands, and Guam, which provided more than 22,000 burials in fiscal year 2007. Since the program began in 1980, the VA has awarded 162 grants, totaling more than $312 million.

CHAPTER 17

STATE & FEDERAL VETERANS FACILITIES

Do you know what veterans' facilities are close to you? You should. They offer a wealth of information, benefits, and services to which you may be entitled. You earned benefits from your service, and you are entitled to those benefits. Learn what is available in your local area, through the federal government, and through your state government. Take advantage of your benefits — you earned them.

FEDERAL VETERANS' FACILITIES

The VA makes it easy for you to find what is available in your local area. Go to the following sites to search for federal facilities:

- Veterans Health Administration: **www1.va.gov/directory/guide/division_flsh.asp?dnum=1**

- Veterans' benefits Administration: **www1.va.gov/directory/guide/division_flsh.asp?dnum=3**

- National Cemetery Administration: **www1.va.gov/directory/guide/division_flsh.asp?dnum=4**

- Vet Centers: **www1.va.gov/directory/guide/division_flsh. asp?dnum=4**

- VA central offices: **www1.va.gov/directory/guide/hq_flsh.asp?**

- Grave site locator: **http://gravelocator.cem.va.gov/j2ee/servlet/ NGL_v1**

- Facilities by state: **www1.va.gov/directory/guide/allstate_flsh. asp?**

- Facility listing: **www1.va.gov/directory/guide/rpt_fac_list. cfm**

STATE VETERANS FACILITIES

State Veterans Facilities are abundant and are surprisingly accessible to most areas in each state. The best way to find those in your local area is to contact your State Veterans Affairs division, visit your state VA Web site, or search the Internet for VA facilities in your area. You will be impressed with what the state has to offer our veterans.

TOLL-FREE VETERANS' BENEFITS SERVICE

For more information about specific benefits, visit the nearest VA regional office or call 1-800-827-1000. For detailed information about all VA benefits and services, visit **www.va.gov**.

Information specific to survivors is available. Select "Benefits," then "Survivors' Benefits." Apply for compensation, pension, healthcare, education, or vocational rehabilitation and employment benefits by selecting "Apply Online." A "Contact VA" link is available for e-mail inquiries.

The VA pledges to:

- Treat you with courtesy, compassion, and respect at all times.

- Communicate with you accurately, completely, and clearly.

    ☡ Provide timely service to you.

    ☡ Make services accessible to you.

    ☡ Fully answer your questions and concerns.

OTHER IMPORTANT PHONE NUMBERS TO KEEP:

Healthcare: 877-222-8387

Education & Training: 888-442-4551

VA Life Insurance: 800-669-8477

Office of SGLI: 800-419-1473

CHAMPVA: 800-733-8387

Helpline: (Agent Orange & Gulf War) 800-749-8387

Direct Deposit: 877-838-2778

Headstones (status of claims only): 800-697-6947

Telecommunication Device for Deaf (TDD): 800-829-4833

"...to care for him who shall have borne the battle and for his widow and his orphan..."

— Abraham Lincoln

CONCLUSION

As a 24-year veteran of the United States Coast Guard, I can tell you the transition from military to civilian life is a hard one. The transition from veteran to disabled veteran, combat-wounded veteran, or severely disabled is significantly more traumatic and life-changing.

It is my sincere hope that this book will be used as a valued reference guide to benefits for our military veterans and provide them with valuable answers surrounding entitlements and benefits. A few more good sources of information about what Congress is proposing for changes in benefits is the House Committee on Veterans Affairs, which can be found at **http://veterans.house.gov**, and the U.S. Senate Committee on Veterans Affairs, which can be found at **http://www.senate.gov/~veterans/public/index.cfm?pageid=19**.

I cannot stress enough the wealth of information on state veterans' Web sites. They are packed with information on benefits and have specific programs and entitlements for your specific state.

This book was not about veterans claims, as that would take up another volume by itself; however, if you are in need of assistance with veterans' claims, there are several nonprofit groups willing to help you out at no cost. I tend to shy away from those who want to charge you a fee for their services. Another reference is the book titled *The Veteran's Survival Guide: How to File and Collect on VA Claims, Second Edition* by John D. Roche. I have found it to be a valuable resource.

Best wishes to all our honored U.S. military veterans, and a heartfelt thank you from the Brown family for your service to our country.

BIBLIOGRAPHY

Budahn, P. J. (2005) *Veteran's Guide To Benefits (Veteran's Guide to Benefits)*, 4th Edition. Mechanicsburg, Pennsylvania: Stackpole Books.

Kaplan. (2007) *Kaplan Scholarships 2008: Billions of Dollars in Free Money for College* (Kaplan Scholarships). New York, New York: Kaplan Publishing

Leyva, Meredith. (2003) *Married to the Military: A Survival Guide for Military Wives, Girlfriends, and Women in Uniform*. New York, New York: Fireside.

Michel, Christopher P. & Norman Schwarzkopf. (2005) *The Military Advantage: A Comprehensive Guide to Your Military & Veterans Benefits*. New York, New York: Simon & Schuster.

U.S. Government. (2007) *Compensation, Appeals, Disability, Medical Care, Insurance Programs, Plans for Families, GI Bill, Home Loan Programs* (Two CD-ROM Set). Publisher: Progressive Management

Roche, John D. (2006) *The Veteran's Survival Guide: How to File and Collect on VA Claims*, Second Edition. Dulles, Virginia: Potomac Books, Inc.

AUTHOR BIOGRAPHY

Bruce C. Brown

Lieutenant Commander Bruce C. Brown is serving his 24th year in the U.S. Coast Guard. He is currently the Deputy Chief, Resource & Performance Management Division of the Seventh Coast Guard District, Miami, Florida. Bruce is married with three sons. He is an award-winning author of five books, including *How to Use the Internet to Advertise, Promote and Market Your Business or Web site with Little or No Money*, winner of a 2007 Independent Publisher Award, *The Ultimate Guide to Search Engine*

Marketing: Pay Per Click Advertising Secrets Revealed, Winner in the USA Best Books 2007 Award program, *The Complete Guide to E-mail Marketing: How to Create Successful, Spam-free Campaigns to Reach Your Target Audience and Increase Sale*s, *The Complete Guide to Google Advertising: Including Tips, Tricks, & Strategies to Create a Winning Advertising Plan,* and *The Secret Power of Blogging: How to Promote and Market Your Business, Organization, or Cause With Free Blogs.* He has been happily married for 24 years to Vonda and holds degrees from both Charter Oak State College and the University of Phoenix.

INDEX